2D Object Detection and Recognition

Yali Amit

2D Object Detection and Recognition

Models, Algorithms, and Networks

The MIT Press
Cambridge, Massachusetts
London, England

This book was set in Times Roman by Interactive Composition Corporation and was printed and bound in the United States of America.

Library of Congress Cataloging-in-Publication Data

Amit, Yali.
    2D object detection and recognition : models, algorithms, and networks / Yali Amit.
      p. cm.
    Includes bibliographical references.
    ISBN 0-262-01194-8 (hc. : alk. paper)
      1. Computer vision. I. Title.

TA1634 .A45 2002
006.3'7–dc21

2002016508

To Granite, Yotam, and Inbal

Contents

Preface   *xi*

Acknowledgments   *xv*

1   Introduction   *1*

    1.1   Low-Level Image Analysis and Bottom-up Segmentation   *1*

    1.2   Object Detection with Deformable-Template Models   *3*

    1.3   Detection of Rigid Objects   *5*

    1.4   Object Recognition   *8*

    1.5   Scene Analysis: Merging Detection and Recognition   *10*

    1.6   Neural Network Architectures   *12*

2   Detection and Recognition: Overview of Models   *13*

    2.1   A Bayesian Approach to Detection   *13*

    2.2   Overview of Object-Detection Models   *18*

    2.3   Object Recognition   *25*

    2.4   Scene Analysis: Combining Detection and Recognition   *27*

    2.5   Network Implementations   *28*

3   1D Models: Deformable Contours   *31*

    3.1   Inside-Outside Model   *31*

    3.2   An Edge-Based Data Model   *40*

    3.3   Computation   *41*

3.4   Joint Estimation of the Curve and the Parameters   *48*

3.5   Bibliographical Notes and Discussion   *51*

4   1D Models: Deformable Curves   *57*

4.1   Statistical Model   *58*

4.2   Computation: Dynamic Programming   *63*

4.3   Global Optimization on a Tree-Structured Prior   *67*

4.4   Bibliographical Notes and Discussion   *78*

5   2D Models: Deformable Images   *81*

5.1   Statistical Model   *83*

5.2   Connection to the Deformable-Contour Model   *88*

5.3   Computation   *88*

5.4   Bernoulli Data Model   *93*

5.5   Linearization   *97*

5.6   Applications to Brain Matching   *101*

5.7   Bibliographical Notes and Discussion   *104*

6   Sparse Models: Formulation, Training, and Statistical Properties   *109*

6.1   From Deformable Models to Sparse Models   *111*

6.2   Statistical Model   *113*

6.3   Local Features: Comparison Arrays   *118*

6.4   Local Features: Edge Arrangements   *121*

6.5   Local Feature Statistics   *128*

7   Detection of Sparse Models: Dynamic Programming   *139*

7.1   The Prior Model   *139*

7.2   Computation: Dynamic Programming   *142*

7.3   Detecting Pose   *147*

7.4   Bibliographical Notes and Discussion   *148*

8   Detection of Sparse Models: Counting   *151*

8.1   Detecting Candidate Centers   *153*

8.2   Computing Pose and Instantiation Parameters   *156*

8.3   Density of Candidate Centers and False Positives   *159*

8.4   Further Analysis of a Detection   *160*

8.5   Examples   *163*

8.6   Bibliographical Notes and Discussion   *176*

9   Object Recognition   *181*

9.1   Classification Trees   *185*

9.2   Object Recognition with Trees   *192*

9.3   Relational Arrangements   *197*

9.4   Experiments   *201*

9.5   Why Multiple Trees Work   *209*

9.6   Bibliographical Notes and Discussion   *212*

10   Scene Analysis: Merging Detection and Recognition   *215*

10.1   Classification of Chess Pieces in Gray-Level Images   *216*

10.2   Detecting and Classifying Characters   *224*

10.3   Object Clustering   *228*

10.4   Bibliographical Notes and Discussion   *231*

11   Neural Network Implementations   *233*

11.1   Basic Network Architecture   *234*

11.2   Hebbian Learning   *237*

11.3   Learning an Object Model   *238*

11.4   Learning Classifiers   *241*

11.5   Detection   *248*

11.6   Gating and Off-Center Recognition   *250*

11.7   Biological Analogies   *252*

11.8   Bibliographical Notes and Discussion   *255*

12   Software   *259*

12.1   Setting Things Up   *259*

12.2   Important Data Structures   *262*

12.3   Local Features   *265*

12.4   Deformable Models   *267*

12.5   Sparse Models   *274*

12.6   Sparse Model—Counting Detector: Training   *276*

12.7   Example—LʌTᴇX   *278*

12.8   Other Objects with Synthesized Training Sets   *280*

12.9   Shape Recognition   *281*

12.10 Combining Detection and Recognition   *284*

Bibliography   *287*

Index   *299*

Preface

This book is about detecting and recognizing 2D objects in gray-level images. How are models constructed? How are they trained? What are the computational approaches to efficient implementation on a computer? And finally, how can some of these computations be implemented in the framework of parallel and biologically plausible neural network architectures?

Detection refers to anything from identifying a location to identifying and registering components of a particular object class at various levels of detail. For example, finding the faces in an image, finding the eyes and mouths of the faces. One could require a precise outline of the object in the image, or the detection of a certain number of well-defined landmarks on the object, or a deformation from a prototype of the object into the image. The deformation could be a simple 2D affine map or a more detailed nonlinear map. The object itself may have different degrees of variability. It may be a rigid 2D object, such as a fixed computer font or a 2D view of a 3D object, or it may be a highly deformable object, such as the left ventricle of the heart. All these are considered object-detection problems, where detection implies identifying some aspects of the particular way the object is present in the image—namely, some partial description of the object *instantiation.*

Recognition refers to the classification among objects or subclasses of a general class of objects present in a particular region of the image that has been isolated. For example, after detecting a face, identify the person, or classify images of handwritten digits, or recognize a symbol from a collection of hundreds of symbols. Both domains have a significant training and statistical estimation component.

Finding a predetermined object in a scene, or recognizing the object present in a particular region are only subproblems of the more-general and ambitious goal of computer vision. In broad terms, one would want to develop an artificial system that can receive an image and identify all the objects or a large part of the objects present in a complex scene from a library of thousands of classes. This implies not only detection and recognition algorithms, but methods for sequentially learning new objects and incorporating them into the current recognition and detection schemes. But perhaps hardest of all is the question of how to start processing a complex scene with no prior information on its contents—what to look for first, and in which particular regions should a recognition algorithm be implemented. This general problem is unsolved, although our visual system seems to solve it effortlessly and very efficiently.

Deformable-template models offer some reasonable solutions to formulating a representation for a restricted family of objects, estimating the relevant parameters and subsequently detecting these objects in the image, at various levels of detail of the instantiation. Each model is defined in terms of a subset of points on a reference grid, *the template,* a set of admissible instantiations of these points, also referred to as *deformations* of the template, and a statistical model for the data—given a particular instantiation of the object is present in the image. A Bayesian framework is used, in that probabilities are assigned to the different instantiations. Bayes's rule then yields a posterior distribution on instantiations. Detections are computed by finding maxima or high values of the posterior. In chapter 2, some general and unifying elements of the Bayesian models used in all the detection algorithms are introduced, together with an overview of the models applied to a simple synthetic example. The details of the detection algorithms are provided in chapters 3–8.

Chapter 9 is devoted to recognition of isolated objects or shapes, assuming some mechanism exists for isolating the individual objects from the more-complex image. The classification schemes can be viewed as a recursive partitioning of the hierarchy of templates using classification trees. Chapter 10 is an exploration into a possible approach to complex scene analysis by merging detection and recognition, both in terms of training and in terms of implementation. Detectors are no longer geared to one particular class, but to object *clusters* containing elements from several classes. Detection can be viewed as a way to quickly choose a number of candidate regions for subsequent processing with a recognition algorithm. An overview of the models of chapters 9 and 10 are also given in chapter 2.

Chapter 11 describes schematic neural network architectures that train and implement detection and recognition algorithms based on the sparse models developed in chapters 6–9. The goal is to show that models based on binary local features, with built-in invariances, simple training procedures, and simple computational implementations, can indeed provide computational models for the visual system. Chapter 12 provides a description of the software and data sets, all of which are accessible through the web at `http://galton.uchicago.edu/~amit/book/`.

The Introduction is used to briefly describe the major trends in computer vision and how they stand in relation to the work in this book. Furthermore, in the last section of each chapter, references to related work and alternative algorithms are provided. These are not comprehensive reviews, but a choice of key papers or books that can point the reader further on.

The emphasis is on simplicity, transparency, and computational efficiency. Cost functions, statistical models, and computational schemes are kept as simple as possible —Occam's razor is too-often forgotten in the computer-vision community. Statistical modeling and estimation play an important role, including methods for training the object representations and classifiers. The models and algorithms are described at a level of detail that should enable readers to code them on their own; however, the readers also have the option of delving into the finest details of the implementations using the accompanying software. Indeed, it is sometimes the case that the key to the success of an algorithm is due to some choices made by the author, which are not necessarily viewed as crucial or central to the original motivating ideas. These will ultimately be identified by experimenting with the software. It is also useful for the readers to be able to experiment with these methods and to discover for themselves the strengths and weaknesses, leading to the development of new and promising solutions.

The images from the experiments shown in the book, and many more, are provided with the software. For each figure in the book, a parameter file has been prepared, allowing the reader to run the program on the corresponding image. This should help jump-start the experimentation stage. Even trying to change parameter settings in these files can be informative, or running them on additional images. Chapter 12 should provide the necessary documentation for understanding the parameters and their possible values.

The examples presented in this book should convince the reader that problems emerging in different computer-vision subcommunities, from the document-analysis community to the medical-imaging community, can be approached with similar tools. This comes at the expense of intensively pursuing any one particular application. Still, the book can be used as a reference for particular types of algorithms for specific applications. These include detecting contours and curves, image warping, anatomy detection in medical images, object detection, and character recognition. There are common themes that span several or all chapters, as well as discussions of connections between models and algorithms. These are, in large part, found in chapter 2 and the introductory comments and the final discussion section of each chapter. It is still possible to study individual models independently of the others.

The mathematical tools used in this book are somewhat diverse but not very sophisticated. Elementary concepts in probability and statistics are essential, including the basic ideas of Bayesian inference, and maximum-likelihood estimation. These can be found in Rice (1995). Some background in pattern recognition is useful but not essential and can be found in Duda and Hart (1973). A good understanding of multivariate calculus is needed for chapters 3 and 5, as well as some basic knowledge of numerical methods for optimization and matrix computation (which can be found in Press and colleagues 1995). The wavelet transform is used in chapters 3 and 5, where a brief overview is provided as well as a description of the discrete wavelet transform. (For a comprehensive treatment of the theory and applications of wavelets, see Wickerhauser 1994.) Some elementary concepts in information theory, such as entropy and conditional entropy, are used in chapters 4 and 9 and are briefly covered in a section of chapter 4. (For a comprehensive treatment of information theory see Cover and Thomas 1991.)

Computer vision is a fascinating subject. On one hand, there is the satisfaction of developing an algorithm that takes in an image from the web or the local webcam and in less than a second finds all the faces. On the other hand are the amazing capabilities of the human visual system that we experience at every moment of our lives. The computer algorithms are nowhere near to achieving these capabilities. Thus, every once in a while, the face detector will miss a face and quite often will select some part of a bookshelf or a tree as being a face. The visual system makes no such mistakes—the ground truth is unequivocal and brutally confronts us at every step of the way. Thus we need to stay humble on one hand and constantly challenged on the other. It is hoped that the reader will become engaged by this challenge and contribute to this exciting field.

Acknowledgments

A large part of the work presented in this book is a result of a long interaction with Donald Geman, to whom I owe the greatest debt. I am referring not only to particular algorithms we developed jointly, but also to endless conversations and exchanges about the subject of computer vision, which have been crucial in the formation of the views presented here. I am deeply thankful to Ulf Grenander for first introducing me to image analysis and deformable-template models. The book as a whole is influenced by his philosophy and also by my interactions with the Pattern Analysis group in the Division of Applied Mathematics at Brown University: Basilis Gidas, Don McClure, David Mumford, and in particular Stuart Geman who, through scattered conversations over the years, has provided invaluable input.

The work on neural network architectures would not have been possible without the recent interaction with Massimo Mascaro. I am indebted to my father Daniel Amit for prodding me to explore the connections between computer vision algorithms and the biological visual system, and for many helpful discussions along the way. Kenneth Wilder contributed immensely to the accompanying software, which would have been unintelligible otherwise. Many thanks to Mauro Piccioni, Kevin Manbeck, Michael Miller, Augustine Kong, Bruno Jedynak, Alejandro Murua, and Gilles Blanchard who have been supportive and stimulating collaborators. I am grateful to the Department of Statistics at the University of Chicago for being so supportive over the past ten years, and to the Army Research Office for their financial support.

2D Object Detection and Recognition

1   Introduction

The goal of computer vision is to develop algorithms that take an image as input and produce a symbolic interpretation describing which objects are present, at what pose, and some information on the three-dimensional spatial relations between the objects. This involves issues such as learning object models, classifiers to distinguish between objects, and developing efficient methods to analyze the scene, given these learned models. Our visual system is able to carry out such tasks effortlessly and very quickly. We can detect and recognize objects from a library of thousands if not tens of thousands in very complex scenes. However, the goal of developing computer algorithms for these tasks is still far from our grasp. Furthermore, there is still no dominant and accepted paradigm within which most researchers are working. There are a number of major trends, briefly described below, relative to which the work in this book is placed.

1.1   Low-Level Image Analysis and Bottom-up Segmentation

Image segmentation is a dominant field of research in the computer vision and image analysis communities. The goal is to extract boundaries of objects or identify regions defined by objects, with no prior knowledge of what these objects are.

The guiding philosophy is that only through such low-level processing is there any chance of identifying more-restricted regions in the scene for further high-level processing, such as recognition. Because these algorithms operate with no higher-level information about the objects, they are referred to as *low-level image analysis*. Another commonly used term is bottom-up image processing.

Many of the early ideas that guided much of the subsequent research can be found in Duda and Hart (1973) and Marr (1982). Motivated by the connections established by Marr and Hilderith (1980) between edge detection algorithms and computations carried out in the primary visual cortex, a significant body of work in computer vision has been devoted to the specific use of edge detection for segmentation. An edge detector is used to identify all edges in the image, after which some type of local rule tells how to group the edges into continuous contours that provide continuous outlines of the objects. Other approaches to segmentation are region based. Regions with similar characteristics are identified, typically through local region-growing techniques. A detailed description of a variety of such approaches can be found in Haralick and Shapiro (1992).

A statistical formulation of the segmentation problem from a Bayesian point of view was introduced in Geman and Geman (1984), combining region and edge information. An extensive review of such statistical approaches can be found in Geman (1990). The statistical model introduces global information in that the full segmentation is assigned a cost or posterior probability, in terms of the "smoothness" of the different regions and their contours. The various algorithms proposed to optimize this global cost are quite computationally intensive. Other approaches to bottom-up image segmentation currently being proposed can be found in Elder and Zucker (1996); Parida, Geiger, and Hummel (1998); Ishikawa and Geiger (1998); and Shi and Malik (2000).

However, there are some persistent problems with the notion of determining a segmentation of an image without any models of the objects that are expected to be present. First, there is no agreement as to what a good segmentation really is. Furthermore, continuous contours are very difficult to determine in terms of local edges detected in an image. Using local-edge information alone, it is very difficult to actually trace the contour of an object—for example, various noise effects and occlusion can eliminate some of the edges along the contour. A local procedure for aggregating or grouping edges would encounter spurious bifurcations or terminations. Homogeneous regions are difficult to define precisely, and at times, lighting conditions create artificial regions that may cause an object to be split or merged with parts of the background.

As a result, people have tried to incorporate a priori information regarding specific objects in order to assist in identifying their instantiations. This involves more-specific modeling and more-restricted goals in terms of the algorithms. Instead of an initial segmentation that provides the outlines of *all* the objects of interest, which then need to be classified, one tries to directly detect specific objects with specific models. Because shape information is incorporated into the model, one hopes to avoid the pitfalls of the bottom-up approach and really identify the instantiation of these objects. This approach, called *high-level image analysis,* is the main theme of chapters 3–8.

It should be emphasized that all high-level models use some form of low-level processing of the data, and often an initial edge-detection procedure is performed. However, such processing is always geared toward some predefined goal of detecting a specific object or class of objects, and hence are presented only within the context of the entire algorithm. In that sense, there is no meaning to the notion of "good" edge detection, or a "good" image segmentation divorced from the outcome of the high-level algorithm.

1.2 Object Detection with Deformable-Template Models

The need to introduce higher-level object models has been addressed in a somewhat disjointed manner in the statistics community on one hand and in the computer-vision community on the other. In this section, we briefly discuss the former, which is the point of origin for the work in this manuscript.

High-level object models, under the name *deformable-template models,* were introduced in the statistics community in Grenander (1970, 1978). A statistical model is constructed that describes the variability in object instantiation in terms of a prior distribution on deformations of a template. The template is defined in terms of generators and bonds between subsets of generators. The generators and the bonds are labeled with variables that define the deformation of the template. In addition, a statistical model of the image data, given a particular deformation of the template, is provided. The data model and the prior are combined to define a posterior distribution on deformations given the image data. The model proposed by Fischler and Elschlager (1973) is closely related, although not formulated in statistical terms, and is quite ahead of its time in terms of the proposed computational tools. Much of the theory relating to these models is presented in Grenander (1978) and revisited in Grenander (1993). Some applications are presented in the latter part of Grenander (1993). The subject matter has been mostly nonrigid objects in particular objects that occur in biological and medical images.

The actual applications described in Grenander (1993) assume that the basic pose parameters, such as location and scale, are roughly known—namely, the detection process is *initialized* by the user. The models involve large numbers of generators with "elastic" types of constraints on their relative locations. Because deformation space— the space of bond values—is high dimensional, there is still much left to be done after location and scale are identified. The algorithms are primarily based on relaxation techniques for maximizing the posterior distributions. These types of elastic models are described in chapters 3 and 5. Chapter 3 draws primarily on the work presented in Grenander, Chow, and Keenan (1991); Zhu and Yuille (1996); and Chesnaud, Réfrégier, and Boulet (1999). Chapter 5 draws on the work in Amit, Grenander, and Piccioni (1991) and Amit (1994), with some new unpublished material.

Some of these ideas were developed in parallel using nonstatistical formulations. In Kass, Witkin, and Terzopoulos (1987) and Terzopolous and colleagues (1987), the idea of 1D deformable contours was introduced, as well as ideas of elastic constraints on deformations, and Bajcsy and Kovacic (1988) introduced the idea of image deformation as an extension of older work on image sequence analysis by Horn and Schunck (1981) and Nagel (1983). In these models, a regularizing term takes the place of the prior, and the statistical model for the data takes the form of a cost function on the fit of the deformed model to the data.

In much of the above-mentioned work, the gray-level distributions are modeled directly. This can be problematic in achieving photometric invariance, invariance to variations in lighting, gray-scale maps, and so on. At the single pixel level, the distributions can be rather complex due to variable lighting conditions. Furthermore, the gray-level values have complex interactions requiring complex distributions in high-dimensional spaces. The options are then to use very simple models, which are computationally tractable but lacking photometric invariance, or to introduce complex models, which entail enormous computational cost.

An alternative is to transform the image data to variables that are photometric invariant—perhaps at the cost of reducing the information content of the data. However, it is then easier to formulate credible models for the transformed data. The deformable curve model in chapter 4 and the Bernoulli deformable image model in section 5.4 employ transforms of the image data into vectors of simple binary variables. One then models the distribution of the binary variables, given a particular deformation rather than the gray-level values. The material in chapter 4 draws primarily from the work in Petrocelli, Elion, and Manbeck (1992) and from Geman and Jedynak (1996).

All the algorithms mentioned above suffer from a similar drawback. Some form of initialization provided by the user is necessary. However, the introduction of binary features of varying degrees of complexity allows us to formulate simpler and sparser models with more-transparent constraints on the instantiations. Using these models, the initialization problem can be solved with no user intervention and in a very efficient way. Such models are discussed in chapters 6, 7, and 8, based on work in Amit, Geman, and Jedynak (1998), Amit and Geman (1999), and Amit (2000).

These ideas do fit within the theoretical pattern-analysis paradigm proposed in Grenander (1978). However, the emphasis on image data reduction does depart from

Grenander's philosophy, which emphasizes image synthesis and aims at constructing prior distributions and data models, which, if synthesized, would produce realistic images. This image-synthesis philosophy has also been adopted by people studying compositional models, as in Bienenstock, Geman, and Potter (1997) and Geman, Potter, and Chi (1998), and by people studying generative models, such as Mumford (1994), Revow, Williams, and Hinton (1996), and Zhu and Mumford (1997). Providing a comprehensive statistical model for the image ensemble is not only a very hard task, it is not at all clear that it is needed. There is a large degree of redundancy in the gray-level intensity maps recorded in an image, which may not be all that important for interpreting the symbolic contents of the image.

1.3   Detection of Rigid Objects

In the computer-vision community, the limitations of straightforward bottom-up segmentation also led to the introduction of object models that enter into the detection and recognition process. Most of the work has concentrated around rigid 3D objects (see Grimson 1990; Haralick and Shapiro 1992; Ullman 1996). These objects lend themselves to precise 3D modeling, and the main type of deformations considered are linear or projective.

Lists of features at locations on the object at reference pose are deduced analytically from the 3D description. The spatial arrangements of these features in the image are also predicted through analytic computations, using projective 3D geometry and local properties of edge detectors. Typical features that are used in modeling are oriented edges, straight contour segments—lines of various lengths, high curvature points, corners, and curved contours. Two complementary techniques for detection are searches of correspondence space and searches through pose space.

1.3.1   Searching Correspondence Space

One systematically searches for arrangements of local features in the image consistent with the arrangements of features in the model. The matches must satisfy certain constraints. Unary constraints involve the relationship between the model feature and the image feature. Binary constraints involve the relationship between a pair of model features and a pair of image features. Higher-order constraints can also be introduced. Various heuristic tree-based techniques are devised for searching all possible matchings to find the optimal one, as detailed in Grimson (1990). Invariance of the detection algorithm to pose is incorporated directly in the binary constraints.

In Haralick and Shapiro (1992), this problem is called the *inexact consistent labeling problem,* and various graph theory heuristics are employed.

Similar to the search of correspondence space, or the inexact consistent labeling problem, is the dynamic programming algorithm presented in chapter 7, which is based on work in Amit and Kong (1996) and Amit (1997). The constraints in the models are invariant to scale and to some degree of rotation, as well as *nonlinear* deformations. Detection is achieved under significant deformations of the model beyond simple linear or projective transformations. The full graph of constraints is pruned to make it decomposable, and hence amenable to optimization using dynamic programming, in a manner very similar to the proposal in Fischler and Elschlager (1973). The local features employed are highly invariant to photometric transformations but have a much lower density than typical edge features.

1.3.2   Searching Pose Space

Searching *pose space* can be done through brute force by applying each possible pose to the model and evaluating the fit to the data. This can be computationally expensive, but we will see in chapter 8 that brute force is useful and efficient as long as it is applied to *very simple structures,* and with the appropriate data models involving binary features with relatively low density in the image.

In some cases, searching parts of pose space can be achieved through optimization techniques such as gradient-descent methods or dynamic programming. This is precisely the nature of the deformable models presented in chapters 3–5. Note, however, that here objects are not assumed rigid and hence require many more pose parameters. These methods all face the issue of initialization.

A computational tool that repeatedly comes up as a way to quickly identify the most important parameters of pose, such as location and scale, is the Hough transform, originally proposed by Hough (1962) and subsequently generalized by Ballard (1981). The Hough transform is effectively also a "brute force" search over all pose space. Because the structures are very simple, the search can be efficiently implemented. The outcome of this computation provides an initialization to the correspondence space search or a more refined pose space search (see Grimson 1990 and Ullman 1996) or, in our case, the more complex deformable template models. In Grimson (1990), a careful analysis of the combinatorics of the Hough transform is carried out in terms of the statistics of the local features. A very appealing and efficient alternative to the Hough transform has recently been proposed in Fleuret and Geman (2001), where a coarse-to-fine *cascade* of detectors is constructed for a treelike decomposition of pose space into finer and finer bins.

The Hough transform, as a method of jump-starting more intensive algorithms, is intuitively very appealing but did not take off as a dominant paradigm in computer vision partly because of the combinatoric problems analyzed in Grimson (1990). Testifying to this is the fact that a significant body of work in the same community did not use this approach for face detection (see, for example, Rowley, Baluja, and Kanade 1998; Sung and Poggio 1998). One reason may be the use of predesigned local features. In chapter 6, we introduce a hierarchy of local-edge arrangements of increasing complexity. Despite being more complex than simple edges, these local features are still very stable on object and quite rare in the background. The features in the model are obtained through training and do not necessarily have a clear semantic interpretation. Sparse object models are then defined as flexible arrangements of a small number of these local features. The construction and training of sparse object models in terms of these local features, and the statistical properties of these features on object and on background are also described in chapter 6.

In chapter 8, an efficient algorithm for detecting such models is presented, where the first step of identifying candidate locations is obtained using the Hough transform. This material is based on work in Amit, Geman, and Jedynak (1998), Amit and Geman (1999), and Amit (2000). The work in Burl, Leung, and Perona (1995) and Burl, Weber, and Perona (1998), is very similar in spirit; however, the features and the statistical models are more complex, and the computation of the detection more intensive.

The dominant view in the computer-vision community is that some form of bottom-up processing involving segmentation is still necessary to jump-start the detection and recognition tasks. In Ullman (1996), a case for this is made in terms of biological processes in the visual system. The point of view put forward here is that one can go a long way with a combination of model-driven detections followed by more-refined processing involving classification and obtaining more-detailed instantiations. This is one of the main conclusions of chapter 6, where we study the statistics of the particular local features employed in the sparse models; of chapter 8, where we implement a version of the Hough transform for initial detection of candidate locations; and of chapter 10, where some ideas on combining object detection and recognition for complex scene analysis are explored.

1.3.3 Rigid versus Nonrigid Objects

Much of the work on object detection is centered around rigid objects. This has led, for example, to detailed analysis of the specific pose space associated with 2D and 3D rigid transformations and their projections (see, for example, Arbter and colleagues 1990, Mundy and Zisserman 1992). There is also an emphasis on complete planar rotation invariance. The rigid nature of the objects has lead to reliance on "predefined features" with labels such as lines, corners, junctions and so on. In recent years, a view-based approach has become widely accepted in which 3D object detection and recognition are treated as 2D problems depending on the particular views of the objects (see Ullman 1996; Riesenhuber and Poggio 2000).

However, even for 2D views of rigid objects, lines and contours or even corners can be ambiguous in the image domain. Moreover, the visual system can detect and recognize rigid objects even if many of the straight lines present on the real object are deformed in the image. The message of chapters 8 and 10 is that all objects should be studied within one framework, based on 2D views, using *nonrigid* 2D models. Views of the object that are substantially different are considered as *different* 2D objects; however, the flexibility (i.e., geometric invariance) introduced in the nonrigid models implies that a *wide range* of views can still be accommodated by one model. This alleviates to some extent the combinatoric problem of the resulting proliferation of 2D objects that need to be modeled, detected, and recognized. Some additional ideas related to this problem are presented in chapter 10.

1.4   Object Recognition

Recognition of isolated objects has been studied extensively in two main contexts: rigid 2D and 3D objects and character recognition. The latter context offers an important test bed for many ideas. Recent extensive reviews can be found in Plamondon and Srihari (2000) and Nagy (2000). The data sets are abundant, different forms of variability are present—rigid for printed characters and nonrigid for handwritten, and one can work with a limited number of classes, say, only the digits, or with large numbers such as all LaTeX symbols, or Chinese characters.

1.4.1   Deformable-Template Models for Object Recognition

The problem of recognizing an image of an isolated object from among several possible classes can be addressed in a Bayesian framework using the deformable-template models. These models have a natural extension to a statistical model for images of the different object classes, once a prior on object classes is determined. The goal is then to compute the Bayes classifier—namely, the class that maximizes the posterior on class, given the data. The deformation parameters are no longer of direct interest but need to be integrated out in order to obtain the posterior on class. This type of computation is very expensive, so that in real applications, one deformation is estimated from *each* of the class templates to best fit the data, and classification is then based on various metrics defined on these deformations. Such a procedure is spelled out in detail in Hastie and Simard (1998). Despite the fact that the distance of the data to each template is computed modulo the deformation, this approach still requires quite careful preprocessing and registration of the images to a standard size. The underlying assumption is that the deformations are small. It also requires explicit modeling of the prototype images, extensive computation at the classification stage, and appears impractical with large numbers of shape classes. A deformable-template-based approach to face recognition is presented in Wiskott and colleagues (1997), although not based on a statistical model. There, the data model is not based directly on the pixel intensities but on local features derived from Gabor filters extracted at multiple scales.

In chapter 9, we present an alternative based on elements of the sparse-detection models. The main tool will be binary classification trees (see Breiman and colleagues 1984), where the splits are defined in terms of flexible arrangements of local features of the same nature as those defining the sparse models. Trees provide a natural mechanism for exploring arrangements of increasing complexity.

Instead of modeling the posterior distribution on deformations and on class, and then computing the posterior on-line, the trees yield partial posteriors conditional on a smaller number of variables, which are obtained off-line during training. Computation during classification is then very fast. An essential element of our approach is to produce multiple randomized classification trees. Individually, the error rates of these trees can be quite large, but when aggregated, a very powerful classifier emerges. The work in chapter 9 is based on Amit and Geman (1997) and Amit, Geman, and Wilder (1997).

1.4.2 Normalization and Registration

In the literature on statistical pattern recognition, it is common to address geometric and photometric variations by preprocessing and normalization. A "standardized" image is produced prior to classification, involving a sequence of operations that brings all images to the same size and then corrects for translation, slant, and rotation. This is not done using some template or model, because the class of the image is unknown. Classification is then performed by one of the standard pattern recognition procedures, based on the gray-level intensities of the standardized image. (For example, penalized discriminant analysis in Hastie, Buja, and Tibshirani 1995, or multilayer neural networks in Bottou and colleagues 1994, or classification trees in Ho, Hull, and Srihari 1994.) Difficulties in generalization are often encountered because the normalization is not robust and does not accommodate nonlinear deformations. This deficiency can only be ameliorated with very large training sets.

An alternative is to define a collection of binary features extracted from the data, such as edges, contours, endings junctions, and so on. The feature/location pairs are collected to make a fixed-size feature vector, which is fed into a standard type of classifier. These features may be designed to be more invariant to geometric deformations than the raw gray-level values, using explicit disjunction (or-ing). Otherwise put, a feature detected at a particular location is "spread" to an entire neighborhood. The features are designed to be photometric invariant, so that no gray-level normalization is required. These matters are investigated in chapter 9.

1.4.3   Geometric Invariants

Another approach, which has been explored in the computer-vision literature, is to search for functions invariant to a family of transformations, such as the affine transformations. Discrimination is possible if the functions have different values for different classes (see, for example, Lamdan, Schwartz, and Wolfson 1988; Forsyth and colleagues 1991; Mundy and Zisserman 1992; Binford and Levitt 1993; Reiss 1993). The explicit introduction of geometric invariance is very appealing and provides an element that is missing in the standard pattern-recognition approaches. The problem, however, is that the invariant functions are defined in terms of precisely located distinguished points on the object. This is not very practical on real gray-level images, or for objects that are deformed nonlinearly. This brings us back to the discussion above regarding rigid versus nonrigid objects. Just as in the case of detection, it is useful to consider shape classification for both categories as one problem. Focusing on invariants associated strictly with rigidity can lead to unstable algorithms. Hence the introduction of looser types of functions—flexible arrangements of local features, which are also explored in chapter 9. With these functions, however, full rotation invariance is lost.

1.5   Scene Analysis: Merging Detection and Recognition

The grand goal of computer vision is to enable the computer to detect and recognize multiple objects in a visual scene. We are still very far from achieving this goal. This is not only a function of computational limitations, it is also a result of the lack of a dominant paradigm agreed upon by most of the research community. As indicated earlier, one paradigm assumes bottom-up image segmentation as a precursor to any high-level processing. At the other extreme are compositional and generative models (see Mumford 1994; Hinton and colleagues 1995; Bienenstock, Geman, and Potter 1997; Geman, Potter, and Chi 1998), where people attempt to provide a comprehensive statistical model of entire scenes, both from the point of view of the components generating the scene—namely, priors on complex scenes—and complex data models of the images, given a particular configuration of objects. The view is that local ambiguities can be resolved only in the framework of a comprehensive explanation of the data. These models appear diametrically opposed to the segmentation models. The only way to unambiguously determine the boundary of an object is by identifying the object, its pose, all the objects in its neighborhood, and their respective positions. Conceptually, these models are appealing in their attempt to pose the scene analysis problem in a comprehensive Bayesian framework. Regrettably, they are extremely challenging on all levels: formulating the prior models, the data models, estimating the relevant parameters, and ultimately computing the optimal interpretation given the image data.

Chapter 10 is an initial exploration into a possible middle path between these two extremes, based on a combination of the sparse-detection models described in chapter 8 and the recognition algorithms of chapter 9. Local features in the image are not grouped in a bottom-up manner as in standard segmentation; rather, the grouping is an outcome of the detection of a particular model, and comes with an estimated pose and some additional instantiation parameters. These model-driven groupings of local features can be viewed as elements of a compositional model. Recent implementations of compositional models have used very gradual compositions, from edgelets to lines or curves to small combinations of these, and so on. The compositions proposed here are very coarse and there is a direct jump from the local to the global model.

If the detection models are created to be less specific, either by directly training on a collection of classes or by training on one class and then using lower thresholds, they define object clusters, as opposed to being dedicated to one particular class. This means that classification must follow detection. Detecting instances of several coarse models and subsequently classifying them is a very efficient way to obtain a relabeling of the image into detections (involving some pose parameters) and class labels. This labeling in no way provides a final scene interpretation. There could be multiple labels at the same location, overlapping detections, and so on. From the point of view of the compositional and generative models, this can be taken as a crude first pass, which provides the higher-level models with multiple possible scene interpretations for evaluation. In chapter 10, we discuss possible strategies for generating this basic map of labeled detections. How to then analyze this information and produce coherent scene interpretations is beyond the scope of this book.

1.6   Neural Network Architectures

There have been a number of attempts to formulate parallel network architectures for higher-level vision tasks such as detection. Some examples are the work in Fukushima (1986) and Fukushima and Wake (1991), Olshausen, Anderson, and Van Essen (1993), and recent models, such as Riesenhuber and Poggio (1999). Each of these models touches upon certain important aspects of the problem. In Fukushima and Wake (1991), hard wiring of invariance is achieved through or-ing or *spreading,* which is an important component of the algorithms described in this book. However, the proposed network depends too heavily on a long sequence of processing layers and on learning more and more complex features. In Olshausen, Anderson, and Van Essen (1993), mechanisms for shifting data from the periphery to the center for further processing are studied, but the training of classifiers or implementing object detection as a component of visual selection are not discussed. In Riesenhuber and Poggio (1999), invariant recognition is achieved through a combination of or-ing as in Fukushima and Wake (1991), generalized to continuous variables through a MAX (maximization) operation, and predefined pair-wise conjunctions of features. The MAX operation is taken to an extreme where all information on the relative locations of features is lost at the highest stage. This is problematic when dealing with even simple data sets such as the NIST (National Institute of Standards and Technology) handwritten character data set. Moreover, this approach cannot produce accurate location information in a detection problem. In chapter 11, we explore how object representations and classifiers, trained using the principles of Hebbian learning, in a central memory module, are able to drive visual selection over the entire scene and at a wide range of scales, as well as classify isolated objects or those present at a selected location. The material ties together the work in Amit (2000) and Amit and Mascaro (2001) into one comprehensive system.

2 Detection and Recognition: Overview of Models

In this chapter, we present an overview of the object-detection and object-recognition models and introduce some notation that will help unify the ideas developed in subsequent chapters.

We will be dealing with gray-level images. An image is defined on a grid L of points $x \in L$, also referred to as pixels, to each of which is assigned a gray-level value $I(x)$. We also use the terms *pixel values* or *intensity values* for $I(x)$. The term *scene* refers to a complex image containing more than one object. At times, the term *image* will refer to the underlying grid as opposed to the gray-level values—for example, when talking about the "size of an image" or "points in the image." By *size of an image,* we mean the size of the grid L on which it is defined. This can vary greatly even for images of an individual object. An image of a face can be as small as 16×16 pixels and as large as 500×500 or more. It is useful then to introduce the notion of a reference grid G of fixed size on which prototypical images of objects are presented. We also use the term *image surface,* which refers to the surface defined by the graph of the function $I(x), x \in L$.

2.1 A Bayesian Approach to Detection

Consider the example illustrated in figure 2.1, where a prototype $\mathcal{E}$ is shown together with a number of deformations, all of which are considered instances of an $\mathcal{E}$. Next is a synthetic scene with an instance of a deformed $\mathcal{E}$ present among other objects. Our goal is to detect instances of the symbol $\mathcal{E}$ in such a scene. How do we go about formulating models and developing the associated algorithms?

Start with an ordered sequence of *model points* $Z = (z_1, \ldots, z_n)$, also called the *template,* defined on the reference grid G. *Detection* is defined as finding a map from

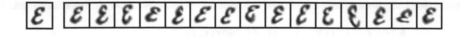

Figure 2.1   (Left) Prototype $\mathcal{E}$. (Right) A sample of randomly deformed $\mathcal{E}$'s. (Bottom) A scene with an $\mathcal{E}$.

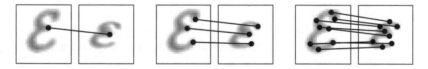

Figure 2.2   Three templates for an $\mathcal{E}$ overlaid on the prototype with a map to an instance of an $\mathcal{E}$.

these model points on the reference grid into a set of points in the image. Because the model points are ordered, the map is uniquely determined by an ordered set of points $\theta = (\theta_1, \ldots, \theta_n)$ in the image, which is also called an *instantiation* of the model. This is illustrated in figure 2.2 for three models of an $\mathcal{E}$ of increasing complexity. The templates are shown overlayed on the prototype image and are mapped into another image of an $\mathcal{E}$.

In some cases, the model points are chosen as points of interest or landmarks on a prototype image—for example, the three "endings" in the second model of figure 2.2. Intuitively, a point of interest is a salient location on the prototype where the image viewed as a surface has some interesting local topography and is not simply planar. In other cases, model points are chosen according to certain statistical properties of the image data in their neighborhood, evaluated on a training population of images of the object, which are presented in the reference scale on the reference grid. Models will vary in complexity in terms of the number of points—the most complex model involving *all* points on the object. An instantiation of a simple model does not provide the information required for determining the instantiation of a more complex model. Knowing the approximate location of the landmark represented by the point in the left-hand model of figure 2.2 does not tell us where to find the other points in the other two models. However, information on the instantiation of the simple model can *restrict* the range of possible instantiations for the more complex models.

2.1.1   The Prior

The model is incomplete without two additional components. The first component involves the definition of the set Θ of *admissible* instantiations. Through the definition of the set Θ, we determine the degree of invariance expected of the associated detector—for example, the range of scales and rotations the detector is expected to cover. It will be convenient to define elements of Θ in terms of a translation coupled with some instantiation around the origin. Specifically, $\Theta^{(0)}$ will denote a collection of admissible instantiations more or less centered at the origin. Each instantiation $\theta \in \Theta$ is of the form $\theta_i = (x + \theta_i')$, $i = 1, \ldots, n$, where x is a location in the image and $\theta' \in \Theta^{(0)}$. Note that x and θ' are *not* uniquely determined by θ. Because we have no prior constraints on locations x, all the constraints are defined on $\Theta^{(0)}$.

A useful example of such a set is given by

$$\Theta^{(0)} = \{(\theta_1, \ldots, \theta_n) : \theta_i = Az_i, A \in \mathcal{A}\}$$

where $\mathcal{A}$ is some subset of linear transformations. Here, we accept only configurations that can be obtained by a linear map from $\mathcal{A}$ applied to the model configuration. A more-general set of constraints is defined as

$$\Theta^{(0)} = \{(\theta_1, \ldots, \theta_n) : \theta_i = vAz_i, v \in \Upsilon, A \in \mathcal{A}\} \tag{2.1}$$

where Υ is some prescribed set of nonlinear deformations in the neighborhood of the identity map. A linear map is applied to the model points and the result is perturbed by a nonlinear deformation $v \in \Upsilon$. A simpler extension of the first definition has the form

$$\Theta^{(0)} = \{(\theta_1, \ldots, \theta_n) : \theta_i \in Az_i + C, A \in \mathcal{A}\} \tag{2.2}$$

where C is some neighborhood of the origin. For C sufficiently large, this last set of admissible instantiations *contains* the second; there are no constraints on the relative locations of the points as long as they are in the proper regions.

A *prior* distribution $P(\theta)$ on Θ determines which instantiations are more likely and which are less. The role of the prior is to penalize certain deviations from the model instantiation defined by the template. It is usually hard to precisely describe the distribution on instantiations, or to reliably estimate it from training data. It is therefore important to define "loose" priors, which do not risk precluding plausible instantiations.

2.1.2   The Data Model and the Posterior

The second component of the model is a description of the image data $I(x), x \in L$, given the object is present in the scene and the specified landmarks on the object are at a particular instantiation θ. Because of the variable nature of image formation, this description comes in the form of a conditional distribution, often called the *likelihood* or *data term*. Given a particular instantiation, there is a range of possible associated images. Lighting can change to produce different gray levels, various noise effects can occur, parts of the object may be occluded. Moreover, even though the instantiation of the model points is fixed, the local and global shape of the object can still vary. For example, many instances of the $\mathcal{E}$ can have the three "endings" at the same location.

The model assigns a probability distribution to the set of possible images given a particular instantiation. It is often easier to describe this probability on *local transforms* of the image data, which are invariant to some of the gray-level variations just mentioned (i.e., transforms that are *photometrically invariant*). The data transform $\hat{I}(x)$ at pixel x will be a vector of local features—namely, functions applied to the gray-level intensities in the neighborhood of x.

$$\hat{I}(x) = (X_1(x), \ldots, X_J(x))$$

$$X_j(x) = X_j\big(I_{N_t(x)}\big), \quad j = 1, \ldots, J \tag{2.3}$$

where $I_{N_t(x)}$ is the image data in the $t \times t$ neighborhood of x, and X_j is a function of that data. In most cases described here, X_j will be binary, and we say that X_j is *on* at x if $X_j(x) = 1$. See, for example, the data transform applied to a sample $\mathcal{E}$ in figure 2.4 next. Four operators are applied at each point. The response of a feature is 1 if the image data in a neighborhood of a point corresponds to a line at a certain range of orientations.

Having chosen a particular data transform, write the likelihood or conditional probability of $\hat{I}(x), x \in L$, given an object is present at instantiation θ, as $P(\hat{I}(x), x \in L \mid \theta)$. In most cases, we will assume that *conditional* on the presence of an object at instantiation θ, the transformed data at the different pixels is *independent*, so that the data term has a simple product form.

$$P(\hat{I}(x), x \in L \mid \theta) = \prod_{x \in L} P(\hat{I}(x) \mid \theta) \tag{2.4}$$

where we emphasize that the distribution $P(\hat{I}(x) \mid \theta)$ could be different for different locations x. The product distributions are usually not very accurate models of the data; however, they allow for efficient computations and, properly used, lead to very useful results.

Once a prior distribution and a likelihood are defined, Bayes' rule allows us to form a posterior distribution on the set of instantiations, given the observed data.

$$P(\theta \mid \hat{I}(x), x \in L) = P(\hat{I}(x), x \in L \mid \theta) P(\theta) \cdot C \qquad (2.5)$$

where C is a constant that does not depend on θ. We typically work with the negative log-posterior, which up to a constant term is given by

$$J(\theta) = -\log P(\theta) - \log P(\hat{I}(x), x \in L \mid \theta) \qquad (2.6)$$

The computational task is to find one or more *minima* of this cost function (hence the use of negative log-posterior)—namely, instantiations that are highly likely given the observed data. Intimately related to the formulation of the model are the computational tools employed to perform this minimization. Chapters 3–8 describe a collection of such models and the associated computational algorithms. In the simple example shown in figures 2.1 and 2.2, the instances of the object are produced through smooth deformations of a single prototype image. However, for real objects in real images this is rarely the case. Consider faces, for example: One can hardly imagine producing all faces using smooth deformations of one or even a small number of prototypes. More detailed instantiations may require specific models for subclasses. Finally, we expect to detect instantiations even if part of the object is hidden or occluded, and this needs to be somehow incorporated in the data models.

In some of the algorithms described below, the underlying assumption is that exactly one object is present in the image, and finding a minimum of the cost function using some optimization procedure, such as gradient descent or dynamic programming, will lead to the instantiation. When more than one object can be present, with a limit of say, K, a more-complex model is needed, involving a prior on

$$\bigcup_{k=1}^{K} \Theta^k$$

where Θ^k is the set of k-tuples of instantiations from Θ. This becomes practical only with the sparse models described below (see chapter 6), where a very loose prior is used with no constraints on the relative locations of the objects. In some cases, more information is available and more structure can be introduced into the prior assumptions on the configurations of multiple objects in the scene. Such matters are beyond the scope of this book.

2.1.3   Statistical Models Versus Cost Functions

Those less familiar with Bayesian modeling can interpret the first term of equation 2.6 as a penalty on deviations from the model instantiation and the second term as a measure of how well the instantiation fits the data. Often in the literature, models are formulated in the form of such a cost function without bothering about the statistical setup. This can work, yet it is hard to ignore the inherent stochastic nature and variability of both the object presentation and the image formation. The same exact physical scene, captured at two consecutive moments by the same camera, can have quite variable gray-level maps simply due to a slight shift in lighting caused by the movement of the tree outside the window.

The advantage of statistical modeling emerges in the formulation of the data term. We are forced to model the distribution of the *entire* image data or transformed image data given an instantiation. This creates a framework in which a proper weighting of different instantiations is possible. The introduction of probabilities into the modeling process forces us to systematically consider the relative weights of different events. In some models that are directly formulated in terms of a cost function, different parts of the image data are used to evaluate different instantiations. This is problematic when it comes to comparing their cost. Finally, the statistical formulation provides a natural framework for estimating the unknown parameters of the model.

On the other hand, it is important to stay faithful to the principle of Occam's razor, and insist on simplicity and transparency of the models. Typically, training data are not really random samples from the populations, and complex statistical models will yield highly biased parameter estimates that do not generalize. Especially with the rise of Monte Carlo–based simulation and Expectation Maximization methods, there is a sense that anything can be estimated. This can be quite misleading. For this reason, most of the statistical models presented below are simple, and the parameters are for the most part simple proportions of individual binary variables.

2.2   Overview of Object-Detection Models

The different detection algorithms described in this book involve variations in the definition of the template—that is, the sequence of model points Z; the set of admissible instantiations Θ and the prior distribution defined on that set; the image transforms $\hat{I}$, together with data model (i.e., the likelihood of the data given an element $\theta \in \Theta$); methods for estimating relevant parameters; and, finally, the computational algorithm for maximizing the posterior. These components are very tightly interlinked. The type of algorithm chosen may constrain the types of data models as well as the definitions of the sets Z and Θ. Typically, the set Θ will cover a limited range of scales, say, $\pm 25\%$, around the reference scale determined by the reference grid; this is the *smallest* scale at which the object is detected. For significantly larger scales, the image is down sampled and the same procedure is implemented.

2.2.1 Deformable Models

These models involve a rather large and dense set Z, and a set $\Theta^{(0)}$, defined using some variation on equation 2.1. The intuition is that a linear transformation of the model is smoothly deformed to produce the instantiation of the object. The set Υ is defined through some finite dimensional parameterization of nonlinear deformations of the set Z, and a prior is defined that penalizes large deviations from the identity map.

The initial location and linear map from $A \in \mathcal{A}$ are provided by the user. This defines an initial instantiation $\theta_{0,i} = x_0 + Az_i, i = 1, \ldots, n$. The aim is to find the instantiation $\theta \in \Theta$, which maximizes the posterior using relaxation methods or other optimization methods in a neighborhood of θ_0.

Deformable Contours

In chapter 3, the set of points Z forms a closed circle in G, or some other closed contour with a specific shape. The set $\Theta^{(0)}$ is a family of smooth perturbations of the model contour. Optimization is done through gradient-descent methods. Under the data model, the pixel values are conditionally independent given the instantiation of the contour—one distribution for the interior of the contour, and another for the exterior. An illustration is given in figure 2.3. The left panel shows the points in the

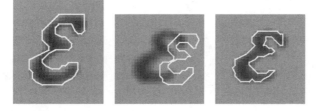

Figure 2.3   (Left) A contour template for the $\mathcal{E}$ (the points of Z) overlaid on prototype. (Middle) Model curve placed in image at initial location. (Right) Final instantiation.

set Z forming a closed curve overlayed on the prototype image. The middle panel shows the initial contour placed in the data image and the right panel shows the final instantiation identified by the algorithm.

Deformable Curves

In chapter 4, the points in Z define an open curve and $\Theta^{(0)}$ represents deformations of the model curve. A prior $P(\theta)$ on $\Theta^{(0)}$ penalizes irregular deviations from the model. The data term is given in terms of a collection of binary local features detecting "ridges" of the image surface at a range of orientations. These are defined in terms of simple comparisons of pixel intensity differences and are highly invariant to photometric transformations (figure 2.4). Under the likelihood model, the binary features are conditionally independent at all locations in the image given the instantiation of the curve. There is a probability associated to finding certain features at certain locations on the curve, and a lower probability of finding these features anywhere else in the image. These probabilities can be estimated from data.

Global optimization over a well-defined neighborhood of the initial instantiation is achieved either by dynamic programming or with a tree-based algorithm in certain cases. Figure 2.4 provides an illustration. In the top left panel is the data image of a deformed $\mathcal{E}$. The next four panels on the top show the locations where the four local "ridge" features are found in the image. In other words, these represent the transformed

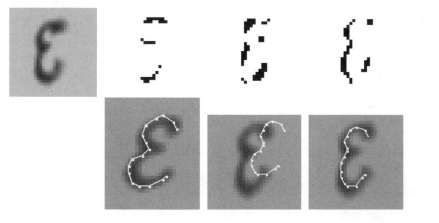

Figure 2.4   (Top) An instance of a deformed $\mathcal{E}$, and the data transform consisting of four oriented ridge detectors. (Bottom) Left: A curve template for the $\mathcal{E}$ (the points of Z) overlaid on the prototype. Middle: The initial curve in the image. Right: Final instantiation.

data $\hat{I}_1, \ldots, \hat{I}_4$. The bottom left panel shows the template points Z overlaid on the prototype image. The middle panel shows the initial curve placed in the data image and the right panel shows the final instantiation identified by the algorithm.

Deformable Images

In chapter 5, Z is the entire reference grid, and $\Theta^{(0)}$ is defined through a finite dimensional parameterization of deformations of the reference grid. The prior is used to penalize irregular nonsmooth deformations. Two data models are discussed. A Gaussian data model simply uses a prototype image of the object and assumes that every image in the class is obtained by first warping the prototype image (as, for example, in figure 2.1) and then adding independent Gaussian noise. *No model for data off the object is provided.* This is the classical image deformation model found in the literature.

The second model, the Bernoulli data model, uses transformed image data defined in terms of binary oriented edge type features, which, like the ridge features, are also defined in terms of comparisons of pixel intensity differences. In training, we identify the probabilities of each edge type at each point in the reference grid, assuming an instance of the object is present at the reference scale and location. There is a lower bound on these probabilities determined by the general density of edges in generic images. There are eight oriented edge types and hence eight probability maps defined on the reference grid. Conditional on a deformation θ, we assume that the edges in the image occur independently according to the deformed probability maps. Optimization in both cases is done with gradient-descent methods.

In figure 2.5, the prototype image is shown in the upper left panel. No points are marked because every point in the reference grid is in the set Z. The upper right panel is the data image. The bottom left panel shows the instantiation obtained by the algorithm in the form of a vector field. Every point in the reference grid is mapped according to the arrow attached to it. The bottom right panel shows the prototype image deformed according to the identified instantiation and should be compared to the data image above it. The Gaussian data model was used in this experiment.

2.2.2   Global Detection with Sparse Models

Sparse models are defined in terms of a smaller set Z and a data transform $\hat{I}$, involving binary local features that are more complex than simple oriented edges. We mainly

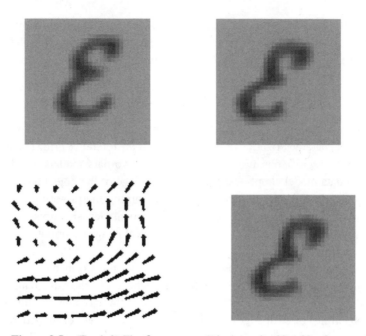

Figure 2.5   (Top left) The $\mathcal{E}$ prototype. Z is the entire 32×32 reference grid. (Top right) The data image. (Bottom left) Vector field describing instantiation. Each point on reference grid is mapped into some point in the image. (Bottom right) Warping of prototype image according to detected instantiation.

make use of *local-edge arrangements*. There is typically a different local feature X_i associated to each model point $z_i \in Z$. This is in contrast to models discussed earlier involving a small number of generic binary features. Again, the features are assumed independent, given the object instantiation. On the background, the local features are of much lower density than oriented edge features, because they involve local conjunctions defined in terms of these edge features. However, the probability of occurrence on particular parts of the object is still relatively high. The object model now has the form of a *flexible arrangement of binary local features*. The degree of flexibility is determined by the set $\Theta^{(0)}$. The conditional independence assumption in this case becomes somewhat more realistic and greatly facilitates the computation of global detections with *no initialization required*. The types of data transforms used to define the local features, methods for training the models, and an analysis of the statistics of the local features on and off the object are presented in chapter 6. Two alternatives for computing the most likely instantiations are provided in chapters 7 and 8.

Sparse Model Detection: Dynamic Programming

In chapter 7, Θ and the prior $P(\theta)$ are defined in terms of constraints and penalties on the spatial arrangements of the points $\theta_1, \ldots, \theta_n$. The constraints are invariant to scale and translation. This is done in terms of relative locations of triples of points in θ. The constraints have a certain decomposable or "peelable" structure, which permits maximization of the posterior through dynamic programming. Constraints on larger subsets of points are possible but greatly increase the computational load. The assumption in this case is that only one instance of the object is present in the image and that given the instantiation is θ, feature X_i is found at θ_i with probability 1. All locations where local feature X_i is found are recorded in a list $S_i, i = 1, \ldots, n$. This is the input to a dynamic programming algorithm that finds the arrangement $\theta \in \Theta$ such that $\theta_i \in S_i, i = 1, \ldots, n$, with highest posterior value.

Sparse Model Detection: Counting

The previous model may be unstable. Even if the object is present at instantiation θ, not all features will be found at their respective points either due to various noise effects or occlusion. In a more realistic model, the probabilities of the individual features on the object are significantly lower than 1. Under simplified assumptions on the probabilities of the features on and off the object, finding instantiations with a high posterior reduces to finding admissible subinstantiations $\theta_{i_1}, \ldots, \theta_{i_m}$, where $m > \tau$ for some $\tau > 0$, and $X_{i_j}(\theta_{i_j}) = 1, j = 1, \ldots, m$. By *admissible subinstantiation* we mean a subsequence for which there exists some element $\hat{\theta} \in \Theta$, such that $\theta_{i_j} = \hat{\theta}_{i_j}, j = 1, \ldots, m$. This approach also allows us to find multiple instances of the object in the image and is studied extensively in chapter 8. The computation is done in two stages, using a coarse-to-fine approach. In the first step, candidate locations are detected using a much looser set of constraints $\Theta_p^{(0)}$, which contains $\Theta^{(0)}$ and which has the form of a product set. Each local feature is constrained relative to a center x, irrespective of the locations of the other features. The structure of this set of constraints allows for very efficient detection of candidate locations using a simple *counting* operation, also known as the Hough transform (Hough 1962). In the second step, at each candidate location—again using a simple counting operation on detected local features—we decide whether to keep the location and simultaneously estimate pose parameters (i.e., scale, translation, and other linear transformations) and identify a full instantiation of the model. The details of this approach are provided in chapter 8.

A sparse model is shown in figure 2.6, consisting of 20 points overlaid on the prototype—top left panel. In the bottom left panel, we show a graphical representation

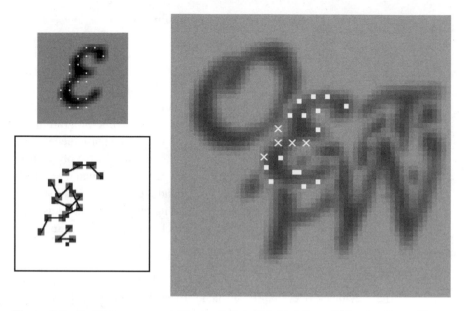

Figure 2.6 (Left) A sparse model for the $\mathcal{E}$. Top: Points of Z overlaid on prototype. Bottom: The edge arrangements corresponding to some of the features in the model. (Right) A detected instantiation, the dots correspond to detected features and the x's to features not found at the expected location.

of seven of the twenty local features, which are defined through local edge arrangements. On the right, we show a scene and one identified instantiation of the sparse model. Note that only a subset of the appropriate features was found, the ones that were not detected are marked as x, and their location is obtained using the estimated pose parameters.

We reiterate that the sparse model represents the object at the smallest scale at which it will be detected. For much larger scales, the image is subsampled and the same algorithm is applied again.

From Deformable Models to Sparse Models

The sparse models can be viewed as coarse approximations to the more-detailed deformable models. In each region, instead of trying to describe the deformation of the template that best fits the data within the family of allowed local deformations, we define a binary local feature that is invariant with respect to these allowable deformations. Loosely speaking, if the local feature is present at some location on the object, then it will also be present at the corresponding location for any admissible deformation of the object. The local feature becomes a rough characterization of that part of the object within the range of admissible deformations. Only if a sufficient number of such features is found in an admissible configuration somewhere in the image is it possible to find a more detailed deformation of the template at that location. This relationship is further discussed in chapter 6.

The reader may have noted that the ordering of the models is not consistent with their logical "algorithmic" ordering. Indeed, the most sensible thing to do is to implement the sparse model first and thus obtain an initial point for the more intensive deformable models described earlier. We show examples of this in chapter 8. The particular ordering here is chosen for historical reasons—deformable contours and deformable images have been around for quite a while and are actively used in many applications. Also, these algorithms present a natural entrance to the field of high-level vision and confront the user with certain problems that help motivate the sparse algorithms.

2.3   Object Recognition

Detection can be viewed as a two-class classification problem. For each possible instantiation, decide if the object is present or not. Namely, at each instantiation, classify *object* or *not-object*. On the other hand, we are also interested in classification among several classes—for example, recognizing images of isolated characters. We assume the image contains only one object but do not know the class. One possibility is to train models for each of the objects, run each one on the image, and find which fits best according to some criterion. This is a difficult path. Some of the models are quite crude and although quite successful in distinguishing between an object and generic background, they may get confused when distinguishing between similar objects. Other models may be more refined but are computationally intensive, and running the associated detection algorithm for each object class would be inefficient.

The alternative is to directly train a classifier based on examples from all the classes. The main difference in training here, compared to training object models for detection, is that now samples from all classes are used simultaneously, and training explicitly identifies properties that discriminate between classes, as opposed to simply creating representations of the individual classes. Classification trees will serve as the classifier of choice. The basic predictors used in growing the classification trees are arrangements of local features, similar in nature to the sparse models. As before, arrangements are not rigid; rather, the locations of the features are constrained in certain regions, either defined absolutely on the reference grid and called *absolute arrangements,* or in terms of relations between features and called *relational arrangements.* This flexibility can be controlled and determines the degree of invariance of the classifier to geometric deformations. In contrast to the detection models, information regarding the *absence* of certain features from certain regions is used as well.

The queries corresponding to deeper nodes involve more-complex arrangements, starting at the top node of the tree with simple queries involving a single or a pair of features. Thus the trees are using models of increasing complexity to recursively partition the population among the different shape classes. All data points at a particular node share some arrangement of some complexity. As an illustration, we show in figure 2.7 a number of $\mathcal{E}$s, all of which reached the same depth-10 node in a classification tree, together with some other symbols that reached the same node. On each image, the instantiation of the relational arrangement associated to that node is shown. The lines connect features that were constrained relative to each other. This tree was made using eight simple oriented edge features as the elements of the arrangements. The observed arrangements are similar to instantiations of a sparse-detection model, although the constraints on the relative locations are defined somewhat differently. The type of edge features at each point in the arrangement is not specified.

Training involves recursively choosing a query at each node of the tree that optimally splits the training data present in that node. A query will simply ask whether a particular feature is present in a certain region, either defined absolutely on the

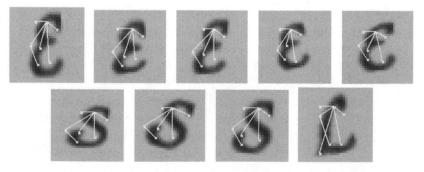

Figure 2.7   Images which reached the same depth 10 node in a decision tree based on eight oriented edge features. The instantiation of the associated arrangement is overlaid on the image. The lines connect features which were constrained relative to each other.

reference grid, or relative to other local features that have already been found in all images present at that particular node. With large numbers of feature types and possible regions, there are many thousands of possible queries at each node. Only a small random sample of these is entertained, and the best query is chosen in terms of some purity criterion on the empirical distribution on class. This randomization allows us to use the same training set to produce multiple trees that are different. Aggregating the information from the multiple trees leads to classification rates by far superior to those of an individual tree produced from the same training data. These issues are discussed in chapter 9.

2.4   Scene Analysis: Combining Detection and Recognition

The detection algorithms we have outlined assume we know what object to find in the image. However, often we are presented with a scene with only very general notions of what we expect to find there. In principle, we could develop a detector for each possible object class and run each such detector on the entire scene. This would of course be highly inefficient. On the other hand, if we are presented with an image with a more or less isolated object, we can train classifiers to recognize the object even from among hundreds of classes. The question is how to obtain isolated objects from a complex scene?

The traditional answer in computer vision assumes some form of bottom-up image segmentation that tries to identify regions of interest—that is, regions corresponding to objects—using no high-level model information, solely based on local information and very generic constraints on the properties of the regions. In chapter 10, we explore an alternative approach, where detection always precedes recognition. Detectors are produced for object clusters from several classes. For example, we may lower somewhat the detection threshold τ in the sparse model for the $\mathcal{E}$s and find that a large fraction of $\mathcal{B}$s, $\mathcal{C}$s, $\mathcal{G}$s, and so on are detected as well. Another possibility is to use nodes of a classification tree. So, for example, a sparse model would be trained for all images in the node represented in figure 2.7.

Using the detected pose, the data in the neighborhood of the detection is registered to a reference grid. This is first done on training images to produce classifiers among detected classes. Then, in a general scene, the data around each detected pose is registered and subsequently classified. The idea is illustrated in figure 2.8 for the cluster of deformed script-style LaTeX symbols hit by the $\mathcal{E}$ detector. Each hit of this detector in the scene is subsequently classified. The main point is that the first step in

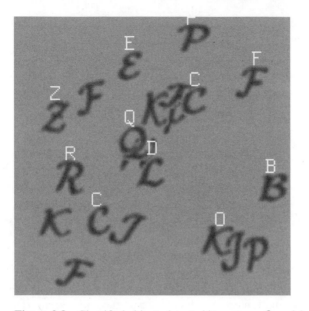

Figure 2.8   Classified objects detected by a sparse $\mathcal{E}$ model.

analyzing a scene is always an efficient counting detector, which provides candidate poses for objects and hence input data for the classifier.

The detector may be quite coarse in that it is not designed to pick out a very specific class and may result in a larger number of hits. However, it is still guiding the low-level processing of the image in terms of a particular set of more complex local features that need to be extracted in a particular configuration.

2.5   Network Implementations

The specific characteristics of the counting detector for the sparse model—the use of binary local features and the simple counting operations involved—make it a natural candidate for trying to model detection in a parallel network of neurons. In chapter 11, we show that both learning and detection can be implemented in such a framework using *minimal* assumptions on the complexity of the units—binary neurons—and the connections between them—bounded positive synapses. The input into the system is the oriented edges detected in the image, which are then processed in local feature layers that detect simple two-edge arrangements. An object-detection task implies evoking a specific object model in a central module. This causes certain intermediate layers to be primed. These also receive input from the local feature layers and can be viewed as the junction between the bottom-up information coming from the local feature layers and the top-down information coming from the central module. Summing the activities in these intermediate layers produces the candidate locations for the object. Training is achieved using simple Hebbian learning on the connections between an "abstract" layer, in which randomly selected populations of units code for each class, and the central module. This architecture does not involve realistic neurons with realistic time dynamics. However, it does offer a global model for how the visual system can learn object representations in a central module and then somehow distribute the information to the entire system in order to compute detections in large scenes. In this framework, we are also able to integrate a classification system that is also trained using Hebbian learning on connections feeding from a copy of the local feature layer and into the abstract layer. Moreover, we show how detection can produce the gating of attention to the selected location, enabling more detailed classification of the data at that location.

3   1D Models: Deformable Contours

Many problems in image analysis require the detection of the closed boundary of an object. In medical imaging, one might need to delineate the boundary of a tumor in an X-ray or MRI image, the boundary of a ventricle of the heart in an angiogram, or any other anatomy of interest. In biological research, boundaries of various microscopic organisms imaged using a variety of techniques may be of interest.

In chapter 1, we discussed possible drawbacks of a purely bottom-up image segmentation approach to determining the regions in the image occupied by objects. A partial solution is to introduce global constraints—in particular, the notion that the "ideal" contour is closed and continuous at all points. One natural idea is then to place a closed contour on the image and allow it to smoothly deform according to some data-driven criterion so as to adjust to the boundary of the desired object present in the image. If the deformations preserve the continuity of the contour and do not tear it apart, these properties will automatically be inherited by the final state, even if parts of the target contour are occluded or missing in the image. Moreover, if the initial contour has a characteristic shape representing some prior knowledge regarding the shape of the target contour, then it is possible to preserve this shape with appropriate deformations. This approach is appealing in its simplicity and is applicable in many contexts. The computations involve gradient-descent techniques, which in this case are quite fast because of the one-dimensional nature of the problem. However, there are serious limitations in the sensitivity to initialization and in parameter settings, as will be illustrated below.

3.1   Inside-Outside Model

In terms of the notation defined in chapter 2, the sequence of model points $Z = (z_1, \ldots, z_n)$ defines a closed contour on the reference grid. This sequence of points is also called the *template*. Because optimization is done with gradient-descent methods, formulating the problem in the continuum facilitates the variational analysis. Thus we consider the points in Z as a discrete sampling of a closed continuous curve $z(t), t \in [0, 1]$, at points $0 = t_0 < t_1 < \cdots < t_n = 1$—that is, $z_i = z(t_i)$, $i = 0, \ldots, n$, with $z_0 = z_n$. Instantiations $\theta \in \Theta$ will similarly be viewed as a discrete sampling of a curve $\theta(t)$ at the same time points—that is, $\theta_i = \theta(t_i), i = 1, \ldots, n$. We abuse notation and use θ to denote both the continuous curve and the discrete instantiation in the image. The deformations of the initial contour $z(t)$ can be described as a parameterized family of continuous contours denoted $\theta(t, u) = (\theta_1(t, u), \theta_2(t, u))$, $t \in [0, 1], u \in \mathcal{U}$, with $\mathcal{U}$ a finite dimensional parameter space. Consequently, the set of instantiations is given by $\Theta = \{\theta : \theta_i = \theta(t_i, u), i = 1, \ldots, n, u \in \mathcal{U}\}$. For each u, the entire contour is denoted $\theta(u)$, and the template contour $z(t) = \theta(t, u_z), t \in [0, 1]$, for some $u_z \in \mathcal{U}$. The curves are assumed oriented counterclockwise, and $\theta_{in}(u)$ denotes the points inside the curve, $\theta_{out}(u)$ the points outside.

We employ the statistical approach outlined in chapter 2. A prior $P(u)$ on $\mathcal{U}$ will assign higher probability to smooth contours that are close to the template contour. The likelihood model will assume that given the contour $\theta(u)$ the pixel intensities inside the contour are independent with distribution $f_{in}(I(x); \eta_{in})$ and the pixel intensities outside the contour are independent with distribution $f_{out}(I(x); \eta_{out})$. First we describe ways to parameterize the contours using orthonormal bases of functions, in particular the periodic Daubechies wavelet basis. The parameters of interest are the coefficients of the contour in this basis. We describe a prior on these coefficients and the likelihood model and obtain a posterior. The negative log-posterior yields a cost function on the coefficients which can be differentiated, allowing for minimization using variants of gradient descent. We then show how the wavelet basis is particularly suited for a coarse-to-fine version of gradient descent. We end with a method to estimate the parameters η_{in}, η_{out} on-line together with the computation of the contour.

3.1.1   Contour Parameterization

A general way to parameterize the contours, which allows us to control their smoothness and control the degree of departure from the template contour, is to separately expand the two components θ_1, θ_2 in a basis of functions $\psi_k(t), k = 0, \ldots, d$ on the interval $[0, 1]$, truncated at some level d. An additional convenience of this parameterization is that it naturally defines a continuous curve defined for all t using a finite number of coefficients. The parameters $u_1 = (u_{1,0}, \ldots, u_{1,d})$ and $u_2 = (u_{2,0}, \ldots, u_{2,d})$

are the basis coefficients. Thus the contours are expressed as

$$
\theta_q(t, u_q) = \sum_{k=0}^{d} u_{q,k} \psi_k(t), \quad \text{and the template } z_q(t) = \theta_q(t, u_z) = \sum_{k=0}^{d} u_{z,q,k} \psi_k(t)
$$

$$(3.1)$$

for $q = 1, 2$, and we assume that $\mathcal{U} = R^{2d}$. This is called a *spectral parameterization* as opposed to a *spatial parameterization,* which directly provides the locations of the points. Different bases of functions can be used depending on the specific application. Standard basis families such as the Fourier basis or wavelets are useful because the particular information conveyed by the coefficients is well understood. Furthermore, there are numerically efficient algorithms for finding the coefficients of a function with respect to these bases.

Wavelets

In the experiments shown here, we use a Daubechies wavelet basis (Daubechies 1988). For convenience, we adopt periodic wavelets. Such bases can be organized in a pyramid with 2^{s-1} functions at each level $s = 1, \ldots, S$. At the top levels, the functions are smooth and supported on a large portion of the interval. The associated coefficients convey information on large-scale properties of the target function. Lower down in the pyramid, the basis functions have smaller support, and the associated coefficients convey local information regarding the target function.

More formally, taking $d = 2^S - 1$, the periodic wavelets on the unit interval are indexed by two parameters $\psi_{s,\ell}, s = 1, \ldots, S$ and $\ell = 0, \ldots, 2^{s-1} - 1$, where s denotes the level in the pyramid. The constant function is denoted $\psi_{0,0}$. At a given level s, the functions $\psi_{s,\ell}$ are shifts of the function $\psi_{s,0}$, covering the entire unit interval:

$$
\psi_{s,\ell}(t) = \psi_{s,0}\big(t - 2^{-(s-1)}\ell\big), \quad \ell = 0, \ldots, 2^{s-1} - 1
$$

Furthermore, depending on the wavelet type, there exists some $\bar{s} > 1$ such that for $s \geq \bar{s}$ we can write

$$
\psi_{s,0}(t) = 2^{(s-S)/2} \psi_{S,0}\big(2^{(s-S)} t\big)
$$

$$(3.2)$$

so that $\psi_{s,0}$ is a scaling and "dilution" of the function $\psi_{S,0}$ defined at the deepest level of the pyramid. In fact, this is true for $s < \bar{s}$ as well, modulo some "wraparound" effects due to periodicity. Thus all basis functions $\psi_{s,\ell}$ can be obtained by scaling, dilution, and shifting of the *mother wavelet* $\psi_{S,0}$. From equation 3.2 it follows that as s

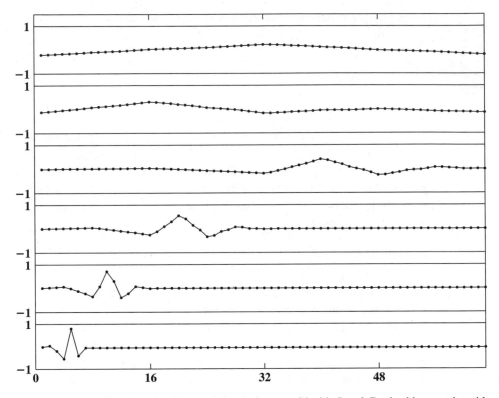

Figure 3.1   One function from each level of a pyramid with $S = 6$. Daubechies wavelet with $R = 3$.

increases, the support of the functions *decreases* (i.e., the *resolution* increases). Thus the level s in the pyramid is also denoted the resolution. This pyramidal structure provides a natural coarse-to-fine mechanism for exploring the deformations of the contour. Figure 3.1 illustrates one function at some shift ℓ, from each resolution of a pyramid with $S = 6$.

Very particular choices of the mother wavelet $\psi_{S,0}$ yield a set $\psi_{s,\ell}$ of orthonormal functions. The family of Daubechies wavelets Daubechies (1988) are parameterized by an integer R, and as R increases, the support of $\psi_{S,0}^{R}$ increases, as does its smoothness. For $R = 1$, one obtains the more classical Haar basis.

The theory of the Daubechies wavelet bases can be found in Daubechies (1988), efficient algorithms for computing the discrete transforms can be found in Mallat (1989). A comprehensive description of the theory and algorithms for the much richer family of wavelet packets can be found in Wickerhauser (1994). Note that the models and algorithms described below will work with other bases such as splines or bases derived from a principle-component analysis.

3.1.2   The Prior

The prior is defined on the parameter space $\mathcal{U}$ taking the $u_{q,k}$ to be independent Gaussian random variables with variance $1/\lambda_k$ and means $u_{z,q,k}$. This completely defines a prior on curves $\theta(t, u)$ and hence a prior on discrete instantiations. However, the latter is harder to write explicitly because many different curves can produce the same discrete instantiation. The role of the prior in this setting is simply to impose smoothness and prevent large deviations from the model curve $z(t)$. The log-prior has the form of a weighted quadratic penalty on the deviations of the coefficients.

$$\log P(u) = -\frac{1}{2} \sum_{q=1}^{2} \sum_{k=0}^{d} \lambda_k (u_{q,k} - u_{z,q,k})^2 + C \qquad (3.3)$$

where C does not depend on θ.

Basis functions of higher index are usually of higher frequency or less smooth. The corresponding variances should be smaller, implying that λ_k should increase with k. For the Fourier basis

$$\psi_k(t) = \frac{1}{\sqrt{2\pi}} \exp 2\pi i k t, \quad t \in [0, 1] \qquad (3.4)$$

for $k = 0, \ldots, d$ and we set $\lambda_k = \alpha k^\rho$ for some $\rho > 1$.

For the wavelet basis, take $k = (s, \ell)$ to be the two-parameter index described above, with $s = 1, \ldots, S$ and $\ell = 0, \ldots, 2^{s-1} - 1$. Then $\lambda_k = \rho^s$ for some $\rho > 0$. All coefficients of functions at the same resolution s have the same variance $1/\rho^s$. In both cases, Fourier and wavelet bases, the larger the parameter ρ the more concentrated the prior on smooth functions.

3.1.3   The Data Model and the Posterior

We assume that if the curve $\theta(u)$ defines the contour of the object, the gray-level values at each pixel inside the curve are independent and identically distributed according to a distribution $f(\cdot; \eta_{in})$, and outside they are distributed according to $f(\cdot; \eta_{out})$, where

η_{in} and η_{out} are parameters. Hence the name *inside-outside model*. The log likelihood of the data, given the curve u and the parameters η_{in}, η_{out}, is given by

$$\log P(I(x); x \in L \mid u, \eta_{in}, \eta_{out}) = \sum_{x \in \theta(u)_{in}} \log f(I(x); \eta_{in}) + \sum_{x \in \theta(u)_{out}} \log f(I(x); \eta_{out})$$

$$(3.5)$$

This assumption of conditional independence of the gray-level values inside and outside the true contour is clearly unrealistic. First, nearby locations will typically be strongly correlated; furthermore, the distributions cannot be identical unless the interior and exterior are very homogeneous. This precludes any particular structures in the interior that actually may be characteristic of the object in question. Nevertheless, in some contexts this model is meaningful, and its simplicity allows us to implement the types of algorithms described here.

The negative log-posterior on $\mathcal{U}$ can be written as

$$-\log P(u \mid I(x); x \in L; \eta_{in}, \eta_{out}) = \frac{1}{2} \sum_{q,k} \lambda_k (u_{q,k} - u_{z,q,k})^2$$

$$- \sum_{x \in \theta(u)_{in}} \log f(I(x); \eta_{in})$$

$$- \sum_{x \in \theta(u)_{out}} \log f(I(x); \eta_{out}) + C \qquad (3.6)$$

In the continuum formulation, the second and third sums become integrals over the interior and exterior of the contour. Writing $F_{in}(x) = -\log f(I(x); \eta_{in})$ and $F_{out}(x) = -\log f(I(x); \eta_{out})$, the negative log-posterior on $\mathcal{U}$ has the form of a cost function

$$J(u) = \mathcal{E}(u) + \mathcal{D}(\theta(u), I) \qquad (3.7)$$

where

$$\mathcal{E}(u) = \frac{1}{2} \sum_{q,k} \lambda_k (u_{q,k} - u_{z,q,k})^2$$

$$\mathcal{D}(u) = \int_{\theta(u)_{in}} F_{in}(x)\,dx + \int_{\theta(u)_{out}} F_{out}(x)\,dx$$

This continuum formulation is useful for computing the derivatives of J with respect to u. One important point, which is at times ignored in the literature, is that $\mathcal{D}(\theta, u)$ should not depend on the *time* parameterization of the curve $\theta(u)$, it should be a quantity depending on the image and the physical curve determined by the parameter u.

The simplest example for f_{in} and f_{out} is the Gaussian distribution with means μ_{in}, μ_{out}, respectively, and the *same* variance σ. The data model is then

$$\mathcal{D}(\theta(u), I) = \frac{1}{2\sigma^2} \int_{\theta(u)_{in}} (I(x) - \mu_{in})^2 \, dx + \frac{1}{2\sigma^2} \int_{\theta(u)_{out}} (I(x) - \mu_{out})^2 \, dx + C$$

(3.8)

where again C does not depend on u. The data model in this case tries to drive the mean gray-level value inside the curve toward μ_{in} and outside the curve toward μ_{out}. The cost function is

$$J(u) = \frac{1}{2} \sum_{q,k} \lambda_k (u_{q,k} - u_{z,q,k})^2 + \frac{1}{2\sigma^2} \int_{\theta(u)_{in}} (I(x) - \mu_{in})^2 \, dx$$

$$+ \frac{1}{2\sigma^2} \int_{\theta(u)_{out}} (I(x) - \mu_{out})^2 \, dx$$

(3.9)

If the variances inside and outside the contour are different, the data model has a more complex form involving the different normalizing constants of the respective densities. In the discrete setting, up to an additive constant, the log likelihood is given by

$$- \sum_{x \in \theta(u)_{in}} \left[\frac{1}{2\sigma_{in}^2} (I(x) - \mu_{in})^2 + \log \sigma_{in} \right] - \sum_{x \in \theta(u)_{out}} \left[\frac{1}{2\sigma_{out}^2} (I(x) - \mu_{out})^2 + \log \sigma_{out} \right]$$

which translates in the continuum to a data term

$$\mathcal{D}(u) = \frac{1}{2\sigma_{in}^2} \int_{\theta(u)_{in}} (I(x) - \mu_{in})^2 \, dx + A_{in} \log \sigma_{in}$$

$$+ \frac{1}{2\sigma_{out}^2} \int_{\theta(u)_{out}} (I(x) - \mu_{out})^2 \, dx + A_{out} \log \sigma_{out}$$

where A_{in}, A_{out} are the areas of the interior and exterior domains defined by the curve.

3.1.4   Variational Analysis

The cost functions in equations 3.7 and 3.9 depend on the parameters u in a complex way. They are not guaranteed to be quadratic or even convex. All we can hope to find is a local minimum of the cost function somewhere in the neighborhood of the initial value. This is achieved by following the downward gradient flow of the cost function. Specifically, we solve the equations

$$\frac{du_{q,k}(\tau)}{d\tau} = -\frac{\partial J(u(\tau))}{\partial u_{q,k}}, \quad q = 1, 2, \quad k = 0, \dots, d \tag{3.10}$$

Here τ is a time variable used for the gradient flow and has nothing to do with the parameter t defining the curve. The next step is to compute the derivatives of the cost function in the variables $u_{q,k}, q = 1, 2, k = 0, \dots, d$.

Let F be a function defined on the domain and let $C_{in}(u) = \int_{\theta_{in}(u)} F(x)\, dx$. We assume the curve $\theta_{in}(u)$ is parameterized as in equation 3.1 and employ the following equality, the proof of which is provided in the next section.

$$\frac{\partial C_{in}(u)}{\partial u_{1,k}} = \int_0^1 F(\theta(t, u))\dot\theta_2(t, u)\psi_k(t)\, dt$$

$$\frac{\partial C_{in}(u)}{\partial u_{2,k}} = -\int_0^1 F(\theta(t, u))\dot\theta_1(t, u)\psi_k(t)\, dt \tag{3.11}$$

Because the integral over the entire domain—$\int_L F(x)$—is fixed and does not depend on u, $\partial C_{out}(u)/\partial u_{q,k} = -\partial C_{in}(u)/\partial u_{q,k}$, and the derivative of the cost function J is given by

$$\frac{\partial J(u)}{\partial u_{1,k}} = \lambda_k(u_{1,k} - u_{z,1,k}) + \int_0^1 (F_{in}(\theta(t, u)) - F_{out}(\theta(t, u)))\dot\theta_2(t, u)\psi_k(t)\, dt \tag{3.12}$$

$$\frac{\partial J(u)}{\partial u_{2,k}} = \lambda_k(u_{2,k} - u_{z,2,k}) - \int_0^1 (F_{in}(\theta(t, u)) - F_{out}(\theta(t, u)))\dot\theta_1(t, u)\psi_k(t)\, dt \tag{3.13}$$

Observe that the derivatives of $\mathcal{D}$ with respect to $u_{1,k}$ are simply the coefficients of $(F_{in} - F_{out})(\theta(t, u))\dot\theta_2$, in the basis $\psi_k, k = 0, \dots, d$. Similarly, the derivatives of $\mathcal{D}$ with respect to $u_{2,k}$ are the coefficients of $-(F_{in} - F_{out})(\theta(t, u))\dot\theta_1$, in the same basis. Thus the gradient of $\mathcal{D}$ is obtained from the forward transforms of two functions with respect to the chosen basis of functions.

This gradient can be interpreted as follows. If ψ_k is a locally supported function at t then $u_{1,k}, u_{2,k}$ describe the curve $\theta(u)$ in a neighborhood of t. Because the curve is oriented counterclockwise, $(-\dot\theta_2, \dot\theta_1)$ is the *inward*-pointing normal, and if $F_{in} > F_{out}$ in the vicinity of t, the minimization, which proceeds along $(-\partial\mathcal{D}/\partial u_{1,k}, -\partial\mathcal{D}/\partial u_{2,k})$, is trying to pull the point $\theta(t)$ *outward* along the normal. The reason being that locally, the inside of the curve fits the data better than the outside, and an improved fit should involve enlarging the curve.

Proof of Equality 3.11

The area integrals are rewritten as curvilinear integrals along $\theta(u)$ as follows. Define

$$Q(x_1, x_2) = \frac{1}{2} \int_0^{x_1} F(t, x_2)\, dt$$

$$P(x_1, x_2) = -\frac{1}{2} \int_0^{x_2} F(x_1, t)\, dt \tag{3.14}$$

Then $\partial Q/\partial x_1 - \partial P/\partial x_2 = F(x_1, x_2)$, and by Green's theorem we can rewrite the integral of F over the interior of the curve as an integral along the curve.

$$C_{in}(u) = \int_{\theta_{in}(u)} F(x)\, dx = \int_0^1 P(\theta(t, u))\dot{\theta}_1(t, u) + Q(\theta(t, u))\dot{\theta}_2(t, u)\, dt \tag{3.15}$$

Writing $\partial_q P$ for $\partial P/\partial x_q$, for $q = 1, 2$, and differentiating in $u_{1,k}$ we get

$$\frac{\partial C_{in}(u)}{\partial u_{1,k}} = \int_0^1 \partial_1 P(\theta(t, u)) \frac{\partial \theta_1(t, u)}{\partial u_{1,k}} \dot{\theta}_1(t, u) + P(\theta(t, u)) \frac{\partial \dot{\theta}_1(t, u)}{\partial u_{1,k}}$$

$$+ \partial_1 Q(\theta(t, u)) \frac{\partial \theta_1(t, u)}{\partial u_{1,k}} \dot{\theta}_2(t, u)\, dt \tag{3.16}$$

Interchanging the order of differentiation in the second term and then integrating by parts, we have

$$\int_0^1 P(\theta(t, u)) \frac{\partial \dot{\theta}_1(t, u)}{\partial u_{1,k}}\, dt = \int_0^1 P(\theta(t, u)) \frac{d}{dt} \frac{\partial \theta_1(t, u)}{\partial u_{1,k}}\, dt$$

$$= -\int_0^1 \frac{d P(\theta(t, u))}{dt} \frac{\partial \theta_1(t, u)}{\partial u_{1,k}}\, dt$$

$$= -\int_0^1 [\partial_1 P(\theta(t, u))\dot{\theta}_1(t, u)$$

$$+ \partial_2 P(\theta(t, u))\dot{\theta}_2(t, u)] \frac{\partial \theta_1(t, u)}{\partial u_{1,k}}\, dt \tag{3.17}$$

From equation 3.1 $\partial\theta_q/\partial u_{q,k} = \psi_k(t)$, and plugging equation 3.17 in 3.16, some terms cancel out and we get

$$\frac{\partial C_{in}(u)}{\partial u_{1,k}} = \int_0^1 [\partial_1 Q(\theta(t,u)) - \partial_2 P(\theta(t,u))]\dot{\theta}_2(t,u)\psi_k(t)\,dt$$

$$= \int_0^1 F(\theta(t,u))\dot{\theta}_2(t,u)\psi_k(t) \tag{3.18}$$

The second part of equation 3.11 is obtained in the same manner. A change in the orientation of the curves would change the signs in both equations.

3.2   An Edge-Based Data Model

The original work on deformable contours in the computer-vision literature, Kass, Witkin, and Terzopoulos (1987), did not employ a statistical model. Rather, a cost function was directly formulated in which the data term evaluates how consistent the curve is with the edges in its neighborhood. The original approach simply integrated the magnitude of the image gradient along the curve. The cost there ignores the issue of whether the direction of the edge is consistent with the direction of the curve—moreover, it is not invariant to the time parameterization of the curve. In other words, the cost function does not depend on the physical curve in the plane, rather, on the particular way the curve is described. An alternative is to parameterize the curve between 0 and 1 and to write

$$\mathcal{D}(u) = -\int_0^1 (-\partial_2 I(\theta)\dot{\theta}_1 + \partial_1 I(\theta)\dot{\theta}_2)(1 + \partial_1 I^2 + \partial_2 I^2)^{-1/2}(\theta)\,dt \tag{3.19}$$

where $\partial_1 I, \partial_2 I$ are the partial derivatives of I. If the curve is oriented counter-clockwise, this integrand is positive if the normalized gradient of the image has similar direction to the outward normal. Because we are minimizing, there is a negative sign before the integral. This cost is invariant to curve parameterization and is equivalent to

$$\oint_\theta (1 + \partial_1 I^2 + \partial_2 I^2)^{-1/2}\nabla I \cdot n$$

where n is the outward normal to the curve. The gradient of $\mathcal{D}$ with respect to the parameters is

$$\frac{\partial \mathcal{D}}{\partial u_{1,k}} = \int_0^1 K(\theta)\dot{\theta}_2 \psi_k \, dt, \qquad \frac{\partial \mathcal{D}}{\partial u_{2,k}} = -\int_0^1 K(\theta)\dot{\theta}_1 \psi_k \, dt \qquad (3.20)$$

where $K(x)$ is the mean curvature of the surface defined by the function I—namely,

$$K(x) = \frac{\partial_{22}I \cdot (1 + (\partial_1 I)^2) + \partial_{11}I \cdot (1 + (\partial_2 I)^2) - 2\partial_1 I \cdot \partial_2 I \cdot \partial_{12} I}{(1 + (\partial_1 I)^2 + (\partial_2 I)^2)^{3/2}}$$

Once again, the gradient of the data part of the cost function is the forward transform in the chosen basis of an easily calculated function. If I is not a smooth function, it is possible to smooth it with some kernel and then differentiate. Note that the derivatives need to be precalculated only once at every point in the image and stored.

Edge-based cost functions do not correspond to real statistical data models. The data used to evaluate the cost function changes with the curve, and it is not clear how different curves are weighted. Any local structure with clear boundaries will stop the evolution of the contour in its neighborhood, even if the local structure is irrelevant to the object we are seeking to fit. On the other hand, the inside-outside model can in some cases overcome such obstacles, as illustrated in some of the examples.

3.3 Computation

The computation of the minimizer of equation 3.7 is obtained through some form of gradient-descent algorithm. Because the cost function is nonlinear, this simply leads to a local minimum. The simplest form of gradient descent uses a discrete approximation to the downward gradient flow. For a given function $f(t)$ on $[0, 1]$ let

$$\Psi(f) = \left\{ \int_0^1 f \psi_k \, dt, k = 0, \dots, d \right\}$$

denote the forward transform of f, namely, the coefficients of f in the basis ψ_k, $k = 0, \dots, d$. For a given vector of coefficients $u = (u_0, \dots, u_d)$, let $\Psi^{-1}(u)$ denote the backward transform—that is,

$$\Psi^{-1}(u) = \sum_{k=0}^{d} u_k \psi_k$$

Let $u_{q,k,m}, k = 0, \ldots, d,\ q = 1, 2$ denote the mth iterate of the coefficients of the curve.

A time step Δ is determined (see below) and using the expression in equation 3.12, we obtain the following algorithm.

Algorithm 3.1: Deformable Contour

1. Choose a scale s and translation x for the initial contour $\theta^{(0)}(t) = sz(t) + x$. Initialize $u_{q,0} = \{u_{q,k,0},\ k = 0, \ldots, d\} = \Psi(\theta_q^{(0)}), q = 1, 2,$

   Set $m = 0$.

2. Calculate $\theta_1 = \Psi^{-1}(u_{1,m}), \theta_2 = \Psi^{-1}(u_{2,m})$, and $\dot{\theta}_1, \dot{\theta}_2$.

3. Set $\beta_q(t) = (F_{in} - F_{out})(\theta(t)) \cdot \dot{\theta}_q(t),\ q = 1, 2.$ Compute

   $$v_1 = \Psi(\beta_2(t)), \qquad v_2 = \Psi(-\beta_1(t))$$

4. Set $u_{q,k,m+1} = u_{q,k,m} - \Delta \cdot [\lambda_k(u_{q,k,m} - u_{q,k,0}) + v_{q,k}]$ for $q = 1, 2,\ \ k = 0, \ldots, d.$

5. If a stopping criterion is satisfied, exit, otherwise $m \leftarrow m + 1$ go to 2.

Note that the means $u_{z,q,k}$ of the coefficients in the prior term from equation 3.9 have been changed to the coefficients $u_{q,k,0}$ of the initial contour $\theta^{(0)}$, which is a scaled and translated version of the template $z(t)$.

3.3.1   Discretization

In a real implementation, the curve is discretized using the points $\theta(t_i, u), i = 1, \ldots, n$, which also define the instantiation. The gradient of the curve calculated in step 2 is approximated using differences $\dot{\theta}(t_i) = \theta(t_{i+1}) - \theta(t_i)$, and β_q in step 3 are evaluated only at the points t_i, yielding two n dimensional vectors. A discrete version of the original basis functions is used. For wavelets or the Fourier basis, the discrete version has discrete forward and backward transforms, which we again denote as Ψ and Ψ^{-1}. For the Fast Fourier Transform implementation of the discrete Fourier transform, see Press and colleagues (1995). For a fast discrete wavelet transform, see Mallat (1989) and Wickerhauser (1994). In the examples shown in this chapter, we have used periodic Daubechies wavelets and, for the sake of completeness, we briefly describe the discrete wavelet transform, omitting any proofs.

3.3.2   Discrete Wavelet Transform

Associated to various choices of the mother wavelet $\psi_{s,0}$ (see equation 3.2), there is an even integer R and two vectors of coefficients $g = (g_0, \ldots, g_R)$ and $h = (h_0, \ldots, R)$, with

$$\sum_{k=0}^{R} g_k = \sqrt{2}, \qquad \sum_{k=0}^{R} h_k = 0$$

Let $n = 2^S$, and start with an n-dimensional data vector $x^{(S)} = x = (x_0, \ldots, x_{n-1})$. The transform starts from the deepest level of the pyramid, obtaining the coefficients $u_\ell^{(s)}$ as follows. Set $s = S$ and write

$$u_\ell^{(s)} = \sum_{j=0}^{R} h_j x_{(2\ell+j) \bmod 2^s}^{(s)}, \qquad \text{for } \ell = 0, \ldots, 2^{s-1} - 1 \qquad (3.21)$$

Note that there are only 2^{s-1} coefficients $u_\ell^{(s)}$ due to the scaling by 2 in the summation index. Thus $u_\ell^{(s)}$ is obtained by convolving $x^{(s)}$ with the filter h and subsampling. Because the coefficients of h sum to zero, h is like a difference operator, and this convolution has the flavor of a high-pass filter. It has higher response at locations where the data is discontinuous or changes rapidly.

The coefficients of g add to a positive value so that convolving with g amounts to smoothing, namely, g is a low-pass filter. It has higher response at locations where the data are smooth. The remaining levels of the transform are then obtained recursively in precisely the same way, by defining a subsampled low-pass version $x^{(s-1)}$ of $x^{(s)}$ using the filter g and then reapplying equation 3.21 for $s - 1$. Specifically,

$$x_\ell^{(s-1)} = \sum_{j=0}^{R} g_j x_{(2\ell+j) \bmod 2^s}^{(s)}, \qquad \text{for } \ell = 0, \ldots, 2^{s-1} - 1 \qquad (3.22)$$

The vector $x^{(s-1)}$ has dimension 2^{s-1} and equation 3.21 can be reapplied to obtain $u_\ell^{(s-1)}$, $\ell = 0, \ldots, 2^{s-2} - 1$, which are the coefficients corresponding to level $s - 1$ of the pyramid. Note that due to the wraparound effect of the modulo operation in the index, the same element of $x^{(s)}$ can enter the sum more than once. This procedure continues until the single coefficient $u_0^{(1)}$ is obtained from $x^{(1)}$, which is a vector with only 2 elements. Furthermore, $x^{(0)}$ is a weighted sum of these 2 elements, determined by applying equation 3.22 at $s = 1$, and corresponds to the coefficient $u_0^{(0)}$. The full transform consists of the vector of coefficients

$$u_\ell^{(s)}, s = 1, \ldots, S, \text{ with } \ell = 0, \ldots, 2^{s-1} - 1, \text{ and } u_0^{(0)}$$

Each $u_\ell^{(s)}$ is the coefficient corresponding to the basis function $\psi_{s,l}$.

The inverse transform takes coefficients $u_0^{(0)}$ and $u_\ell^{(s)}$, $s = 1, \ldots, S, \ell = 0, \ldots,$ $2^{s-1} - 1$ and reproduces the original data vector x. This is now done recursively from the top of the pyramid. Set $x^{(0)} = u_0^{(0)}$ and recursively define $x^{(s)}$ as

$$x_{2k}^{(s)} = \sum_{j=0}^{R/2} \left(h_{2j} x_{(2k+j) \bmod 2^{s-1}}^{(s-1)} + g_{2j} u_{(2k+j) \bmod 2^{s-1}}^{(s)} \right)$$

$$\tag{3.23}$$

$$x_{2k+1}^{(s)} = \sum_{j=0}^{R/2} \left(h_{2j+1} x_{(2k+1+j) \bmod 2^{s-1}}^{(s-1)} + g_{2j+1} u_{(2k+1+j) \bmod 2^{s-1}}^{(s)} \right)$$

for $k = 1, \ldots, 2^{s-1}$. The coefficients of h and g are chosen in such a way that the procedure of equation 3.23 inverts that of equations 3.21 and 3.22 so that at each stage the same vector $x^{(s)}$ is reconstructed from $x^{(s-1)}$ and $u^{(s)}$. In fact, the step described in equations 3.21 and 3.22 can be viewed as a matrix multiplication

$$y^{(s)} = W x^{(s)} \tag{3.24}$$

where W is a square $2^s \times 2^s$ matrix. The first 2^{s-1} elements of $y^{(s)}$ are $u^{(s)}$ and the second 2^{s-1} elements are $x^{(s-1)}$. The step described in equation 3.23 is then simply computing $W^t y^{(s)}$. The fact that this reproduces $x^{(s)}$ means that W is an orthogonal matrix. Identifying filters g and h, which allow for such simple inversion of the forward transform, involves a very sophisticated analysis and can be found in Daubechies (1988), including the coefficients identified for a range of values of R. For example, for $R = 2$ we have $g = (1/\sqrt{2}, 1/\sqrt{2})$ and $h = (1/\sqrt{2}, -1/\sqrt{2})$, and for $R = 4$

$$g = \frac{1}{4\sqrt{2}}(1 + \sqrt{3}, 3 + \sqrt{3}, 3 - \sqrt{3}, 1 - \sqrt{3})$$

$$h = \frac{1}{4\sqrt{2}}(1 - \sqrt{3}, -3 + \sqrt{3}, 3 + \sqrt{3}, -1 - \sqrt{3})$$

3.3.3   Time Step

Determining the appropriate time step Δ is a nontrivial problem. On one hand, it should be large enough so that the algorithm proceeds at a reasonable rate; on the other hand, if it is too large, the algorithm becomes unstable. Assuming the cost function is quadratic, the time step could be taken as the inverse of the largest eigenvalue of the Hessian matrix of J. This can be bounded from above by the trace of the Hessian of J. Assuming that the functions F_{in}, F_{out} are bounded by 1, this in turn is bounded by $l(\theta) + \sum_k \lambda_k$, where $l(\theta) = \sum_{i=0}^{n-1} |\dot{\theta}(t_i)|$, is the length of θ. The time step is then taken to be $\Delta = 1/(l(\theta) + \sum_k \lambda_k)$.

It is possible to avoid the approximation of the time step by carrying out a conjugate gradient algorithm. It is then necessary to carry out searches for the minimum along a line, and hence directly evaluate the cost function that involves 2D integrals. Using equation 3.15, these can be reduced to one-dimensional integrals along the contour. The functions P and Q defined in equation 3.14 need only be computed and stored at the beginning of the procedure.

3.3.4   Coarse to Fine

In all examples of bases mentioned above, the low-index elements of the basis are smooth functions with a large support. These describe global smooth variations of the curve. The higher indices describe higher frequency or more local variations. It turns out that minimizing first on the low-index coefficients until some convergence is observed and then gradually adding in new coefficients leads to a more stable algorithm. Choose $\mathcal{N}_1 < \mathcal{N}_2 < \cdots < \mathcal{N}_A \leq d$. Apply algorithm 1 but in item 4 update only $k = 0, \ldots, \mathcal{N}_1$. When convergence is observed, update in 4 up to $\mathcal{N}_2$, and so on. This procedure will often avoid local minima in the vicinity of the initial curve. If all coefficients are updated at once, the high-index coefficients dominate the cost function and local fits of the curve to noise and small elements of clutter cause it to get stuck very far from the true fit. In fact, when proceeding to minimize in stages, it is often possible to omit the penalty term $\mathcal{E}(u)$ altogether.

For example, when a wavelet basis is used, update all coefficients corresponding to resolutions $s \leq a$. Thus for small values of a, only coefficients of the smoother basis elements $\psi_{s,l}$ with large support are updated. Taking $d = n - 1 = 2^S - 1$ we use $\mathcal{N}_a = 2 \cdot 2^a$, $a = 1, \ldots, A$, for some $A \leq S$. The factor 2 comes from the two components of the contour. The results shown in this chapter were all obtained in this fashion.

In figure 3.2, the detection of the boundary of the left heart ventricle is shown, and in figure 3.3, we show some detections of the contour of a chess piece. In both, the template contour is a generic circular curve. In figure 3.3, two successful detections are shown alongside a failed match in which the object merges with the background. In figure 3.4, we show 3 steps in the coarse-to-fine process corresponding to the outcome of the algorithm for $\mathcal{N}_1 = 2 \cdot 2, \mathcal{N}_2 = 2 \cdot 4, \mathcal{N}_3 = 2 \cdot 8$.

In figure 3.5, we show the detection of the deformable contour algorithm in a case where the initial curve has a particular shape, that of the posterior ventricles in an

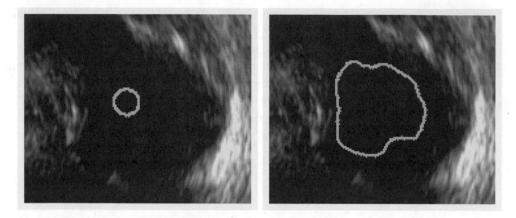

Figure 3.2   An ultrasound image of the left heart ventricle, with the outcome of the deformable contour algorithm. (Left) Initial contour. (Right) Final fit.

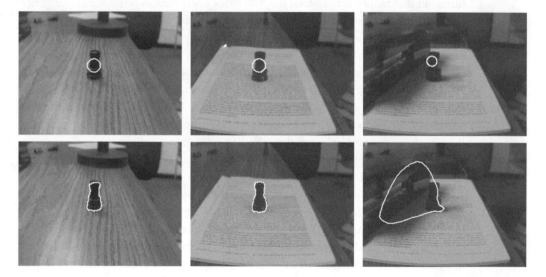

Figure 3.3   Three examples of the deformable contour algorithm trying to fit the boundary of the rook. (Top) Initial position. (Bottom) Final state. The experiment on the right shows how the algorithm can fail when the background is similar in intensity to the object.

Figure 3.4 Three stages in the coarse to fine deformable contour algorithm corresponding to the final state for $\mathcal{N}_1 = 2 \cdot 2$, $\mathcal{N}_2 = 2 \cdot 4$, $\mathcal{N}_3 = 2 \cdot 8$.

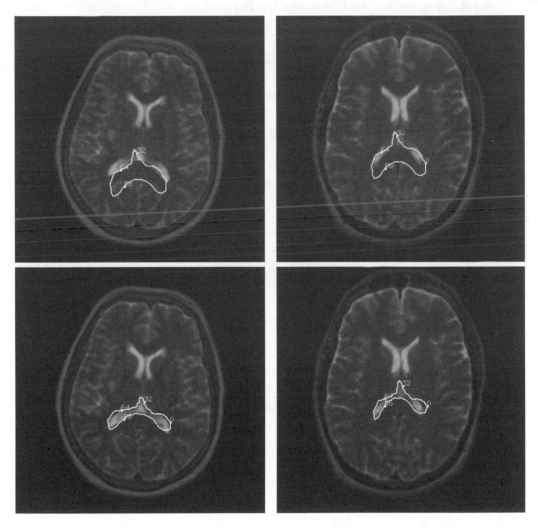

Figure 3.5 Initial and final state of a deformable contour for detecting the posterior ventricles in two axial MRI brain scans. (Top) Initial state. (Bottom) Final state.

axial MRI brain scan. Initialized in the vicinity of the correct position, the contour detects the boundaries of the ventricles. Similar experiments using an initial curve with a shape determined by a particular object class are shown in figures 2.3 and 8.17. The enumerated points on the initial curve and on the final detection provide an explicit instantiation of the shape. Such a match is meaningless in the previous examples where a generic circle is deformed into some region.

3.4   Joint Estimation of the Curve and the Parameters

In the statistical model presented in section 3.1, we assumed the parameters η_{in}, η_{out} in the data model were known—namely, estimated *off-line,* by computing means and variances in various regions identified by the user, as inside and outside, on some training images of contours. It is also possible to model the case where these parameters are unknown and are estimated *on-line.* We define a prior on the parameters as well, and our task is to maximize the joint posterior on η_{in}, η_{out}, u. For simplicity, we assume a flat prior on these parameters in some bounded domain. Then the log of the joint posterior on u, η_{in}, η_{out}—that is, $P(u, \eta_{in}, \eta_{out} \mid I(x), x \in L)$ has the same form as in equation 3.6, with a different constant. For fixed value of u, namely, a fixed curve, maximizing in η_{in} and η_{out} produces the maximum likelihood estimates of these parameters, given the data inside and outside the contour, respectively. For many models, these estimates have analytic expressions in terms of the data. They are plugged into the log-posterior and yield a function that depends only on u. It then remains to maximize this function with respect to u. We provide the details in the case where $f(\cdot; \eta)$ are Gaussian with unknown mean and variance.

3.4.1   Gaussian

To simplify notation, let r denote one of the regions $\theta_{in}(u)$, $\theta_{out}(u)$. Set N_r to be the number of pixels in r, and write the log-density of the Gaussian as

$$\log f(I(x), \mu_r, \sigma_r) = -\frac{1}{2\sigma_r^2}(I(x) - \mu_r)^2 - \frac{1}{2}\log 2\pi - \frac{1}{2}\log \sigma_r^2$$

The cost function to be minimized is given by the negative log-posterior on instantiation and distribution parameters together,

$$J(u, \mu_{in}, \sigma_{in}, \mu_{out}, \sigma_{out}) = -\log P(u, \mu_{in}, \sigma_{in}, \mu_{out}, \sigma_{out} \mid I(x), x \in L)$$

$$= \mathcal{E}(u) + \frac{1}{2\sigma_{in}^2} \sum_{x \in \eta_{in}} (I(x) - \mu_{in})^2 + \frac{N_{in}}{2} \log \sigma_{in}^2$$

$$+ \frac{1}{2\sigma_{out}^2} \sum_{x \in \eta_{out}} (I(x) - \mu_{out})^2 + \frac{N_{out}}{2} \log \sigma_{out}^2 + C$$

$$(3.25)$$

where C does not depend on u, η_{in}, η_{out}, and incorporates the uniform prior on the parameters on some bounded interval.

Fixing $\theta(u)$, for each of the regions, minimizing equation 3.25 in the corresponding parameters μ_r, σ_r yields

$$\hat{\mu}_r = \frac{1}{N_r} \sum_{x \in r} I(x)$$

and

$$\hat{\sigma}_r^2 - \frac{1}{N_r} \sum_{x \in r} I^2(x) - \hat{\mu}_r^2$$

These are precisely the maximum likelihood estimates of the mean and variance in the region. Using the fact that

$$\sum_{x \in r} (I(x) - \hat{\mu}_r)^2 / \hat{\sigma}_r^2 = 1$$

and because $N_{\theta_{in}} + N_{\theta_{out}}$ is constant (the total number of pixels in the lattice L), we have

$$\max_{\mu_{in}, \sigma_{in}, \mu_{out}, \sigma_{out}} J(u, \mu_{in}, \sigma_{in}, \mu_{out}, \sigma_{out}) = \mathcal{E}(u) + \frac{N_{in}}{2} \log \hat{\sigma}_{in}^2 + \frac{N_{out}}{2} \log \hat{\sigma}_{out}^2 + C'$$

For the continuum formulation, define

$$\mathcal{N}_r(u) \doteq \int_r 1 \, dx, \qquad H_r(u) \doteq \int_r I(x) \, dx,$$

$$G_r(u) \doteq \int_r I^2(x) \, dx$$

Then $\mathcal{N}_r$ substitutes N_r, and $\hat{\mu}_r$ and $\hat{\sigma}_r^2$, respectively, become

$$\mathcal{M}_r(u) \doteq \frac{H_r(u)}{\mathcal{N}_r(u)}, \qquad \mathcal{S}_r(u) \doteq \frac{G_r(u)}{\mathcal{N}_r(u)} - \mathcal{M}_r^2(u)$$

The cost function to be minimized is then

$$J(u) = \mathcal{E}(u) + \frac{\mathcal{N}_{in}(u)}{2} \log \mathcal{S}_{in}(u) + \frac{\mathcal{N}_{out}(u)}{2} \log \mathcal{S}_{out}(u)$$

The derivative of the second and third terms with respect to $u_{q,k}$ has the form

$$\frac{1}{2} \frac{\partial \mathcal{N}_r(u)}{\partial u_{q,k}} \log \mathcal{S}_r(u) + \frac{1}{\mathcal{S}_r(u)} \left[\frac{\partial G_r(u)}{\partial u_{q,k}} - \mathcal{S}_r(u) \frac{\partial \mathcal{N}_r(u)}{\partial u_{q,k}} \right.$$
$$\left. - 2\mathcal{M}_r \frac{\partial H_r(u)}{\partial u_{q,k}} + \mathcal{M}_r^2(u) \frac{\partial \mathcal{N}_r(u)}{\partial u_{q,k}} \right] \qquad (3.26)$$

At first glance, this appears a very complex derivative to compute. However, each of the partial derivatives has the form given in equation 3.11 with the argument F replaced by I^2, I, or 1, and can therefore be obtained by taking the forward transform of the appropriate one-dimensional functions.

The other terms in this expression are composed of simple algebraic operations on integrals of I^2, I, or 1 over the domains $\theta_{in}(u)$ and $\theta_{out}(u)$. Again, using Green's theorem (equation 3.15), these can be reduced to one-dimensional integrals, along the contour, of the functions

$$\mathcal{I}_{p,1}(x_1, x_2) = -\frac{1}{2} \int_0^{x_2} I^p(x_1, t)\, dt$$

$$\mathcal{I}_{p,2}(x_1, x_2) = \frac{1}{2} \int_0^{x_1} I^p(t, x_2)\, dt$$

for $p = 0, 1, 2$. Specifically,

$$\int_{\theta(u)_{in}} I^p(x)\, dx = \int_0^1 \mathcal{I}_{p,1}(\theta(t, u))\dot{\theta}_1(t, u) + \mathcal{I}_{p,2}(\theta(t, u))\dot{\theta}_2(t, u)\, dt, \quad p = 0, 1, 2$$

The functions $\mathcal{I}_p$ do not depend on u and can be precalculated and stored once and for all at the start of the computation. This leads to the following algorithm.

Algorithm 3.2: Deformable Contour—on-Line Parameter Estimation

1. Compute $\mathcal{I}_{p,j}(x_1, x_2)$, $p = 0, 1, 2$ $j = 1, 2$ (simple summation), and total integrals of I^p over entire domain: T_p, $p = 0, 1, 2$.

2. Initialize $u_{q,0} = \{u_{q,k,0}, \ k = 0, \ldots, d\}, q = 1, 2$. Set $m = 0$.

3. Calculate $\theta_1 = \Psi^{-1}(u_{1,m})$, $\theta_2 = \Psi^{-1}(u_{2,m})$, and $\dot{\theta}_1, \dot{\theta}_2$.

4. Calculate

   Integrals:

$$N_{in} = \sum_{i=0}^{n-1} \mathcal{I}_{0,1}(\theta(t_i))\dot{\theta}_1(t_i) + \mathcal{I}_{0,2}(\theta(t_i))\dot{\theta}_2(t_i),$$
$$H_{in} = \sum_{i=0}^{n-1} \mathcal{I}_{1,1}(\theta(t_i))\dot{\theta}_1(t_i) + \mathcal{I}_{1,2}(\theta(t_i))\dot{\theta}_2(t_i),$$
$$G_{in} = \sum_{i=0}^{n-1} \mathcal{I}_{2,1}(\theta(t_i))\dot{\theta}_1(t_i) + \mathcal{I}_{2,2}(\theta(t_i))\dot{\theta}_2(t_i).$$
$$N_{out} = T_0 - N_{in}, \ H_{out} = T_1 - H_{in}, \ G_{out} = T_2 - G_{in}.$$
$$\mu_{in} = H_{in}/N_{in}, \ \mu_{out} = H_{out}/N_{out}.$$
$$\sigma_{in}^2 = G_{in}/N_{in} - \mu_{in}^2, \ \sigma_{out}^2 = G_{out}/N_{out} - \mu_{out}^2.$$

   Transforms: $v^{p,1} = -\Psi(I^p(\theta)\dot{\theta}_2)$, $v^{p,2} = -\Psi(I^p(\theta)\dot{\theta}_1)$, $p = 0, 1, 2$.

5. Set $d_{q,r,k} = \frac{1}{2}\log(\sigma_r^2)v_k^{0,q} + \frac{1}{\sigma_r^2}[v_k^{2,q} - \sigma_r^2 v_k^{0,q} - 2\mu_r v_k^{1,q} + \mu_r^2 v_k^{0,q}]$, $q = 1, 2, \ k = 0, \ldots, d$ and $r = in, out$.

6. Set $u_{q,k,m+1} = u_{q,k,m} - \Delta \cdot (\lambda_k u_{q,k,m} + d_{q,in,k} + d_{q,out,k})$ $i = 1, 2, \ k = 0, \ldots, d$.

7. If a stopping criterion is satisfied, exit, otherwise $m \leftarrow m + 1$ go to 3.

The outcomes for the two approaches, off-line and on-line parameter estimation, are compared in figures 3.6 and 3.7. We see that if the parameters are fixed off-line at unreasonable values, the first approach yields erroneous results, whereas on-line parameter estimation is successful at finding the contour of the heart ventricle. On the other hand, if the on-line method is initialized at a starting point with higher interior mean than that of the desired region, it may converge to something entirely wrong, whereas the first method, driven by the correct parameters, obtains a good detection.

3.5 Bibliographical Notes and Discussion

The idea of deformable contours goes back to Grenander (1970, 1978). In Grenander, Chow, and Keenan (1991), the details of the implementation are described together

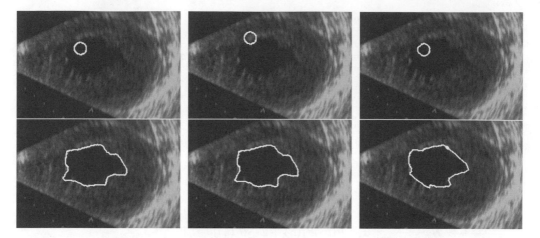

Figure 3.6 (Top) Initial curves. (Bottom) Final detection. (Left and middle) Gaussian model with equal variances and means estimated off-line, $\mu_{in} = 0$, $\mu_{out} = .2$ (Pixel values are scaled between 0 and 1). (Right) Gaussian model with on-line parameter estimation.

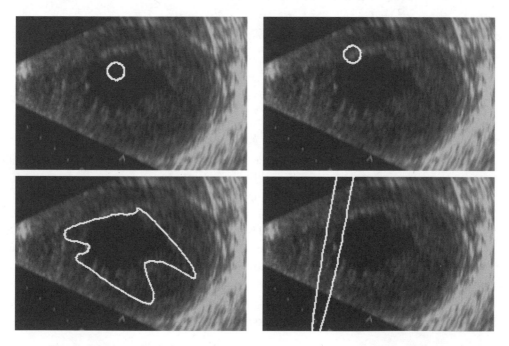

Figure 3.7 (Top) Initial curves. (Bottom) Final detections. (Left) Using fixed parameters. Gaussian model with equal variances, $\mu_{in} = 0$, $\mu_{out} = .3$ (as opposed to $\mu_{out} = .2$ in figure 3.6). The contour grows beyond the boundaries of the ventricle chamber. (Right) Gaussian model with on-line parameter estimation, initialized outside the ventricle.

with theoretical aspects of the statistical formulation. The curve there is parameterized directly in terms of the locations of the n points, also known as the lattice parameterization. This can be viewed as one extreme example of the spectral parameterization, where the basis functions are shifts of some "smoothed delta" function. In this case, all elements of the basis are of equal support and in order to enforce smoothness, it is necessary to introduce penalties in terms of sums of squared differences of the point locations or, in the continuum formulation, integrals of squared derivatives of some order. In this parameterization, one loses a natural way to proceed from coarse to fine. Starting with a small number of points and gradually increasing their number is a possibility; however, it is then necessary to determine the type of interpolation to use between the point positions in order to define the continuous curve, and how additional points are placed along the curve. Still, most formulations in the literature appear in this form. The idea of on-line estimation of the parameters appears in Zhu and Yuille (1996), and is worked out in further detail in Chesnaud, Réfrégier, and Boulet (1999).

A deformable-contour model, called *snakes,* based only on an edge-data term was originally proposed in Kass, Witkin, and Terzopoulos (1987). However, using only an edge-data model is problematic. The contours tend to perform only local adjustments unless artificially forced by additional terms in the cost function to grow or shrink (see Cohen 1991). In such models, the initial contour shown, for example, in figure 3.5, would have trouble crossing the boundary encountered by the top part of the curve on the lower part of the ventricle. When a specific data model is expected in the interior and exterior, and the coarse-to-fine algorithm is implemented, the curve is able to find the correct region.

Note that when initialized with a small contour, the algorithms presented here can be viewed as smoothed-region-growing algorithms (see, for example, figure 3.2). The gradient of the data term is locally looking for directions in which more pixels satisfying the "inside model" can be found, and the penalty term is constraining this growth to be smooth. Region growing is a very old methodology in pattern recognition (see, for example, Duda and Hart 1973 or Haralick and Shapiro 1992). In Zhu and Yuille (1996), there is further discussion on the relation between region growing and deformable contours. In this work, several contours are grown simultaneously using a systematic model incorporating several closed regions, a prior on the number of regions and on the *shape* of the region contours. The data model is based on conditional independence of the gray-level intensities in the different regions. There is also the option to merge adjacent regions. Such region-growing techniques can hardly be viewed as object detection—rather, as image-segmentation tools. On the other hand, when the deformable contour has a particular shape that is more or less preserved during the detection process, there is meaning to the match obtained between the model points on the curve and those in the image, as illustrated by the enumerated points along the model curve and matched curve in figure 3.5.

One of the problems of the algorithm presented above is that there is no inherent mechanism to prevent the self-intersection of the deforming curve; moreover, there is no straightforward way to extend the work to deformable 2D surfaces embedded in 3D. An interesting computational approach that overcomes these limitations can be found in the level set methods (Malladi, Sethian, and Vemuri 1995; Caselles and colleagues 1997; Caselles, Kimmel, and Sapiro 1997). The idea is to view the deforming contour as the 0-level set of a "virtual" function on the entire 2D domain. The gradient-descent motion of the curve translates into an evolution of the virtual function based on a time-dependent partial differential equation. At each step, the estimated curve corresponds to the 0-level set of the evolved virtual function. There is never any need to define the virtual function in the entire domain. In numerical implementations, it suffices to define it locally around the current estimated curve. An interesting advantage of this approach is that the topology of the curve can change in a natural way. A smooth evolution of the virtual function can produce, at some point, a change from one closed curve to two or more. These models have all been implemented using an edge-data model and inherit the drawbacks of this type of data model. Also, in the presence of noisy data, their increased topological flexibility can become a liability, because it allows the algorithm to produce multiple isolated curves, instead of finding the one region of interest.

There are numerous other papers in the literature on deformable contours. The variations involve different data models, different forms of curve parameterization, and different forms of smoothing penalties on the curves. (See, for example, Cohen 1991; Cohen and colleagues 1992; Figueiredo and Leitao 1992; Cohen and Cohen 1993; Chuang and Kuo 1996). In Blake and Yuille (1992), several papers describe the use of deformable contours for tracking a contour in time. These ideas are further developed in Blake and Issard (1998), where a statistical model for the curve motion replaces the prior we have used in static images.

Attempts at training the parameterization of the deformations according to the particular shape and its characteristic deformations can be found in Cootes and Taylor (1992). The n points of the instantiation are marked by the user on training images registered to a fixed scale and location, to produce a $2n$ dimensional vector for each training image. The covariance matrix of this data is computed and the eigenvectors (i.e., principal components) of this matrix are used as the basis with which to expand the curve. Most typical variations of the curve around the mean will require only a small number of basis elements with nonzero coefficients. This is an appealing approach, although the resulting basis will not come with a fast-forward and backward transform and hence may be somewhat less efficient. There is also the risk that the covariance matrix and resulting eigenvectors are too dedicated to the training data and result in a prior that does not generalize well to other instances of the object; see Wang and Staib (2000) for a related discussion.

There are certain inherent problems encountered by all implementations, the main one being the initialization of the contour, as clearly emerges from figure 3.6. Some attempts have been made to directly compute a global optimum of a cost function similar to the inside-outside model described above (see Jermyn and Ishikawa 1999; Ishikawa and Geiger 1999) using minimal-cut methods on graphs. These methods are much slower than the iterative algorithms described here. Moreover, they find the global optimum, over the entire image, of a cost function that is very generic and hence this optimum may not be anywhere near the desired object.

The pose-initialization problems, the sensitivity of the deformable contours to noise, and the need to derive more-specific data models motivate the algorithms developed in chapters 6–8.

4   1D Models: Deformable Curves

The deformable-contour model described in chapter 3 is based on a nonlinear cost function that is optimized using a gradient-descent method. At best, the algorithm will reach a satisfactory local minimum. It is easily confused by clutter. If the interior of the object, or the exterior, are not homogeneous, the data models for the deformable contour are grossly incorrect and the minima are nowhere near the desired object contours.

An alternative approach involves more detailed modeling of the data along the curve. The template is again defined in terms of a sequence of points $Z = (z_1, \ldots, z_n)$ on the reference grid. The instantiation is described directly in terms of a sequence $(\theta_1, \ldots, \theta_n)$ of locations in the image grid L, and the constraints are explicitly defined in terms of a set $\Theta \subset L^n$ and a prior $P(\theta)$ penalizing nonsmooth deformations of the model curve. The data model is again based on a conditional independence assumption. In contrast to chapter 3, the problem is no longer considered in the continuum, rather, the discrete aspect is emphasized in the computational methods. The cost function has the form of a sum of costs on pairs or triples of consecutive points, and therefore lends itself in principle to global optimization. One method of optimization is dynamic programming. The other is a tree-based optimization technique from Geman and Jedynak (1996). It should be noted that in order for this approach to be computationally feasible, in terms of time and memory requirements, it is necessary to introduce some hard constraints on the locations of the n points, as detailed below. In other words, some user initialization is still required although the algorithms are much less sensitive to the initial configuration.

4.1 Statistical Model

Here we use a transform of the gray-level pixel data into a vector of binary local image features $X_a(x), a = 1, \ldots, A$, and write $\hat{I}(x) = (X_a(x); a = 1, \ldots, A)$. The main advantage is that such features can be chosen to be robust to monotone gray-level transformations, and changes in the contrast of the data along the curve will not affect the detection. Otherwise put, such features are *photometrically invariant*. This is in contrast to the data models of chapter 3, which assumed a fixed mean intensity inside the object. Such data models would be very sensitive to global changes in the range of gray-level values. Furthermore, the discrete nature of the transformed data allows for simple estimation of model parameters.

4.1.1 Local Features

We assume the curve can either traverse a pixel x at one of A different angles $a\pi/A, a = 1, \ldots, A$, in which case we write $ang(x) = a$; or no curve traverses the pixel, in which case we write $ang(x) = \phi$. For example, take $A = 4$ and assume that locally each curve is either horizontal, vertical, or at $\pm 45°$. The notion of curve angle is quite loose and covers quite a wide range. The feature X_a is expected to be "on" at x—that is, $X_a(x) = 1$, if $ang(x) = a$. We list here two possible definitions, $\hat{X}_a$ and $\tilde{X}_a$, for these features, but many others exist. In the experiments below, we use the conjunction of these two conditions, namely, $X_a(x) = \hat{X}_a(x) \cdot \tilde{X}_a(x)$. If the curve is expected to be "ridgelike," and say, brighter than its surroundings, define

$$\hat{X}_a(x) = 1, \quad \text{if } I(x) > I(x + \mu_a) \quad \text{and} \quad I(x) > I(x - \mu_a) \tag{4.1}$$

where μ_a is the vector of length μ pixels in the direction orthogonal to a, for some small μ.

If the curve can be brighter or darker than its surroundings but relatively constant in intensity, we require the intensity differences within the curve to be smaller than those between the pixels on the curve and those alongside it.

$$\tilde{X}_a(x) = 1, \quad \text{if } |I(x + \nu_a) - I(x)| < \min(|I(x) - I(x + \mu_a)|, |I(x) - I(x - \mu_a)|) \tag{4.2}$$

where ν_a is a vector of ν pixels in the direction of a. In figure 4.1, we show the points obtained using the conjunction of conditions 4.1 and 4.2, on an axial MRI brain scan. The original image can be found in the top right panel of figure 4.3 (in section 4.2 Computation: dynamic programming).

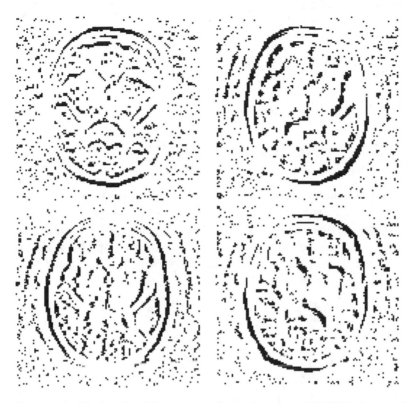

Figure 4.1   The four local feature types detected on the axial MRI brain scan shown at the top right of figure 4.3, we use $A = 4$, $\mu = 3$, $\nu = 1$.

4.1.2   The Likelihood

Clearly, the probability that $X_\alpha(x) = 1$ will tend to be larger if a curve of angle α passes through x—that is, $ang(x) = \alpha$. For angles a that are different from α we would expect the probability that $X_a(x) = 1$ to be smaller. Denote these probabilities $p_{\alpha,a}, \alpha, a = 1, \ldots, A$. Finally, if no curve passes through the neighborhood of x—that is, x is a "background" pixel, the probability of $X_a(x) = 1$ is denoted p_b and is the same for all a. Assume that given that the curve passes through the pixel x at angle α, the variables $X_a(x), a = 1, \ldots, A$ are independent, and given no curve passes through the pixel, they are also independent. The conditional distribution of

$\hat{I}(x)$ at pixel x given $ang(x) = \alpha$—is then

$$P(\hat{I}(x) \mid ang(x) = \alpha) = \prod_{a=1}^{A} p_{\alpha,a}^{X_a(x)} (1 - p_{\alpha,a})^{1-X_a(x)} \tag{4.3}$$

and given no curve passes through the pixel

$$P_b(\hat{I}(x)) = P(\hat{I}(x) \mid ang(x) = \phi) = \prod_{a=1}^{A} p_b^{X_a(x)} (1 - p_b)^{1-X_a(x)} \tag{4.4}$$

Given an instantiation $\theta = (\theta_1, \ldots, \theta_n)$ of the curve, we assume the data $\hat{I}(x)$, $x \in L$ to be conditionally independent. Let L_i be the pixels on the segment connecting the points θ_i, θ_{i+1} and let $L(\theta)$ be the union of the sets L_i. Also, let α_i denote the angle of the ith segment. Associated to each $x \in L(\theta)$ there is a specific angle $ang(\theta, x)$—the angle of the segment to which the pixel x belongs. The conditional distribution of $\hat{I}$, on the entire lattice, given the instantiation θ is then

$$P(\hat{I} \mid \theta) = \prod_{x \in L(\theta)} P(\hat{I}(x) \mid ang(\theta, x)) \cdot \prod_{x \notin L(\theta)} P_b(\hat{I}(x))$$

$$= \prod_{i=1}^{n-1} \prod_{x \in L_i} P(\hat{I}(x) \mid \alpha_i) \prod_{x \notin L(\theta)} P_b(\hat{I}(x)) \tag{4.5}$$

Dividing 4.5 by $\prod_{x \in L} P_b(\hat{I}(x))$, which can be interpreted as the probability of $\hat{I}$ given *no* curve is present, and does not depend on θ, and substituting 4.4 and 4.3, we obtain a likelihood ratio of the form

$$\frac{P(\hat{I} \mid \theta)}{P_b(\hat{I})} = \prod_{x \in L(\theta)} \frac{P(\hat{I}(x) \mid ang(\theta, x))}{P_b(\hat{I}(x))}$$

$$= \prod_{i=1}^{n-1} \prod_{a=1}^{A} \left[\frac{p_{\alpha_i,a}}{p_b} \right]^{N_{ia}} \left[\frac{1 - p_{\alpha_i,a}}{1 - p_b} \right]^{(N_i - N_{ia})} \tag{4.6}$$

where N_{ia} is the number of times $X_a(x) = 1$ along the segment L_i and N_i denotes the total number of pixels along this segment. The log-likelihood is thus up to a constant given by a sum of functions of the counts along the segments of the curve.

$$\log \frac{P(\hat{I} \mid \theta)}{P_b(\hat{I})} = \sum_{i=1}^{n-1} \sum_{a=1}^{A} \left[N_{ia} \log \left(\frac{p_{\alpha_i,a}(1 - p_b)}{p_b(1 - p_{\alpha_i,a})} \right) + N_i \log \left(\frac{1 - p_{\alpha_i,a}}{1 - p_b} \right) \right]. \tag{4.7}$$

We are again making strong conditional independence assumptions that are clearly a gross simplification. However, the data model is simple and transparent and does depend on the angle of the curve in a direct way. Furthermore, as in the previous chapters, the model is created with the computational task in mind. The log-likelihood is simply a linear function of the counts. In this equation, the dependence on the data $\hat{I}$ is through N_{ia}. It is also useful to note for later computational considerations that the log-likelihood can be written in the form

$$\sum_{i=1}^{n-1} \psi(\hat{I}, \theta_i, \theta_{i+1}) \tag{4.8}$$

where the functions ψ depend only on the two consecutive points θ_i, θ_{i+1} and on the data $\hat{I}$ along the segment connecting them.

Under this data model, the maximum likelihood estimates of the parameters are obtained from training sample proportions. Take training subimage samples from each of the categories: $\alpha = 1, \ldots, A$. For each α, obtain the proportion for which $X_a(x) = 1, a = 1, \ldots, A$ to produce an estimate $\hat{p}_{\alpha,a}$. An estimate of p_b is obtained from subimages with no curve, estimating one pooled probability for $P(X_a(x) = 1 \mid ang(x) = \phi)$, for all as.

The model can be simplified by setting $p_{\alpha,a} = p_c$ if $\alpha = a$, meaning that $P(X_a(x) = 1 \mid ang(x) = a) = p_c$ for any $a = 1, \ldots, A$ and $p_{\alpha,a} = p_b$ if $a \neq \alpha$, meaning that the probability of $X_a(x) = 1$ if $ang(x) \neq a$ is the same as the background probability. The likelihood ratio then has the simpler form

$$\frac{P(\hat{I} \mid \theta)}{P_b(\hat{I})} = \prod_{i=1}^{n-1} \left[\frac{p_c}{p_b}\right]^{N_{i\alpha_i}} \left[\frac{(1 - p_c)}{(1 - p_b)}\right]^{(N_i - N_{i\alpha_i})} \tag{4.9}$$

In this case, parameter estimation also simplifies. Estimate one parameter $p_c = p_{a,a}$ for all $a = 1, \ldots, A$, pooling together all subimage samples containing a curve of any angle. For each a let n_a be the number of training subimages labeled with angle a, and let $n_{a,1}$ be the number of these for which $X_a(x) = 1$. Then estimate p_c as

$$p_c = \frac{\sum_{a=1}^{A} n_{a,1}}{\sum_{a=1}^{A} n_a}$$

The parameter p_b is estimated from training subimages identified as not having any curve.

Training samples are either obtained by hand with the user pointing out pixels with curves of the A different angles and pixels with no curve. Alternatively, one can start with initial parameter settings, detect the curve, and use pixels on and off the detected curve to update the parameters.

4.1.3   The Prior and the Posterior

The curve is parameterized directly through the locations of the n points $\theta_1, \ldots, \theta_n$. It is important to include a prior penalizing irregular nonsmooth curves. This can have a variety of forms. For example, a penalty on high curvature can be written as

$$P(\theta_1, \ldots, \theta_n) \propto \exp\left[-\left(\sum_{i=1}^{n-2} \phi_i(\theta_i, \theta_{i+1}, \theta_{i+2})\right)\right]$$

where $\phi_i(\theta_i, \theta_{i+1}, \theta_{i+2})$ is the modulus of the difference between the angle of the segment θ_i, θ_{i+1}, and that of the segment $\theta_{i+1}, \theta_{i+2}$. Each such term depends on a triple of consecutive points and is entirely scale invariant. Such penalties are useful when there are no particular prior assumptions on the shape of the curve. If the model or template has a particular shape and we do not expect significant variations in scale or rotation, the functions ϕ_i can be simplified to depend only on consecutive pairs. In the examples below, we compare angles and lengths between a pair of consecutive points in the instantiation and the corresponding pair in the model sequence:

$$\phi_i(\theta_i, \theta_{i+1}) = A|\text{ang}(\theta_{i+1} - \theta_i, z_{i+1} - z_i)| + B|\log(|\theta_{i+1} - \theta_i|/|z_{i+1} - z_i|)|$$

$$(4.10)$$

and

$$P(\theta_1, \ldots, \theta_n) \propto \exp\left[-\left(\sum_{i=1}^{n-1} \phi_i(\theta_i, \theta_{i+1})\right)\right] \quad (4.11)$$

This is a simple prior that independently penalizes deviations in angle and length of individual segments of the deformed curve from their counterparts on the template curve. The higher-probability instantiations will tend to have a shape similar to the model curve $(z_1, \ldots, z_n)$.

Putting the data model from equation 4.8 together with the prior of equation 4.11, we write a negative log-posterior of the form

$$J(\theta) = -\log P(\theta_1, \ldots, \theta_n \mid \hat{I}) = \sum_{i=1}^{n-1} \Phi_i(\theta_i, \theta_{i+1}) + C \quad (4.12)$$

where

$$\Phi_i(\theta_i, \theta_{i+1}) = \phi_i(\theta_i, \theta_{i+1}) - \psi_i(\hat{I}, \theta_i, \theta_{i+1}), \quad i = 1, \ldots, n-1$$

with ψ_i defined in equation 4.8 and ϕ_i defined in 4.10.

4.2 Computation: Dynamic Programming

The structure of the cost function—a sum of terms each depending on two consecutive variables—lends itself to efficient minimization using dynamic programming. Each point θ_i along the curve is assigned a state space $S_i \subset L$ of possible values. It is not necessary to try all possible n-tuples of points from S_i, $i = 1, \ldots, n$. Rather, the computation reduces to trying all possible pairs of points of consecutive indices, $i, i+1$ for $i = 1, \ldots, n-1$. Even with this reduction it is impractical to assume that S_i is the entire image lattice. However, if some hard constraints on the location and variability of the curve are introduced, the computation becomes tractable.

One approach to limiting the state space is to assume that the first and last points are given within small neighborhoods S_1, S_n in the image. Then, using some heuristic, determine regions $S_2, \ldots, S_{n-1}$ such that for any reasonable configuration $\theta_1, \ldots, \theta_n$, we would have $\theta_i \in S_i$, $i = 1, \ldots, n$. Alternatively, set an initial curve $\theta^{(0)}$, determined by an affine map A applied to the model configuration—that is, $\theta_i^{(0)} = Az_i$, and define S_i as neighborhoods of the points $\theta_i^{(0)}$, of some size.

Dynamic programming is based on the following simple observation. Let $J^{(0)}(\theta) = J(\theta)$, as defined in equation 4.12. For each point $\theta_{n-1} \in S_{n-1}$, define

$$\theta_n^*(\theta_{n-1}) = argmin_{S_n} \Phi_{n-1}(\theta_{n-1}, \theta_n)$$

$$f^*(\theta_{n-1}) = \min_{S_n} \Phi_{n-1}(\theta_{n-1}, \theta_n)$$

Then define

$$J^{(1)}(\theta_1, \ldots, \theta_{n-1}) = \sum_{i=1}^{n-2} \Phi_i^{(1)}(\theta_i, \theta_{i+1})$$

with $\Phi_i^{(1)} = \Phi_i$ for $i = 1, \ldots, n-3$ and

$$\Phi_{n-2}^{(1)}(\theta_{n-2}, \theta_{n-1}) = \Phi_{n-2}(\theta_{n-2}, \theta_{n-1}) + f^*(\theta_{n-1})$$

A simple argument shows that $(\theta_1^*, \ldots, \theta_{n-1}^*)$ minimizes $J^{(1)}$ if and only if

$$(\theta_1^*, \ldots, \theta_{n-1}^*, \theta_n^*(\theta_{n-1}^*))$$

minimizes $J^{(0)}$. If $\theta_n^*(\theta_{n-1})$ is stored for all values of $\theta_{n-1} \in S_{n-1}$ as well as the values $f^*(\theta_{n-1})$ then the n-dimensional problem has been reduced to an $n-1$-dimensional problem of the same form, although one of the functions has been modified. These reductions continue until we are left to find $\theta_2^*(\theta_1)$ for every possible $\theta_1 \in S_1$. This leads to the following algorithm.

Algorithm 4.1: Curve Detection with Dynamic Programming

1. For $i = 1, \ldots, n$, define arrays H_i indexed by elements $x \in S_i$, and with 5 columns: the first two giving the coordinates of x are merely for convenience. The last three columns get updated as the algorithm proceeds.

2. Set $H_n(x, 5) = 0$ for all $x \in S_{n-1}$. Set $i = n - 1$.

3. While $i > 0$, do
   For every $x \in S_i$ find the point $z^*(x)$ in S_{i+1}, which minimizes $\Phi_i(x, z) + H_{i+1}(z, 5)$. Store the coordinates of $z^*(x)$ in columns 3 and 4 of the x entry in H_i. Column 5 is used to store the value of $f^*(x) = \Phi_i(x, z^*(x)) + H_{i+1}(z^*(x), 5)$. Set $i = i - 1$.

4. Loop over the array H_1 and find the row with lowest value Φ^* of column 5. Let θ_1^* be the point given by the first two columns of that row. Set $i = 1$.

5. While $i < n - 1$, do
   Set θ_{i+1}^* to be the point given in columns 3 and 4 of H_i at the row indexed by θ_i^*. Set $i = i + 1$.

6. The configuration θ_i^*, $i = 1, \ldots, n$ is the optimal configuration satisfying $\theta_i \in S_i$ and the associated cost is Φ^*.

If the sets S_i are large, the computation and memory requirements of the algorithm get out of hand. For example, for square regions of size 20×20, which is the size used below, each step takes approximately .25 seconds on the Pentium III 700 MHz. However, computation here grows quadratically with the size of the state space. So, for example, using 10×10 regions, the time reduces to 10 milliseconds per iteration. In figure 4.2, we show some of the stages of the dynamic programming for detecting an $\mathcal{E}$ in a cluttered scene. The initial curve is shown in the left panel. The optimal result of the first two stages is shown in the second panel. This would be the result if the model consisted only of the first two segments corresponding to the bottom ending of the $\mathcal{E}$. This optimal solution is clearly misplaced, and is

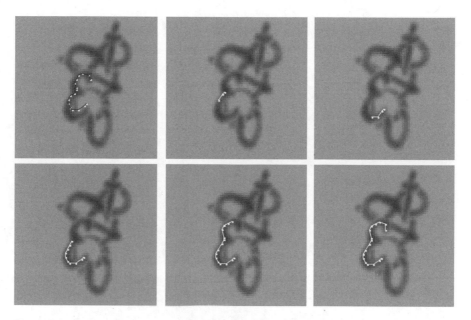

Figure 4.2   Stages of dynamic programming. The initial curve which determines the regions S_i is shown in the top left panel. Then at four stages of the dynamic programming the corresponding optimal curve is shown. Final detection is in the bottom right panel.

corrected in the next stage where the optimum corresponding to the first three segments of the model is shown. A few additional stages are shown together with the final detection.

The outcome of dynamic programming for detecting the deformable-curve algorithm on an axial MRI brain scan is shown in figure 4.3. The aim is to identify the exterior boundary, which corresponds to the scalp. The initial curve, which has the form of a semicircle, is shown in black, and the final curve is shown in white. The regions S_i were 21×21 neighborhoods of each of the points along the initial black curve. In the lower left-hand panel, the final segment of the curve is off the correct path, most likely because the neighborhood around the last point in the initial curve did not intersect the scalp. It is important to note that there is significant clutter in these images that is not easily visible. This can be seen in figure 4.1, where plenty of hits of the four local features are found inside as well as outside the scalp. These local features are the only input to the detection algorithm, and due to their photometric invariance, they detect ridges even in very-low-contrast regions.

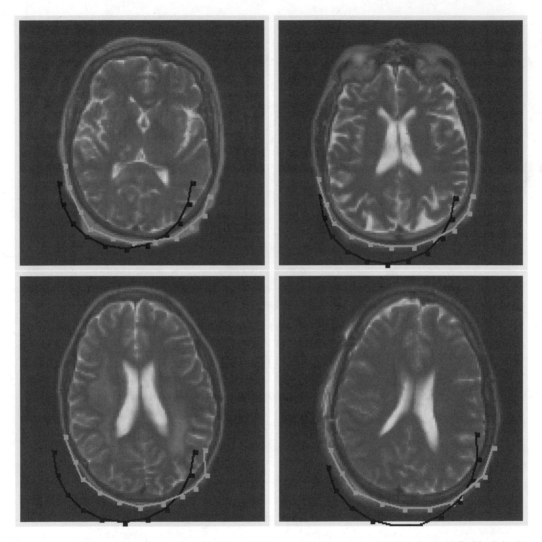

Figure 4.3 Examples of deformable curve detection on an MRI brain scan: In black is the original curve used to define the search regions, and in white are shown the stages of the dynamic programming.

When there is no particular prior shape to the curve and the only constraint is that of smoothness, priors involving consecutive triples are essential. Even with prior shape information, such constraints may be needed. Curves detected with the simpler prior can have sharp turns because there is no constraint on the curvature. The dynamic programming procedure is similar but requires computations over *triples* of consecutive points. The computational and memory requirements increase, and at times it is necessary to implement heuristics to prune the lists of optimal states to avoid an explosion in the computation time. In chapter 7, we return to dynamic programming as a technique for matching a sparse model with no prior initialization. There, we indeed use functions depending on triples of points in the model and provide the algorithmic details. A more efficient alternative to dynamic programming is described in the next section in the case where the curves are assumed to have low curvature.

4.3   Global Optimization on a Tree-Structured Prior

When the curve changes direction very slowly, we can assume that the change in angle between two consecutive segments is limited to three possible values, $-\beta, 0, \beta$, where $\beta = \pi/A$ for some large A. The distance N between consecutive points is taken to be constant. If the first two points θ_1, θ_2 are given, the path of the curve can be described as a sequence of symbols from the space $\{-1, 0, 1\}$ according to whether the next segment turns $-\beta, 0$, or β degrees. The entire space of possible curves emanating from the initial segment can be represented as a ternary tree $\mathcal{T}$, of depth n, with each node representing a possible segment. The root node of the tree is the segment θ_1, θ_2, which is fixed. Each node is connected to three children nodes representing the three possible segments following it. A curve is represented by a path from the root node to a terminal node of the tree, and is thus completely determined by that terminal node.

Starting at the initial segment, the path on the tree up to a node t provides a sequence of turns on consecutive segments of angle $\beta, 0$, or $-\beta$, all of equal length. Thus each interior node t in the tree corresponds to a physical segment L_t in the image, and has an associated angle α_t. If the initial segment is assigned angle 0, the angle of α_t can be any multiple of β. The node t also determines a set $\Theta_t \subset \Theta$ of curves passing through it. We freely interchange the use of θ for a terminal node of the tree, the path it determines in the tree, and the corresponding physical path in the image. Thus the set of possible instantiations Θ is given by the set of paths or terminal nodes of the tree. Note that certain points in the image can be traversed by two different segments represented in the tree $\mathcal{T}$. This is ignored in the model developed next.

4.3.1   The Data Model

We employ the simpler model of equation 4.9, where $P(X_a(x) = 1 \mid ang(x) = a) = p_c$ and $P(X_a(x) = 1 \mid ang(x) \neq a) = p_b$, for all $a = 1, \ldots, A = \pi/\beta$. Let $Y_t = N_{t\alpha_t}$ denote the counts along the segment L_t, of the corresponding feature X_{α_t}. Recall that α_t is the angle of L_t. The likelihood ratio of the transformed image data is now written as

$$\frac{P(\hat{I} \mid \theta)}{P_b(\hat{I})} = \prod_{t \in \theta} [p_c/p_b]^{Y_t} [(1 - p_c)/(1 - p_b)]^{N - Y_t}$$

where N is the fixed number of points along each segment. Given the true curve is θ, this data model expects a higher count of the feature X_{α_t} on the segments L_t for $t \in \theta$ than on background segments, $t \notin \theta$. Multiply the above expression by $\prod_{t \in T} p_b^{Y_t} (1 - p_b)^{N - Y_t}$, which is constant, and write the likelihood of the data, *only at pixels corresponding to segments of the tree,* conditional on the curve as

$$P(\hat{I}(x), x \in \cup_{t \in T} L_t \mid \theta) = C \cdot \prod_{t \in \theta} p_c^{Y_t} (1 - p_c)^{N - Y_t} \cdot \prod_{t \notin \theta} p_b^{Y_t} (1 - p_b)^{N - Y_t} \qquad (4.13)$$

Through some simple algebraic manipulation, we have reformulated a *restricted* likelihood only in terms of the data along $\cup_{t \in T} L_t$, namely, the collection of image segments corresponding to the tree nodes. Recall that we are ignoring the fact that these segments may have nontrivial intersections. This likelihood depends on the data along each segment L_t only in terms of the count Y_t. Moreover, in our particular setting, the distribution of Y_t is binomial $B(N, p_c)$ or $B(N, p_b)$ depending on whether the curve passes through t or not. Because the data along the segments are still considered independent given the curve, we can write a simplified likelihood of the *counts Y_t* along the segments as

$$P(Y_t, t \in T \mid \theta) = \prod_{t \in \theta} P_1(Y_t) \prod_{t \notin \theta} P_0(Y_t) \qquad (4.14)$$

where P_0 and P_1 are the binomial distributions $B(N, p_b)$ and $B(N, p_c)$, respectively. A simple computation shows that the relative weighting of the likelihood for two curves will not change using 4.13 or 4.14. Because the prior on the tree is uniform, the posterior on curves given the counts along the segments of the tree is again

$$P(\theta \mid Y_t, t \in T) = C \cdot \prod_{t \in \theta} P_1(Y_t) \prod_{t \notin \theta} P_0(Y_t) \qquad (4.15)$$

Thus in the current setting one can start with a model that only considers the image data along the tree of paths. Assume conditional independence of the counts Y_t, given θ corresponds to the true curve, with some distribution P_1 for the counts on segments in θ, and another distribution P_0 for the counts on segments in the tree not in θ. This is a somewhat weaker assumption than conditional independence of the data at each pixel, and is the approach taken in Geman and Jedynak (1996). One can then use a nonparametric form of P_1 and P_0 as opposed to the binomial model. The distribution P_1 is estimated from a sample of subimages in which a curve is passing through the center. If the angle in a subimage is α, obtain N_α along the appropriate segment. These counts are then pooled into a histogram to estimate the distribution P_1. On subimages with no curve, find the counts N_a *for each of the angles* $a = 1, \ldots, A$ and pool these into a histogram to obtain an estimate of P_0.

Before proceeding to describe the details of this algorithm, we make a brief digression to define the notion of entropy, conditional entropy, and mutual information, which will be used in the following sections as well as in chapter 9 in the context of classification trees. A comprehensive exposition of the theory of entropy, also called *information theory,* can be found in Cover and Thomas (1991).

4.3.2 Entropy

Given a random variable X with values in a finite discrete set S and with probability distribution $p(s) = P(X = s)$, we define the *entropy* of X as

$$H(X) = -\sum_{s \in S} p(s) \log p(s) \tag{4.16}$$

Because $x \log x = 0$ if $x = 0$, this sum is well defined even if some of the probabilities are 0. This quantity is one way to express how "random" X is, or the degree of "uncertainty" in X. If X is uniform on S, then $H(X) = \log(|S|)$. This can easily be seen to be the highest attainable value for any distribution on S. Indeed, the uniform distribution is the most "random." At the other extreme, if X is concentrated at one point (i.e., $p(s) = 1$ for some $s \in S$), then $H(X) = 0$, which is the lowest attainable value, because $-x \log x \geq 0$ for $0 \leq x \leq 1$. Note that $H(X)$ depends only on the distribution p and not on the values of X, so we can also write $H(p)$.

Let X_1 and X_2 be two random variables with values in S, so that the pair (X_1, X_2) has values in $S \times S$ with a joint distribution $p(s_1, s_2) = P(X_1 = s_1, X_2 = s_2)$. The *joint entropy* of X_1 and X_2 is defined in the same way as

$$H(X_1, X_2) = -\sum_{s_1 \in S, \, s_2 \in S} p(s_1, s_2) \log p(s_1, s_2) \tag{4.17}$$

Let $p_i(s_i) = P(X_i = s_i), i = 1, 2$ denote the marginal distributions of p. Let $p(s_1 \mid s_2)$ denote the conditional probability $P(X_1 = s_1 \mid X_2 = s_2)$. We can ask what is the randomness in X_1, given we know that $X_2 = s_2$, written as the entropy of the distribution $p(\cdot \mid s_2)$—that is,

$$H(X_1 \mid X_2 = s_2) = -\sum_{s_1 \in S} p(s_1 \mid s_2) \log p(s_1 \mid s_2) \tag{4.18}$$

This could be greater or less than the original entropy of X_1. If we average over all possible values s_2 in terms of the distribution p_2, we get the *conditional entropy* of X_1 given X_2

$$
\begin{aligned}
H(X_1 \mid X_2) &= -\sum_{s_2 \in S} p_2(s_2) \sum_{s_1 \in S} p(s_1 \mid s_2) \log p(s_1 \mid s_2) \\
&= -\sum_{s_1, s_2} p(s_1, s_2) \log p(s_1 \mid s_2)
\end{aligned}
\tag{4.19}
$$

Using the fact that $p(s_1 \mid s_2) = p(s_1, s_2)/p_2(s_2)$, and that $H(X_2) = -\sum_{s_1, s_2} p(s_1, s_2) \log p(s_2)$, we get the following relation between conditional entropy and joint entropy.

$$H(X_1 \mid X_2) = H(X_1, X_2) - H(X_2) \tag{4.20}$$

Furthermore, using the fact that $-\log x$ is convex, we get

$$
\begin{aligned}
H(X_1) - H(X_1 \mid X_2) &= -\sum_{s_1, s_2} p(s_1, s_2) \log \frac{p(s_1)p(s_2)}{p(s_1, s_2)} \\
&\geq -\log \left(\sum_{s_1, s_2} p(s_1, s_2) \frac{p(s_1)p(s_2)}{p(s_1, s_2)} \right) \\
&= \log 1 = 0
\end{aligned}
$$

In other words, the conditional entropy of a variable (conditioned on any other variable) is always less than the entropy. On average, the randomness in X_1 decreases if the value of X_2 is known. Except when the variables are independent—that is, $p(s_1, s_2) = p_1(s_1)p_2(s_2)$, in which case it is easy to see that

$$H(X_1 \mid X_2) = H(X_1) = H(X_1, X_2) - H(X_2) \tag{4.21}$$

Note that by equation 4.20,

$$H(X_1) - H(X_1 \mid X_2) = H(X_1) + H(X_2) - H(X_1, X_2) = H(X_2) - H(X_2 \mid X_1)$$

The quantity

$$\Delta(X_1, X_2) = H(X_1) - H(X_1 \mid X_2) = H(X_2) - H(X_2 \mid X_1) \tag{4.22}$$

is symmetric in X_1, X_2 and is called the *mutual information* of X_1 and X_2.

In our context, if we want to obtain a good guess on θ in terms of an observation X, we would pick one for which the conditional entropy of θ given X is low, or the *mutual information is high*. Not much randomness is left in θ once X is observed. This will guide us in the development of the algorithm below.

4.3.3 Sequential Updating of the Partial Posterior

Trying to directly find the maximum of the posterior in equation 4.15 is computationally impossible for trees of depth on the order of several tens. The state space is huge and even evaluating Y_t along each segment L_t corresponding to a node t of $\mathcal{T}$ is nontrivial. The idea behind the algorithm described below is to evaluate a sequence of partial posteriors conditioning only on the data at a small subset of nodes of $\mathcal{T}$, as opposed to conditioning on all the data, and evaluating the probabilities of a limited number of coarse subsets of Θ. Gradually, the size of the conditioning set increases and the subsets at which the posterior is evaluated become more refined.

At step m, assume we already have chosen a subtree T_m rooted at the root node of $\mathcal{T}$, and m nodes $t_1, \ldots, t_m \in T_m$ at which Y_t has been computed, with values $y_1, \ldots, y_m$. Let B_m denote the event $\{Y_{t_1} = y_1, \ldots, Y_{t_m} = y_m\}$. Each $t \in T_m$ determines a subset Θ_t of paths, and we calculate the partial posterior

$$\pi_t^{(m)} \doteq P(\theta \in \Theta_t \mid Y_{t_i} = y_i, i = 1, \ldots, m) \tag{4.23}$$

for all $t \in T_m$. Typically, there are more than m nodes in T_m, but the number of segments at which we actually observe Y_t is given by m and is increased by 1 at each step. The subtree T_m is sequentially updated, and typically the partial posterior in equation 4.23 becomes more and more peaked at some node t of the current subtree. There is a recursive method to calculate $\pi_t^{(m+1)}$ in terms of $\pi_t^{(m)}$.

Moreover, as discussed in the previous section, the next segment to "query" (i.e., the choice of t_{m+1} at which to observe $Y_{t_{m+1}}$) is chosen as the variable maximizing the mutual information with θ, *given the data already observed*—that is, given the event B_m. At some stage, the partial posterior is sufficiently peaked at, say, $t^* \in T_m$, the true curve can be assumed to pass through t^* (i.e., $\theta \in \Theta_{t^*}$) and the search is reinitialized at t^*.

Choosing the Next Segment to Query

Assume $m - 1$ segments have been queried, determining an event B_{m-1}, and that the current set T_m from which to choose t_m is already determined. We are seeking $t \in T_m$ for which the mutual information of θ and Y_t given B_{m-1} is largest. Due to the conditional independence assumptions, the most informative node is identified solely in terms of the current partial posterior $\pi_t^{(m-1)}$.

For $0 \leq \pi \leq 1$ define the mixture distribution $P_\pi = \pi P_1 + (1 - \pi) P_0$ and let

$$\phi(\pi) = H(P_\pi) - \pi H(P_1) - (1 - \pi) H(P_0) \tag{4.24}$$

where $H(P)$ is the entropy of the distribution P. Because $-x \log x$ is concave, the function

$$H(P_\pi) = \sum_{k=0}^{N} [\pi P_1(k) + (1 - \pi) P_0(k)] \log[\pi P_1(k) + (1 - \pi) P_0(k)]$$

is concave in π. The rest of the expression in 4.24 is linear in π so that ϕ is a concave function of $\pi \in [0, 1]$ and has a unique maximum at π_{max}. It depends on the particular distributions P_0, P_1. *The mutual information is maximized at a the node $t \in T_m$ for which $\pi_t^{(m-1)}$ is closest to π_{max}.*

This is seen as follows: The distribution of Y_t given θ depends only on whether the curve defined by θ passes through t ($\theta \in \Theta_t$) and therefore the mutual information between Y_t and θ is the same as the mutual information between Y_t and the indicator function $1_{\Theta_t}(\theta)$. Setting $\pi_t^{(m-1)} = P(\Theta_t \mid B_{m-1}) = P(1_{\Theta_t}(\theta) = 1 \mid B_{m-1})$, and letting Δ denote mutual information and H the entropy, we have

$$\Delta(Y_t, \theta \mid B_{m-1}) = \Delta(Y_t, 1_{\Theta_t} \mid B_{m-1}) = H(Y_t \mid B_{m-1}) - H(Y_t \mid 1_{\Theta_t}, B_{m-1}) \tag{4.25}$$

The conditional distribution of Y_t given B_{m-1} can be written as a mixture distribution

$$
\begin{aligned}
P(Y_t = k \mid B_{m-1}) &= \pi_t^{(m-1)} P(Y_t = k \mid \Theta_t, B_{m-1}) \\
&\quad + \left(1 - \pi_t^{(m-1)}\right) P(Y_t = k \mid \Theta_t^c, B_{m-1}) \\
&= \pi_t^{(m-1)} P_1(k) + \left(1 - \pi_t^{(m-1)}\right) P_0(k)
\end{aligned}
$$

where the second equality follows from the conditional independence. The second term in 4.25 is rewritten as

$$
\begin{aligned}
H(Y_t \mid 1_{\Theta_t}, B_{m-1}) &= H(Y_t \mid \Theta_t, B_{m-1}) \pi_t^{(m-1)} + H\left(Y_t \mid \Theta_t^c, B_{m-1}\right)\left(1 - \pi_t^{(m-1)}\right) \\
&= \pi_t^{(m-1)} H(P_1) + \left(1 - \pi_t^{(m-1)}\right) H(P_0)
\end{aligned}
$$

where again the second equality follows from the conditional independence of Y_t and B_{m-1} given 1_{Θ_t}. Therefore the mutual information reduces to

$$
\begin{aligned}
\Delta(Y_t, \theta \mid B_{m-1}) &= H\left(\left(1 - \pi_t^{(m-1)}\right)P_0 + \pi_t^{(m-1)}P_1\right) \\
&\quad - \pi_t^{(m-1)}H(P_1) - \left(1 - \pi_t^{(m-1)}\right)H(P_0) \\
&= \phi\left(\pi_t^{(m-1)}\right)
\end{aligned}
\tag{4.26}
$$

as defined in equation 4.24. We therefore need to pass through all the nodes in T_m and set t_m to be the one with π_t closest to π_{max}.

Updating from $\pi_t^{(m-1)}$ to $\pi_t^{(m)}$

Once the next node $t_m \in T_m$ at which to observe the data is chosen, we update the partial posterior given the larger conditioning set B_m, for every node in T_m. In the next section, we will see how the set T_m is chosen.

Recall that the partial posterior given B_{m-1} (i.e., $\pi_t^{(m-1)}$) has already been computed and stored for every node in $t \in T_m$. Let t be a *terminal* node of T_m, because all the nodes $t_1, \ldots, t_m$ are in T_m, knowing that the curve passes through t—that is, $\theta \in \Theta_t$— completely determines whether or not each of the nodes $t_i, i = 1, \ldots, m$ is on the curve or not. Thus Y_{t_m} is conditionally independent of B_{m-1} given Θ_t. We can then write

$$
\begin{aligned}
\pi_t^{(m)} &= P(\Theta_t \mid B_{m-1}, Y_{t_m} = y_m) \\
&= P(Y_{t_m} = y_m \mid \Theta_t, B_{m-1})P(\Theta_t \mid B_{m-1})\frac{P(B_{m-1})}{P(B_m)} \\
&= P(Y_{t_m} = y_m \mid \Theta_t)\pi_t^{(m-1)}\frac{P(B_{m-1})}{P(B_m)}
\end{aligned}
\tag{4.27}
$$

The first factor can be expressed as

$$
P(Y_{t_m} = y_m \mid \Theta_t) = \begin{cases} P_1(y_{t_m}) & \text{if } t_m \text{ is an ancestor of } t \\ P_0(y_{t_m}) & \text{otherwise } t_m \in \theta_t \end{cases}
$$

and the ratio is given by

$$
\begin{aligned}
\frac{P(B_m)}{P(B_{m-1})} &= P(Y_{t_m} = y_m \mid B_{m-1}, \Theta_{t_m})P(\Theta_{t_m} \mid B_{m-1}) \\
&\quad + P\left(Y_{t_m} = y_m \mid B_{m-1}, \Theta_{t_m}^c\right)(1 - P(\Theta_{t_m} \mid B_{m-1})) \\
&= P_1(y_m)\pi_{t_m}^{(m-1)} + P_0(y_m)\left(1 - \pi_{t_m}^{(m-1)}\right)
\end{aligned}
\tag{4.28}
$$

Thus for any terminal node $t \in T_m$, the calculation of $\pi_t^{(m)} = P(\Theta_t \mid B_m)$ is given entirely in terms of $\pi_t^{(m-1)}, \pi_{t_m}^{(m-1)}$, and $P_i(y_m), i = 0, 1$—all of which are known.

For every *internal* node t of the tree T_m, write $\pi_t^{(m)} = \pi_{t_1}^{(m)} + \pi_{t_2}^{(m)} + \pi_{t_3}^{(m)}$, where t_1, t_2, t_3 are the three child nodes of t, so that $\pi_t^{(m)}$ can be recursively updated going from the terminal nodes upward.

Defining the Subtree T_{m+1}

The partial posterior $\pi_t^{(m)}$ has been computed for all $t \in T_m$. The set T_{m+1} is obtained from the set T_m, keeping in mind the fact that subsequently we will be looking for informative nodes—that is, nodes with $\pi_t^{(m)}$ close to π_{max}. First include all nodes in T_m. For any terminal node $t' \in T_m$ satisfying $\pi_{t'} > \pi_{max}$, add the three children to T_{m+1}. For these children nodes write

$$\pi_t^{(m)} = P(\Theta_t \mid B_m) = \frac{1}{3} P(\Theta_{t'} \mid B_m) = \frac{1}{3}\pi_{t'}^{(m)} \tag{4.29}$$

This is due to the uniform prior and the fact that we are conditioning on observed data at nodes in T_m, so that $t \neq t_1, \ldots, t_m$. On the other hand, if $\pi_t^{(m)} < \pi_{max}$ there is no point in adding the children because their value would be further away from π_{max}. Even if $\pi_t^{(m)} > \pi_{max}$, the value for the three children themselves will have to be less than π_{max} again because of the factor of $1/3$ and because π_{max} is typically between .4 and .6. Therefore this extension occurs *only for one level*—that is, all new nodes are children of terminal nodes of T_m. An important conclusion is that *the most informative segment in the entire tree given the information in B_m has to be in the set T_{m+1}*.

The procedure now repeats. The next query t_{m+1} will be that segment t in T_{m+1} for which $\pi_t^{(m)}$ is closest to π_{max}. The new probability $\pi_t^{(m+1)}$ is computed from $\pi_t^{(m)}$ for all elements of T_{m+1} and T_{m+1} is extended to T_{m+2}. To start, we set T_0 as the root node and therefore necessarily T_1 consists of the root node and its three children, one of which is picked at random as t_1. At some stage, the partial posterior is sufficiently peaked at some $t^* \in T_m$. We then assume the true curve passes through t^* (i.e., $\theta \in \Theta_{t^*}$) and the search is reinitialized at t^*.

The entire algorithm is summarized as follows:

Algorithm 4.2: Curve Detection—Tree-Based Algorithm
A node t in the tree is an object with variables used to store the following information:

- First and second point of segment: $t.p_1, t.p_2$
- The count: $t.Y$
- Pointers to 3 children and parent: $t.ch_1, t.ch_2, t.ch_3, t.par$

- The current approximate posterior: $t.\pi$
- Depth in tree: $t.depth$

π_{max} The minimum of ϕ defined in equation 4.26.

TM Pointer to node with π value closest to π_{max}

Δ Store $|TM.\pi - \pi_{max}|$

TMS Node at which algorithm reinitializes

π^* Lower threshold for posterior at node t to reinitialize algorithm from the corresponding segment assuming $t.depth$ is greater then d_{min}

1. Initialize π^*, π_{max}, d_{min} Get two initial points from user: x_1, x_2
2. Initialize $\Delta = 1$, $TM = null$, $TMS = null$

   top is the top node of the tree. $top.p_1 = x_1$, $top.p_2 = x_2$

   Call $birth(top)$
3. For $step = 0 : step_{max}$

   Evaluate data at TM and store in $TM.Y$

   Compute $R = 1/(TM.\pi \cdot P_1(TM.Y) + (1 - TM.\pi) \cdot P_0(TM.Y))$. (eq. 4.28)

   Sweep through nodes of current tree

   - If (t is terminal)

     (Apply eq. 4.27)

     if (t descendent of TM) $t.\pi \leftarrow t.\pi \cdot R \cdot P_1(TM.y)$

     else $t.\pi \leftarrow t.\pi \cdot R \cdot P_0(TM.y)$

     if ($t.\pi > \pi_{max}$) Call $birth(t)$

   - If (t is not terminal)

     $t.\pi = t.ch_1.\pi + t.ch_2.\pi + t.ch_3.\pi$

   - Call $update(t)$: Check if time to reinitialize, and update current choice of TM

Function $update(t)$

  if ($t.\pi > \pi^*$) and ($t.depth > d_{min}$)

    $TMS = t$

    $x_1 = t.p_1$, $x_2 = t.p_2$

    Go to 2.

  if ($|t.\pi - \pi_{max}| < \Delta$)

    $\pi_\Delta = |t.\pi - \pi_{max}|$, $TM = t$

Function $birth(t)$

  Create $t.ch_j$, $j = 1, 2, 3$

  Calculate p_1, p_2 for each,

  and set $ch_j.\pi = t.\pi/3$

  if ($|ch_j.\pi - \pi_{max}| < \Delta$)

    $\Delta = |ch_j.\pi - \pi_{max}|$

    $TM = ch_r$ (r -random)

The $m + 1$th segment at which the data is observed (i.e., Y_t is measured) can be characterized as one of the following possibilities. If the posterior on t_m is very high, it could be a randomly chosen child of t_m. This corresponds to asking whether the curve continues down the path determined by t_m. If the posterior on t_m is low, the next segment could be one of the *interior* elements of T_m for which the updated posterior is closer to π_{max}, recall that not all nodes of T_m have been queried. The information at that node may actually indicate where the curve *does not* pass. This is useful information. If there is accumulated evidence that the curve does not pass through certain parts of the tree, the posterior on other parts increases and the next query may be a randomly chosen child of some element of T_m, which has high updated posterior, but which is not close to t_m. The last two options are specifically what allow for backtracking and choosing a new direction of search. It is also possible to "jump ahead." Assume t_j is somewhere near the root and that $t_{j+1}, \ldots, t_m$ are not descendents of t_j, and that T_m includes some subtree $\mathcal{T}_j$ rooted at t_j. (This is possible because descendents of t_j could have been added to the sets without having been queried.) It may be that t_{m+1} is some element of $\mathcal{T}_j$, which is not a direct child of t_j.

This algorithm performs essentially in *real time*. The key component of this efficiency is the very small number of segments at which the data is actually accessed and processed, and the simple recursive way in which the posterior can be updated. In figure 4.4, we illustrate the workings of the algorithm in detecting the scalp in an axial MRI scan used in figure 4.3. The parameters p_b, p_c were not estimated but set manually to .4 and .7, respectively. The angle β was set to $10°$ and the length of each segment is set to 10. The algorithm tracks the entire scalp with only the two initial points provided and marked in white. In the top image this track is shown in white and in black are shown those segments in the tree for which the image data were accessed. In the bottom image, we see the tracked curve with two different initial points. The computation time is a fraction of a second. In figure 4.5, a similar experiment is done to track the artery in an angiogram.

Although the tree grows exponentially with the depth, the number of nodes actually involved in the algorithm (i.e., the size of T_m) never grows above several hundreds. It is also possible to prune terminal nodes for which the posterior falls below a very low threshold. Although it is hard to see, there is plenty of clutter in the background, which is able to "distract" the algorithm for rather extensive periods (see figure 4.1).

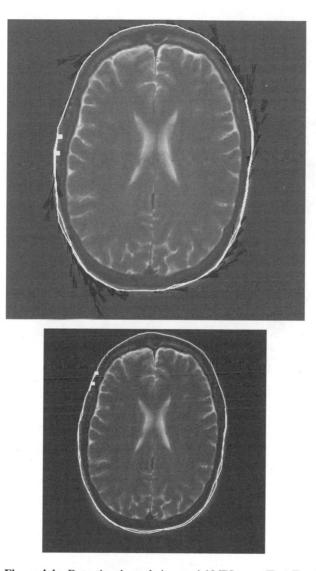

Figure 4.4   Detecting the scalp in an axial MRI scan. (Top) Two initial points shown as larger squares. In black every segment that was queried, i.e., at which image data was accessed. In white the track leading to the terminal node of highest posterior at each step. (Bottom) Final contour with two different initial points.

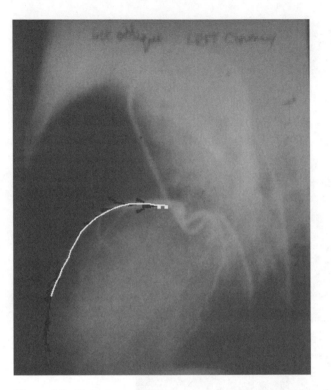

Figure 4.5   Detecting an artery in an angiogram using tree based algorithm.

4.4   Bibliographical Notes and Discussion

The motivation for the dynamic programming algorithm comes from Petrocelli, Elion, and Manbeck (1992), and similar work can also be found in Geiger and colleagues (1995). The tree-based algorithm is taken from Geman and Jedynak (1996) and has been implemented with great success for tracking roads in remote-sensing images. It is very fast and outperforms any computationally feasible implementation of dynamic programming. Whereas the deformation algorithms described in chapter 3 had a region-growing flavor to them, and hence in some coarse sense expected the initial contour to expand around a more or less homogeneous region, the curve detection algorithms described in this chapter perform some form of "tracking," in that they attempt to proceed along a curve with some particular image statistics in its neighborhood. The curve-detection algorithms need some form of initialization but

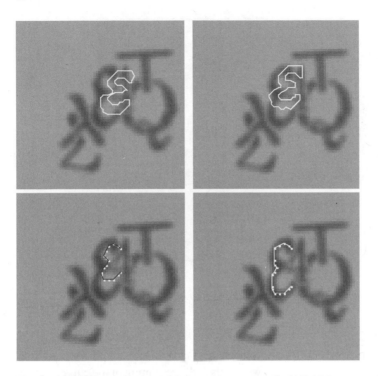

Figure 4.6 (Top) Detection of deformable contour. (Left) Initial contour. (Right) Detection. (Bottom) Detection of deformable curve with dynamic programming. (Left) Initial curve. (Right) Detection.

are much more robust to clutter and noise both due to the more systematic model-ing of the data along the curve and the fact that within some restricted region the actual *global optimum* is found. In figure 4.6, we show an example of a randomly perturbed LaTeX $\mathcal{E}$ in a cluttered environment. Using a closed contour of the proto-type $\mathcal{E}$, we run a deformable contour algorithm initialized with the contour shown in the top left panel. The final detection is shown in the top right panel. Due to the cluttered environment, the contour reaches some local minimum that does not reflect the correct instantiation. For comparison, we initialize the dynamic programming algorithm for curve detection with a curve also produced from the prototype $\mathcal{E}$. The initial curve is even further removed from the correct instantiation, and yet the final detection shown in the bottom right panel has identified a correct instantiation of the deformed $\mathcal{E}$.

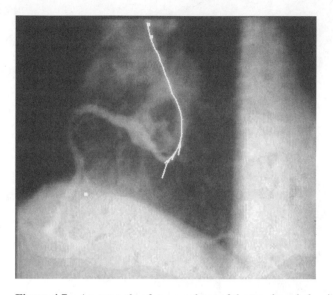

Figure 4.7   An example of an overshoot of the tree based algorithm at a severe bend of the curve.

Tree-based curve detection is much faster than dynamic programming and only requires an initialization of two points at the beginning of the curve. It is very successful in detecting long smooth curves of low curvature. However, it is hard to incorporate prior shape information in this setting and it risks overshooting if the true curve does have large curvature at some point. This is the effect of the very strong prior. See, for example, the tracking of the artery in the angiogram of figure 4.7. When the artery has a strong bend, the detection overshoots.

5   2D Models: Deformable Images

In chapters 3 and 4, we explored the idea of fitting a one-dimensional model to the boundary of an object. Prior information regarding the shape of the object is represented in terms of the initial template contour or template curve. In most cases, when we analyze images of a particular object class, there is much more information available than the mere shape of one contour. Any two images of the object class viewed as surfaces would exhibit many topological and geometric similarities that are ignored when the contour alone is computed. The variations between objects often appear to be smooth, in the sense that with some pulling and stretching and squeezing, one could take one image from such a collection and transform it into another. This form of stretching and squeezing, which we call image deformation, deforms not only the contour of one object to the contour of the other, it deforms the entire image surface.

Consider the image domain D as a continuum, typically the unit square, and let the prototype image be a function $F(x)$, $x \in D$. Let ϕ denote a smooth deformation of D onto itself. What can we say about the image $\tilde{F}(x) = F(\phi(x))$? If ϕ is smooth, extremal points are preserved, maxima are mapped onto maxima, minima onto minima, saddle points onto saddle points, level curves onto level curves. Loosely speaking, the topography of the surface remains the same, although the shapes of the hills and valleys may change. If ϕ is sufficiently close to the identity, we seem to be observing a different version of the same object. For example, in figure 5.1, 25 smooth, random nonlinear deformations of a face still look like a face—although not necessarily of the same person. The various points of interest, which are characterized by some peculiar topography of the image surface, are mapped to points with the same local topography and they maintain their relative spatial arrangement. Moreover, if the boundary of the object or any part of the object is marked in the prototype image F, then ϕ^{-1} will deform it to the corresponding boundary in the image $\tilde{F}$.

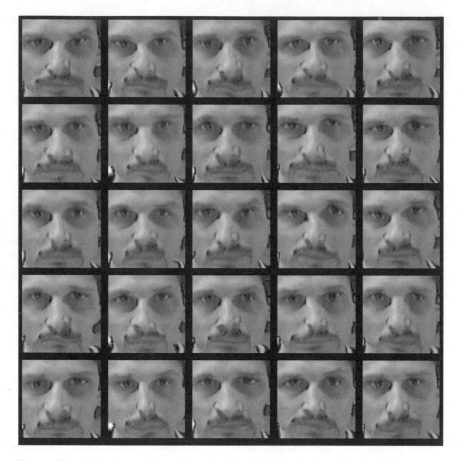

Figure 5.1   25 random deformations of a face (yours truly) using the 8×8 lower resolution coefficients of a Daubechies wavelet basis for a 64×64 lattice.

We have reparameterized the images of the object class in terms of the deformations ϕ and have established a correspondence to the prototype image. This is illustrated by picking several points on the prototype image and plotting $\phi^{-1}(x)$ on the data image for each such point. For example, note that in figure 5.2 the mapping ϕ^{-1} maps the eyes in the prototype image to the eyes in the data image, as well as the tips of the mouth or other points on the boundary of the face.

Our goal in this section is to describe techniques for computing ϕ given a prototype image F and a new data image I of the same object class.

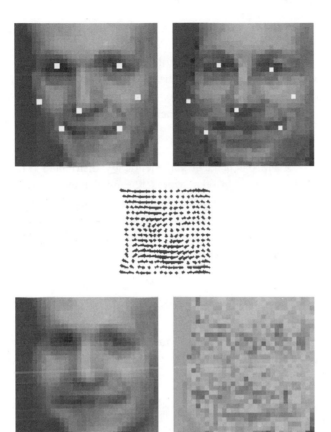

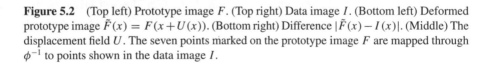

Figure 5.2   (Top left) Prototype image F. (Top right) Data image I. (Bottom left) Deformed prototype image $\tilde{F}(x) = F(x + U(x))$. (Bottom right) Difference $|\tilde{F}(x) - I(x)|$. (Middle) The displacement field U. The seven points marked on the prototype image F are mapped through ϕ^{-1} to points shown in the data image I.

5.1   Statistical Model

In terms of the formulation in chapter 2, we take the template points Z to cover the entire reference grid G, and assume the data images are defined on a lattice L, which is the same size as G. The set of instantiations Θ is then a collection of smooth one-to-one maps of $Z = G$ onto the image lattice $L = G$.

5.1.1   Gaussian Data Model

Let $F(z)$, $z \in Z$ be a prototype image of the object. We distinguish here between the template, which is simply the lattice structure of points Z that are mapped onto the image grid L, and the prototype image, which is used to define the data model. Assume that any image of the object is generated as

$$I(\theta(z)) = F(z) + N(z), z \in Z \tag{5.1}$$

where $N(z)$, $z \in Z$ are independent and identically distributed (i.i.d) Gaussians with some fixed variance σ. In other words, the pixel intensity of the prototype image at point z is moved to $\theta(z)$, and some noise is added, independently at each pixel. This is not a realistic model but is very simple and leads to interesting results. Under this model, the data $I(x)$, $x \in L$ given the instantiation θ is again independent, because the additive noise is independent. It will be more convenient to write this equation as

$$I(x) = F(\phi(x)) + N(x)$$

where $\phi = \theta^{-1}$. Every pixel $x \in L$ grabs the value of the prototype image F at $\phi(x)$. The gray-level intensities given $\phi = \theta^{-1}$ are assumed to be independent Gaussians with variance σ, and mean given by $F(\phi(x))$. Up to a constant, the log-likelihood therefore has the simple form

$$\mathcal{D}(\phi) = -\frac{1}{2\sigma^2} \sum_{x \in L} |F(\phi(x)) - I(x)|^2 \, dx \tag{5.2}$$

Because we will be optimizing through gradient-descent methods, we consider the data image and the prototype image as defined on the continuum—that is, as $I(x)$, $F(x)$, $x \in D$ where D is the unit square. The map ϕ defines a smooth deformation of the domain D onto itself. The actual instantiation of the grid Z can be recovered by taking $\phi^{-1}(z)$, $z \in Z$.

Define the displacement field as $U(x) = \phi(x) - x$ and denote its two components as $U^{(1)}$ and $U^{(2)}$. Now rewrite $\mathcal{D}(\phi)$ as

$$\mathcal{D}(U) = -\frac{1}{2\sigma^2} \int_D |F(x + U(x)) - I(x)|^2 \, dx \tag{5.3}$$

The field $U(x)$ is easier to work with because the value 0 corresponds to the identity map. To simplify notation and computation, we will henceforth assume that U is periodic on the unit square.

Section 5.4 describes an alternative data model based on transforming the image data into binary local features similar to those used in chapter 4. This data model will have some advantages in terms of photometric invariance and in terms of parameter estimation.

5.1.2   The Prior and Posterior

There are many solutions U that will yield $\mathcal{D}(U) = 0$. However, such solutions will typically be highly irregular, discontinuous, and noninvertible. The topography of the image surface would no longer be conserved. In order to rule out the discontinuous and irregular solutions, we introduce a prior on the set of displacement fields that implicitly defines a prior on the maps $\phi(x) = x + U(x)$ of the image onto the reference grid. As in chapter 3, we adopt a spectral parameterization of the displacement fields in terms of their expansion in some basis of functions. Again, such a representation defines a map on the continuum in terms of a finite number of parameters, and using wavelet or Fourier functions, we obtain a natural coarse-to-fine parameterization of the deformations. Write

$$U^{(q)}(x) = \sum_{k=0}^{d} u_k^{(q)} \psi_k(x), \quad q = 1, 2 \tag{5.4}$$

for some finite d where ψ_k is some basis of functions on the unit square. This parameterization allows for a direct approach to enforcing the smoothness if we assume the coefficients $u_k^{(q)}$ are independent Gaussian, with mean zero and variance $1/\lambda_k$, with λ_k an increasing sequence of positive values. The log-prior is then up to a constant given by

$$\mathcal{E}(U) = -\frac{1}{2} \sum_{k=0}^{d} \lambda_k \left[\left(u_k^{(1)} \right)^2 + \left(u_k^{(2)} \right)^2 \right] \tag{5.5}$$

One drawback of this parameterization is that $\phi(x) = x + U(x)$ is not guaranteed to be one-to-one, and $\phi(x)$ may not necessarily be in the domain D. This does not cause major problems in applications, as will be seen below.

Fourier Basis

For the two-dimensional Fourier basis $k = (k_1, k_2)$ is a two-parameter index, and each basis element has the form

$$\frac{1}{2\pi} \psi_k(x) = \exp[2\pi i (k_1 x_1 + k_2 x_2)]$$

As k_1, k_2 increase, the functions ψ have derivatives of increasing magnitude. In order to ensure smoothness, the variances must decrease. Thus we set $\lambda_k = (k_1^2 + k_2^2)^\rho$ for some positive ρ. The larger ρ, the smoother the resulting functions will be.

Wavelets

As in one dimension, the two-dimensional wavelet basis on the unit square is also arranged in a pyramid. The structure is somewhat more complex. At each level s, there are three functions $\psi_{\alpha, s, 0, 0}$, $\alpha = 1, 2, 3$ and all other functions of that level are given as shifts of one of these three functions:

$$\psi_{\alpha, s, \ell_1, \ell_2}(x) = \psi_{\alpha, s, 0, 0}\left(x_1 - 2^{-(s-1)} \ell_1, x_2 2^{-(s-1)} \ell_2\right)$$

for $\alpha = 1, 2, 3$ and $\ell_1, \ell_2 = 0, \ldots, 2^{s-1}$. Thus k is a four-parameter index $k = (\alpha, s, \ell_1, \ell_2)$ where the index s defines the resolution. The constant function is denoted $\psi_{0,0,0,0}$. For $s \geq \bar{s}$ the function $\psi_{\alpha, s, 0, 0}$ is a scaling and dilution of $\psi_{\alpha, S, 0, 0}$. Specifically

$$\psi_{\alpha, s, 0, 0}(x) = 2^{(s-S)} \psi_{\alpha, S, 0, 0}\left(2^{(s-S)} x\right)$$

Again, this is also true for $s < \bar{s}$ modulo some wraparound effects.

At the highest resolution S, the functions $\psi_{\alpha, S, 0, 0}$ have very small support. The support increases as the resolution s decreases. For higher values of s, the information conveyed by the coefficients is more local. Also, as s increases, the derivatives of the functions increase in magnitude and a smaller variance needs to be set for the coefficients to maintain the smoothness of the function. Thus we set

$$\lambda_k = \lambda_{(\alpha, s, \ell_1, \ell_2)} = 2^{\rho s} \tag{5.6}$$

for all $0 \leq \ell_1, \ell_2 < 2^s$, $\alpha = 1, 2, 3$. The same variance is assigned to coefficients of all functions at the same resolution. This particular form of decrease of the variance with resolution is motivated by the theory relating rates of decay of wavelet coefficients to smoothness properties of the corresponding functions, which can be found in Meyer (1990) and Wickerhauser (1994).

Smoothing with Differential Operators

Often in the literature, the smoothness of the deformations is obtained by a regularizing term in the cost function. A common practice is to penalize the magnitude of the derivatives of the function. In the discretized world, this corresponds to penalizing large distances between the mapping under U of two nearby lattice points. Nearby pixels should be mapped to nearby locations. If on the lattice we want to minimize

$$\mathcal{E}_L(U) = \sum_{|x-y|=1} |U(x) - U(y)|^2 \tag{5.7}$$

in the continuum, this translates to a penalty term of the form

$$\mathcal{E}(U) = \int_D \left|\nabla U^{(1)}(x)\right|^2 + \left|\nabla U^{(2)}(x)\right|^2 dx \tag{5.8}$$

Higher-order differences or derivatives lead to higher degrees of smoothness. Any penalty of the form appearing in equation 5.8 involving differential operators can be directly translated into a penalty of the form appearing in equation 5.5, with the Fourier basis, taking $d = \infty$ and using particular choices of λ_k. For example, for the penalty in equation 5.8, take $\lambda_k - (k_1^2 + k_2^2)$. However, the spectral parameterization offers a much richer collection of possible penalties, because other values of λ_k can be chosen as well as other bases, such as wavelets or wavelet packets. As in chapter 3, this representation also has the advantage of offering a natural way to implement a coarse-to-fine computation, and a built-in interpolation of the map ϕ to the continuum.

Combining the likelihood and the prior, and ignoring the constant, which does not depend on the unknowns, the negative log-posterior has the form of a cost function of the form

$$J\left(u^{(1)}, u^{(2)}\right) = \frac{1}{2} \sum_{k=0}^{d} \lambda_k \left[\left(u_k^{(1)}\right)^2 + \left(u_k^{(2)}\right)^2\right]$$

$$+ \int \left(F\left[x_1 + \sum_{k=0}^{d} u_k^{(1)} \psi_k(x), x_2 + \sum_{k=0}^{d} u_k^{(2)} \psi_k(x)\right] - I(x) \right)^2 dx \tag{5.9}$$

which is now rewritten as a function of the coefficients $u^{(q)} = \{u_k^{(q)}\}_{k=0}^d, q = 1, 2$. The variance coefficient $1/\sigma^2$ from the data term has been absorbed into the coefficients λ_k.

5.2   Connection to the Deformable-Contour Model

It is of interest to point out the relation of this model to the inside-outside deformable-contour model presented in chapter 3. Given the initial contour $\gamma^{(0)}$, define a prototype image that has constant value μ_{in} inside the initial contour and constant value μ_{out} outside. The data term for the two-dimensional model is now identical to the data term for the one-dimensional model. The difference in applying the two-dimensional model is in the way the deformations of the initial contour are parameterized. Now the contour, which is the boundary between the two intensity levels, is deforming together with the entire 2D unit square. If $\phi(x) = x + U(x)$ is the two-dimensional deformation, then $\gamma(t, \phi) = \phi^{-1}(\gamma^{(0)}(t))$. Because ϕ is smooth, $\gamma(t, \phi)$ is a smooth deformation of $\gamma^{(0)}$. One way of illustrating the difference between these two forms of parameterization is to imagine the one-dimensional model as a deforming elastic rubber band and the two-dimensional model as a curve drawn on a deforming elastic sheet. It is clear, for example, that in the second case there is a much smaller chance of getting self-intersections of the curve. In the one-dimensional model, even if the perturbation is smooth, it is easy to obtain self-intersections.

On the other hand, the advantage of the one-dimensional model is that even though it uses a data term involving the entire two-dimensional domain, the actual gradient-descent algorithm only uses data in the immediate vicinity of the curve and is therefore less sensitive to whether the global data model is appropriate or not. Thus, for example, in figure 3.2, the outside model that assumes the outside is brighter is obviously wrong, except locally at the boundaries of the ventricle. By contrast, the two-dimensional algorithm always integrates over the entire domain, and tries to match the two surfaces.

5.3   Computation

The cost function is optimized using a gradient-descent algorithm. The derivative of the cost function J, of equation 5.9, in the coefficients $u_k^{(q)}$, is obtained by interchanging integration and differentiation and applying the chain rule. This yields

$$\frac{\partial J\left(u^{(1)}, u^{(2)}\right)}{\partial u_k^{(q)}} = \lambda_k u_k^{(q)} + \int \frac{\partial F}{\partial x_q}(x + U(x))[F(x + U(x)) - I(x)]\psi_k(x)\,dx$$

$$(5.10)$$

for $q = 1, 2$ and $k = 0, 1, \ldots, d$. As in chapter 3, the derivative of the data term is a forward transform of a function in terms of the chosen basis. In this case, the function is

$$\partial_q F(x + U(x))[F(x + U(x) - I(x)]$$

where $\partial_q F, q = 1, 2$ are the two partial derivatives of F. In chapter 3, we already introduced the idea of gradually increasing the number of updated coefficients. This idea proves to be very useful in the context of deformable images as well. Minimizing in the first few coefficients in a wavelet or Fourier basis provides large and smooth coarse deformations. Once these converge to a local minimum, increase the number of coefficients and obtain more detailed matches.

Let Ψ denote the forward transform of a function and Ψ^{-1} denote the backward transform applied to a sequence of coefficients with respect to the chosen basis.

$$\Psi(f) = \left\{ \int_D f\psi_k dx, k = 0, \ldots, d \right\}$$

$$\Psi^{-1}(u) = \sum_{k=0}^d u_k \psi_k$$

Choose $\mathcal{N}_1 < \mathcal{N}_2 < \cdots < \mathcal{N}_A \le d$. The coarse-to-fine gradient-descent algorithm has the following form:

Algorithm 5.1: Image Deformation—Coarse to Fine

1. Normalize F and I to have range of values in $[0, 1]$.
   Initialize $u_0^{(q)} = \{u_{k,0}^{(q)}, k = 0, \ldots, d\}, q = 1, 2$. (Typically $u_0 = 0$).
   Set $m = 0, a = 1$.

2. Calculate $U^{(1)} = \Psi^{-1}(u_m^{(1)}), U^{(2)} = \Psi^{-1}(u_m^{(2)})$,

3. Calculate

   $$W_q(x) = \partial_q F(x + U(x))[F(x + U(x) - I(x)], \quad q = 1, 2.$$

4. Calculate $v^{(q)} = \Psi(W_q), q = 1, 2$.

5. Set $u^{(q)}_{k,m+1} = u^{(q)}_{k,m} - \Delta \cdot (\lambda_k u^{(q)}_{k,m} + v_{q,k})$ *only* for $k = 0, \ldots, \mathcal{N}_a$, and $q = 1, 2$

6. If stopping criterion satisfied go to 7. Otherwise $m \leftarrow m + 1$, go to 2.

7. If $a < A$, $a \leftarrow a + 1$, go to 2. Otherwise exit.

For the Fourier basis, we take $0 < k_1, k_2 < a$, for each of the two field components, so that $\mathcal{N}_a = 2 \cdot a^2$, and $a = 1, \ldots, A$. The index a corresponds to the highest frequency being updated. For the wavelet basis, take $\psi_{\alpha,s,\ell_1,\ell_2}$ such that $1 \leq s \leq a$ and $0 \leq \ell_1, \ell_2 < 2^{s-1}$. In this case, $\mathcal{N}_a = 2 \cdot 2^a$, $a = 1, \ldots, A$. The index a corresponds to the highest *resolution* currently being updated.

The choice of initial point 0 is motivated by the fact that the mapping generated by the solution is expected to be in some neighborhood of the identity map.

5.3.1   Discretization and the 2D Wavelet Transform

The functions F and I are defined only on the grid L. When $x + U(x)$ does not lie on the grid, set the value of $F(x + U(x))$ as the linear interpolation of the four nearest lattice points around $x + U(x)$. The derivatives of F are calculated using finite differences and stored before the iteration procedure begins. When $x + U(x)$ lies outside the domain D, set $F(x + U(x))$ to 0. These are the ingredients needed to compute $W_1(x)$, $W_2(x)$ step 3, at each $x \in L$.

Discretizing involves replacing the continuous basis with its discrete counterpart and applying discrete forward and backward transforms, also denoted Ψ, Ψ^{-1}. Let the image lattice be $2^S \times 2^S$. When using discrete wavelets, the largest possible value for A is S.

The discrete 2D wavelet transform is easily obtained from the 1D transforms. Given a $2^s \times 2^s$ data array $F^{(s)}$, compute one step as described in equations 3.21 and 3.22 for each row to obtain $\hat{F}^{(s)}$. Then compute the same for each column of $\hat{F}$ to obtain $Y^{(s)}$. The result is a $2^s \times 2^s$ array

$$Y^{(s)} = \begin{pmatrix} u_1^{(s)} & u_2^{(s)} \\ u_3^{(s)} & F^{(s-1)} \end{pmatrix}$$

where $u^{(s)}_{\alpha,\ell_1,\ell_2}$, $0 \leq \ell_1, \ell_2 \leq 2^{s-1} - 1$ and $\alpha = 1, 2, 3$ are the coefficients corresponding to resolution s—that is, the functions $\psi_{\alpha,s,\ell_1,\ell_2}$. The same type of operation is again repeated on $F^{(s-1)}$, and so on.

The filters h and g of equations 3.21 and 3.22 can be combined through tensor products to define the following four $R \times R$ filters: $H^{(1)}_{i,j} = h_i \cdot h_j$, $H^{(2)}_{i,j} = h_i \cdot g_j$,

$H_{i,j}^{(3)} = g_i \cdot h_j$, $G_{i,j} = g_i \cdot g_j$, for $i, j = 1, \ldots, R$. Then for each $\alpha = 1, 2, 3$, the matrices $u_\alpha^{(s)}$ are simply the subsampled convolution of $F^{(s)}$ with $H^{(\alpha)}$. These are high-pass filters of $F^{(s)}$. The matrix $F^{(s-1)}$ is the subsampled convolution of $F^{(s)}$ with G, which is a low-pass filter.

The inverse transform is obtained in the same way. Apply equation 3.23 to each row of $Y^{(s-1)}$ and then apply the same to each column of $Y^{(s-1)}$. This reconstructs $F^{(s)}$, again due to the particular properties of h and g.

5.3.2 Time Step

The time step is given as the inverse of an approximation to the trace of the Hessian matrix of J. The second derivative of $\mathcal{D}$ with respect to the coefficient $u_k^{(q)}$ is a sum of two integrals. One has the difference of $F(x + U(x))$ and $I(x)$ in the integrand and is ignored assuming that $F(x + U(x))$ is relatively close to $I(x)$. The other term is $\int \partial_q F^2 \psi_k^2(x) dx$, $q = 1, 2$. Assuming a uniform bound M on ψ_k, $k = 0, \ldots, d$, we bound the trace of J by

$$T = dM \int |\nabla F|^2 \, dx + \sum_k \lambda_k$$

and set the time step $\Lambda = T^{-1}$.

5.3.3 Smoothing

In some cases, it is useful to smooth and subsample the prototype image and the data image. First, this tends to single out global geometric structures and eliminate local ones. Second, lowering the dimension of the data speeds up the algorithm. Finally, if I and F have disjoint support—for example, two "humps" supported on disjoint parts of the domain—there is really no reason for these two structures to attract. Smoothing can increase the support size of the two functions and create some interaction between the two.

5.3.4 Other Optimization Algorithms

The minimization algorithm is a discrete approximation to the downward gradient flow. Other more sophisticated approaches are described in the literature (see Press and colleagues 1995). The first alternative would be to implement the conjugate gradient method. This involves line searches, and turns out to yield comparable results to the gradient-descent algorithm at about the same speed. Note that the computation involved in the forward or backward wavelet transform is on the order of a few evaluations of the cost itself and thus very inexpensive. A second alternative involves Newton or quasi-Newton methods. These can be rather computationally intensive. In section 5.5, we discuss the linearization of the cost function and the associated least-square solution. Implementing this procedure at any iteration of the gradient-descent algorithm corresponds to a quasi-Newton type step and may speed convergence.

5.3.5   Computing Pose Parameters

The standard bases mentioned in this chapter rarely express the affine pose parameters other than translation in a direct way. Some initial updating of these parameters could be useful to improve on the initial pose parameters provided by the user. In the context of the minimization problem posed above, write

$$D(A) = \min_{A \in \mathcal{A}} \int |F((I + A)x) - I(x)|^2 \, dx$$

where $\mathcal{A}$ is the set of affine maps. If this set is directly parameterized in terms of the four entries of the linear matrix and the two entries of the translation, the problem is equivalent to defining three basis functions $\psi_1(x) = 1$, $\psi_2(x) = x_1$, $\psi_3(x) = x_2$, and minimizing D in terms of their coefficients. The gradient has the same form as in equation 5.10 except that the integral needs to be explicitly calculated and cannot be computed using a fast-forward transform.

Ignoring "shear," A can be parameterized in terms of scaling s_1, s_2 in the two coordinates, a rotation α and a translation (t_1, t_2), writing

$$Ax = \begin{pmatrix} s_x & 0 \\ 0 & s_y \end{pmatrix} \begin{pmatrix} \cos(\alpha) & \sin(\alpha) \\ -\sin(\alpha) & \cos(\alpha) \end{pmatrix} x + (t_1, t_2)$$

One can either simultaneously optimize in all five parameters, calculating the respective partial derivatives, or iterate by first adjusting for translation, then scale, and finally rotation. This cycle can be repeated several times. This is used in the Bernoulli model below.

5.3.6   Lattice Parameterization

In order to enforce smoothness, the low dimensionality of the deformation space, and a natural coarse-to-fine procedure, we used a spectral parameterization of the deformations in terms of some orthogonal bases. It is possible to stay with the point-wise parameterization, $U(x)$, $x \in L$, where L is the image lattice. The penalty remains in the form of a differential operator, as in equation 5.8. This procedure is very problematic in terms of obtaining the large coarse deformations and is relatively very slow. It is therefore not recommended for starting. It is, however, possible to use it for fine-detail matching after the spectral approach has converged (this is implemented in Miller and colleagues 1993).

One way to implement the lattice parameterization together with a coarse-to-fine procedure is related to motion estimation algorithms used for image compression. The lattice is divided into large disjoint blocks and a fixed displacement is estimated separately for each block. This is done either through a gradient-descent procedure on the two displacement parameters, or by an exhaustive search for the best match in some constrained region. A smooth interpolation of the displacements identified for each block produces the final displacement field for the current level. This serves as an initial point for the search for displacements for the next level of smaller blocks. Such methods are used in various MPEG implementations (for example, see Chalidabhongse and Kuo 1997). They are very similar to the spectral approach described above if the Haar basis is used, which is a basis of piece-wise constant functions, and is the simplest type of wavelet basis.

5.4   Bernoulli Data Model

One inherent problem in the model discussed thus far is the assumption that the gray levels have a Gaussian distribution with mean given by the deformed prototype image. It is clear that a variety of lighting conditions, such as shadows or nonhomogeneous light, produce a more complex distribution of the gray-level intensities even for a fixed object. In such cases, it is desirable to find forms of the data term $\mathcal{D}$ that are invariant to such changes. Another problem is that it is impossible to model pixel intensities off the object as Gaussians with some fixed mean. However, some form of model for pixels off the object can be helpful when the object does not occupy the entire image. In this section, we will define a data model in terms of photometric invariant binary local features similar to those defined in chapter 4 (see equations 4.1, 4.2). Those were, roughly speaking, "ridge" detectors and were specifically designed to be highly invariant to photometric transformations. We now define discontinuity detectors commonly known in the literature as *edges*, again in terms of simple comparisons of pixel intensity differences.

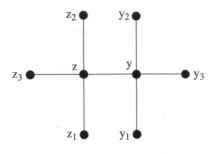

Figure 5.3   The six intensity differences being compared to identify a vertical edge.

5.4.1   Edges

Let v be one of the vectors $(1, 0)$, $(1, 1)$, $(0, 1)$, $(-1, 1)$, and let w be the 90° rotation of v. Let z be a pixel and $y = z + v$, which is one of the eight nearest neighbors of z. Denote $z_1 = z + w$, $z_2 = z - w$, $z_3 = z - v$ and $y_1 = y + w$, $y_2 = y - w$, $y_3 = y + v$. An edge is present at z if

$$|I(z) - I(y)| > \max_{i=1,2,3} (\max (|I(z) - I(z_i)|, |I(y) - I(y_i)|)) \qquad (5.11)$$

The orientation of the edge is v if $I(z) > I(y)$ and $-v$ otherwise. The eight edges correspond to the four possible directions of v multiplied by the two possible signs of $I(z) - I(y)$. The configuration of pixels being compared for a vertical edge is shown in figure 5.3.

All in all, six intensity difference comparisons are involved in defining the edge. These edges can be viewed as local maxima of the modulus of the gradient. It is possible to introduce a lower bound on the size of the gradient to avoid edges in extremely low contrast areas (i.e., $|I(y) - I(z)| > \kappa$).

In a given $b \times b$ block of pixels, several different edges types may be detected. This is even true for $b = 1$. One can decide to allow only n_e edges in each $b \times b$ block, taking those with largest gradient $|I(z) - I(y)|$. Invariance to significant gray-scale transformations is inherent in the definition of these features.

5.4.2   The Data Model

Let $\hat{I}(x) = (X_1(x), \ldots, X_J(x))$ (in this case $J = 8$) denote the transformed image data, namely, the vector of binary outputs of the edge features at point x in the image.

Let $F_1(x), \ldots, F_J(x)$ be functions of value between 0 and 1 and assume that given the object is present at deformation θ, at each location $x \in L$

$$P(X_j(x) = 1 \mid \theta) = F_j(\theta^{-1}x) = F_j(\phi(x)) \tag{5.12}$$

independently of all other locations and features. In other words, given the object is present at deformation θ, the variables $X_j(x), x \in L, j = 1, \ldots, J$ are all independent and have marginal distribution given by $F_j(\phi(x))$. The functions F_j are called probability maps, and because the features are binary, we call this the Bernoulli model. Again, we have a conditional independence model for the transformed image data given the instantiation of the object. The full log-likelihood, in terms of the displacement $U(x) = \phi(x) - x$ has the form

$$\mathcal{D}(U) = \log P(\hat{I}(x), x \in L \mid U)$$
$$= \sum_{j=1}^{J} \sum_{x \in L} \left(X_j(x) \log[F_j(x + U(x))] + (1 - X_j(x)) \log[1 - F_j(x + U(x))] \right)$$
$$\tag{5.13}$$

Adding the prior term of equation 5.5, we have the negative log-posterior

$$J(U) = -\log P(U \mid \hat{I}(x), x \in L)$$
$$= \mathcal{E}(U) - \sum_{j=1}^{J} \sum_{x \in L} \left(X_j(x) \log[F_j(x + U(x))] \right.$$
$$\left. + (1 - X_j(x)) \log[1 - F_j(x + U(x))] \right) + C \tag{5.14}$$

This defines a cost function that needs to be minimized and again this can be achieved using gradient descent. Parameterizing U in terms of the coefficients u, the gradient has the form

$$\frac{\partial J(U)}{\partial u_k^{(q)}} = \lambda_k u_k^{(q)} + \sum_{j=1}^{J} \left[\sum_{x \in L} X_j(x) \frac{\partial_q F_j(x + U(x))}{F_j(x + U(x))} \right.$$
$$\left. - (1 - X_j(x)) \frac{\partial_q F_j(x + U(x))}{1 - F_j(x + U(x))} \right] \psi_k(x) \tag{5.15}$$

for $k = 0, \ldots, d$ and $q = 1, 2$. Again, the gradient is in the form of the forward transform of a function with respect to the basis ψ_k. Maximization can proceed just as in algorithm 5.1. The only change is in step 3. Now

$$W_q(x) = \sum_{j=1}^{J} \left[X_j(x) \frac{\partial_q F_j(x + U(x))}{F_j(x + U(x))} - (1 - X_j(x)) \frac{\partial_q F_j(x + U(x))}{1 - F_j(x + U(x))} \right]$$

and is evaluated at each $x \in L$.

5.4.3   Training

The use of binary features is very convenient from the point of view of parameter estimation or training. At each point in the reference grid, we simply estimate a proportion for each of the features $j = 1, \ldots, J$. Assume we are given a sample of training images of the object, $I^{(t)}, t = 1, \ldots, T$, each with a pose parameter s_t, for example, scale and location. Extract the features $X_j(x), j = 1, \ldots, J$ at all locations $x \in L$ for image t, and register these locations to the reference grid using the pose information s_t for that image. In other words, if $X_j(x) = 1$, add a count to $F_j(z)$ where $z = s_t^{-1}(x)$. Some stability is gained by also adding a count to $F_j(z')$ for $|z - z'| \leq 1$. After normalizing by T the maps $F_j, j = 1, \ldots, J$ are the proportions at each location on the reference grid of the J different features, and serve as estimates of $P(X_j(x) = 1 \mid \theta)$ from equation 5.12. Set a minimal value for F_j at all locations on the reference grid. This is the probability of finding feature X_j in a generic background image not containing the object being modeled.

The probability maps F_j determined in this way will be somewhat "blurred" because the only part of the deformation variability that is "factored out" in training is the pose component s_t. The more variable the instantiations of the object in the training set, beyond pose variability, the lower the probabilities at each location on the reference grid. In other words, the instantiation variability is transferred into probabilities on the reference grid.

The use of a minimal background probability for each of the features offers a form of background model, albeit very primitive, of the data off the object. This is useful in discouraging the template from attempting to match clutter in the immediate vicinity of the object; edge activity outside the object does not incur a high penalty. For regular gray-level prototypes, it is not at all clear what the values of the prototype image outside the object should be.

The top panel of figure 5.4 shows the probability maps for the eight edges. Darker areas correspond to higher probabilities. The middle panels show the eight detected edge features in the data image. We express the estimated instantiation of the face using a collection of reference points that was arbitrarily chosen on the reference grid,

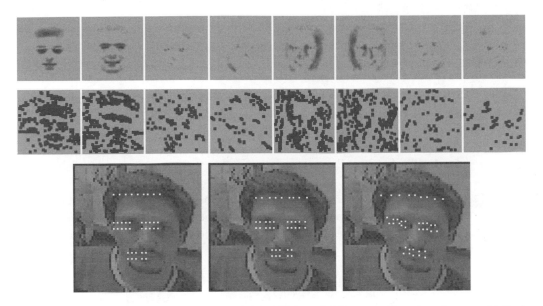

Figure 5.4   Bernoulli data model. (Top) Eight probability maps F_i on the reference grid. Dark denotes high probability. (Middle) Transformed image data, locations of the eight detected edges in the image. The probability maps and transformed data are shown smaller than the original image. They are all 64×64. (Bottom left) Original data image. Overlaid are reference points, chosen by hand on the reference grid which should correspond to the hairline, eyes and mouth if the face is properly detected. (Bottom middle) After estimation of translation and scaling in x and y, the reference points are shown mapped by the estimated scale and translation. (Bottom right) After finding the nonlinear deformation, it is used to map the reference points into the image.

and that are mapped by the estimated ϕ into the data image. The first image shows the initial instantiation, which has some overlap with the background. The second shows an estimated scaling and translation and the third shows the result of computing a nonlinear deformation.

5.5   Linearization

When the deformation U is known to be small in magnitude, the problem can be linearized. We provide the derivations only for the Gaussian data model. The extension to the Bernoulli data model is straightforward. Taking the first-order approximation to $F(x + U(x))$, the cost function becomes

$$J(U) = \mathcal{E}(U) + \int |F(x) + (\nabla F \cdot U)(x) - I(x)|^2 \, dx \qquad (5.16)$$

which is quadratic in U. Computing the minimum of this function is equivalent to solving a least-squares problem. The solution depends on how U is parameterized, however, for each parameterization the solution is unique and easy to compute.

5.5.1   The Spectral Parameterization

With the spectral parameterization, we solve for the first d coefficients of U. Differentiating $J(U)$ from equation 5.16 with respect to the coefficients $u^{(1)}$, $u^{(2)}$ and setting the gradient to equal 0, we obtain the following system of normal equations.

$$\lambda_k u_k^{(q)} + \sum_{\ell=1}^{d} \sum_{p=1}^{2} u_\ell^{(p)} \int \partial_q F \partial_p F \psi_\ell \psi_k dx = \int (I - F) \partial_q F \psi_k \, dx \qquad (5.17)$$

for $k = 0, \ldots, d$, $q = 1, 2$. Assuming the symmetric $2d \times 2d$ matrix with coefficients $\int \partial_p F \partial_q F \psi_\ell \psi_k + diag[\lambda_1, \ldots, \lambda_d, \lambda_1, \ldots, \lambda_d]$ is nonsingular, this can be solved using a Cholesky decomposition (see Press and colleagues 1995).

The solution to the least-squares problem can be obtained without calculating the integrals of equation 5.17. Assume a discrete $N \times N$ lattice L for the spatial variable x and let x_l denote the pixel $(\lfloor \ell/N \rfloor, \ell \bmod N)$, for any $\ell = 0, \ldots, N^2 - 1$. Define the $(N^2 + 2d) \times 2d$ matrix A as

$$A_{l,k} = \begin{cases} (\partial_1 F \cdot \psi_k)(x_\ell) & \text{if } k \leq d \text{ and } \ell < N^2 \\ (\partial_2 F \cdot \psi_k)(x_\ell) & \text{if } d < k \leq 2d \text{ and } \ell < N^2 \\ \sqrt{\lambda_k} & \text{if } k - N^2 = \ell \text{ and } k \leq d \\ \sqrt{\lambda_{k-d}} & \text{if } k - N^2 = \ell \text{ and } d < k \leq 2d \\ 0 & \text{Otherwise} \end{cases}$$

Define the $N^2 + 2d$ vector b as

$$b_\ell = \begin{cases} [I(x_l) - F(x_l)] & \text{if } \ell < N^2 \\ 0 & \text{Otherwise.} \end{cases}$$

The cost function of equation 5.16 becomes $J(u) = \|Au - b\|$, and the least-square problem can be solved using a QR decomposition of A (see Press and colleagues 1995). Note that the penalty term on the coefficients, being quadratic, has been

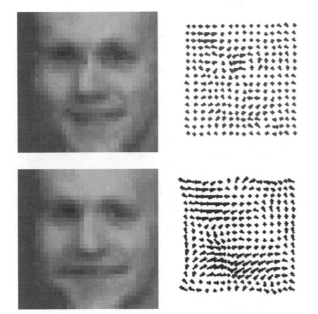

Figure 5.5   (Top left) Deformed prototype image from figure 5.2 using linear cost function and using all 2 × 8 × 8 wavelet coefficients. (Bottom left) Deformed prototype from figure 5.2 using 3 levels of least squares and updating the prototype image. (Bottom right) Deformation field.

incorporated into the least-squares problem by augmenting the "matrix of observations."

For each different value of d we have a different linear problem, and the solutions will change. Although the solution to the linearized problem is obtained directly and has a very simple form, it may be worse than the solution obtained by the coarse-to-fine gradient-descent algorithm for the original nonlinear cost function. In the top left panel of figure 5.5, we show the deformed prototype image of figure 5.2 using the linearized cost function for the first 8 × 8 coefficients, ($a = 3$). A small change is observed but much less than in 5.2.

It is natural to apply the coarse-to-fine idea in this setting by first solving the linearized problem for $d = \mathcal{N}_1$, obtain the estimated displacement field U, then modify the prototype image F to $F(x + U(x))$. Increase d to $\mathcal{N}_2$, recalculate the matrix A and the vector b in terms of the new prototype image, and solve the new linearized problem, and so on. This greatly improves the results, as shown in the bottom left panel of figure 5.5, where the same data as in 5.2 has been used. In both cases, the same Daubechies wavelet basis was used. Starting with one iteration at $\mathcal{N}_1 = 2 \times 2^2$—which corresponds to expanding $U^{(1)}$ and $U^{(2)}$ with the four smoothest elements in the basis—one iteration at $\mathcal{N}_2 = 2 \times 4^2$, and three additional iterations at $\mathcal{N}_3 = 2 \times 8^2$. After each iteration, the prototype image has to be updated, and the derivatives recomputed in order to update A. This is not done in the coarse-to-fine gradient-descent algorithm. The derivatives of F are computed once and for all at the beginning, and only the displacement field is changing at each iteration.

Solving each of the least-squares problems is computationally more intensive than a step of the gradient-descent algorithm but less iterations are needed, and the results can be similar. However, with large numbers of coefficients, the least squares slows down drastically. The outcome of the gradient-descent algorithm shown in figure 5.2 was obtained with 400 iterations and took approximately 1.7 seconds on the Pentium III 700 MHz. The five iterations of the regression problem for the four different dimensions took approximately the same time.

In low dimensions it is possible to implement one least-squares step after the gradient-descent iterations appear to be converging. This can help improve the result. Indeed, this step can be viewed as a quasi-Newton step, where the term $\int \partial_p F \psi_\ell \psi_k \cdot \partial_q F \, dx$, $p, q = 1, 2$ is taken as the typical entry of the Hessian matrix of the original cost function J. There is an additional term $\int (F(x + U(x)) - I(x)) \partial_{qp} F \psi_k \psi_\ell \, dx$ in the true Hessian, which is ignored, as in the time-step approximation in section 5.3.

5.5.2   The Lattice Parameterization

When the deformation is parameterized through the displacement vector $U(x)$ at each of the lattice points, with a smoothing penalty using first-order derivatives, (see equation 5.8), the Euler equations for the linearized cost function are the following:

$$\Delta U^{(1)} + (\nabla F \cdot U) \frac{\partial F}{\partial x_1} = (I(x) - F(x)) \frac{\partial F}{\partial x_1}$$

$$\Delta U^{(2)} + (\nabla F \cdot U) \frac{\partial F}{\partial x_2} = (I(x) - F(x)) \frac{\partial F}{\partial x_2}$$

where Δ denotes the Laplacian operator. These lead precisely to the same equations suggested in the optical flow and image sequence analysis literature (Horn and Schunck 1981). In that context, the problem is to estimate the motion occurring between two consecutive images in a video sequence. Assuming I is the image following F, then $I - F$ is an approximation to the time derivative, and the above equation becomes the same equation derived in Horn and Schunck (1981), using an "image intensity" conservation principle. This form of lattice-based linearization is problematic when dealing with larger deformations and there is no natural coarse-to-fine implementation.

5.6   Applications to Brain Matching

There has been particular interest in applying deformable-image algorithms in brain research (see Friston and colleagues 1995; Sandor and Leahy 1995; Christensen, Rabbitt, and Miller 1996).

Activity in the brain is measured in various ways, the most common being positron emission tomography (PET) and functional magnetic resonance imaging (MRI). In order to study locations of activity in relation to various functions of the brain, it is necessary to align or standardize the data from brains of different patients. One approach has been to match the MRI data of different brains to a standard template. Even if the MRI data does not contain signatures of the activity, the estimated deformation can be applied to the PET data. Note that the PET data itself has very little anatomic information and therefore would not lead to very precise matchings.

Figure 5.6 shows the outcome of a 2D match between two axial brain slices of two different patients, using a wavelet basis. We use this application to illustrate several aspects of the image-deformation algorithm. The images are 128×128, but are processed at a lower resolution of 64×64 as recommended in the discussion on smoothing. Starting at $\mathcal{N}_1 = 2 \times 2^2$ through $\mathcal{N}_6 = 2 \times 64^2$, the coarse-to-fine algorithm is implemented, and the result is shown in figure 5.6 on the bottom left panel. The difference between the data and the deformed template is shown in the top right panel, and the deformation field is shown in the middle. Note that the deformation is able to change some of the local structure of the sulci and giri of the prototype image to match that of the target image, as well as deform and match the shape of the interior ventricles. For comparison, in figure 5.7 we show the outcome of running the algorithm with all coefficients at once (i.e., $\mathcal{N}_1 = 2 \times 64^2$), together with the resulting deformation field. The prototype image is deformed to match certain local structures but the global shapes are not adjusted at all.

Finally, in figure 5.8 we show two other relatively successful matches using the coarse-to-fine algorithm. MRI data is often accessed in 3D form—either as a collection of 2D slices or as a full reconstructed 3D image. The image-deformation algorithm described above is adapted to 3D data in a straightforward way. The deformation field now has three components and is expanded in a 3D wavelet or Fourier basis.

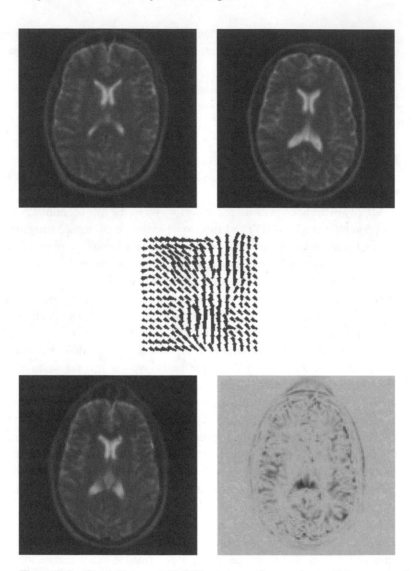

Figure 5.6   (Top left) An axial MRI brain scan of one patient, which serves as the prototype image. (Top right) An axial MRI brain scan of another patient at the same level. (Bottom left) The deformed prototype image. (Bottom right) The residual. (Middle) The displacement field U.

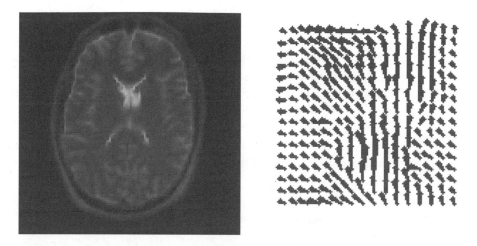

Figure 5.7 The outcome of the deformable image algorithm using all coefficients from the start.

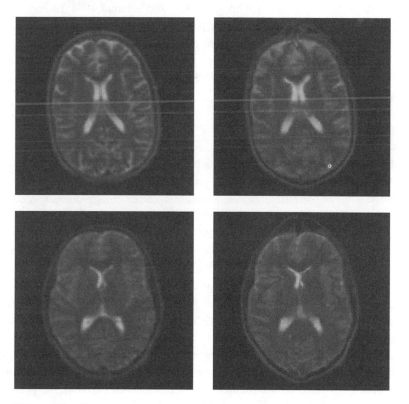

Figure 5.8 Two more experiments with the coarse to fine deformable image algorithm on MRI axial scans. (Left) Data. (Right) Deformed template. Template from figure 5.6.

The question arises as to whether this fine detail matching has any anatomic meaning. Do these locations, which are mapped to each other between two different patients, really correspond to the same anatomy? Beyond the coarse shape matching, is there anything in the data that really justifies a specific deformation of one sulcus or gyrus to another? This is rather debatable because the way in which, say, a short curved gyrus is deformed into a long straight one is rather arbitrary. There is nothing in the actual functionality of the different regions in that gyrus that guides the matching.

5.7   Bibliographical Notes and Discussion

More details on the statistical model can be found in Amit, Grenander, and Piccioni (1991). The computational approach is based on Amit (1994). Similar models in the linear setting were proposed much earlier by several authors in the context of motion estimation from sequences of images. (Horn and Schunck 1981; Huang and Tsai 1981; Nagel 1983). A similar approach is described in Bajcsy and Kovacic (1988), where a spectral parameterization of the deformation is also used. More-recent developments involving more-complex penalty terms and requiring much more computation can be found in Christensen, Rabbitt, and Miller (1996), Grenander and Miller (1998), and Hallinan and colleagues (1999).

5.7.1   Homeomorphisms

In the methods described here, the deformations are not guaranteed to be one-to-one. A number of people have investigated the possibility of constraining the deformations to be invertible homeomorphisms of the image domain onto itself. One approach penalizes large derivatives both of the mapping ϕ and of its inverse ϕ^{-1} (see Hallinan and colleagues 1999). The derivatives of the ϕ^{-1} are computable without actually inverting ϕ using the inverse function theorem. The penalty term involves ratios of derivatives. In this setup, it only makes sense to work with the lattice parameterization—the power of the coarse-to-fine algorithm is lost and the computation becomes very intensive. Another approach exploits the fact that the flow of a continuous field is necessarily a homeomorphism at any time instant, due to the uniqueness properties of solutions to ordinary differential equations (see Grenander and Miller 1998 and references therein). The mathematics is quite involved, but the final practical implementation is essentially the same as the image-deformation algorithm described in this chapter, except that at each iteration, the prototype image is changed according to the current mapping—that is, $F_k(x) = F_{k-1}(\phi_k(x))$. This is related to the procedure described in section 5.5 on linearization. Note that allowing the prototype image to update at each step can lead to drastic changes in the image, without paying a high penalty. The most mathematically complete treatment of this issue is to be found in Trouvé (1998). The diffeomorphisms are treated as a Lie group and the variational formulation is done intrinsically in the Lie group in terms of the associated Lie algebra of smooth vector fields. This yields an interesting modification to the algorithms presented in Grenander and Miller (1998), where the basis functions are implicitly deformed together with the prototype image.

5.7.2 Photometric Invariance

In Hallinan and colleagues (1999), a deformable image model is used to register prototype face images to data images. The algorithm uses intensity-based data models, and the prototype image is obtained by averaging images of several registered and normalized faces. Photometric invariance is addressed by taking several prototypes in the form of principle components of the population of faces imaged at a wide range of illuminations. The images used are very high resolution (512×512), which are carefully normalized, and computational efficiency is not discussed. A question arises here—how much of the photometric invariance is "learned" by observing examples of the object lit in a variety of lighting conditions, and how much can be hardwired into the algorithm by using photometric invariant features, as in the Bernoulli model described above? The answer to this question is not necessarily unique and depends on the type of implementation one is seeking, what type of architecture, how efficient should the algorithm be, and how fast is learning expected to occur. An advantage of the Bernoulli model is the systematic and simple form of parameter estimation—namely, the training of the probability maps. This appears to be more robust than taking means of prenormalized images. There is also the benefit of having some form of model of the data off the object.

5.7.3 Principal Component Bases

Also related to training is the choice-of-function basis. The standard bases will not provide an optimal parameterization of the large-scale deformations typical of the object class. For example, in the case of hands, the individual rotation of the fingers relative to the palm is not easily described in terms of standard bases. One approach to solving this problem has been to calculate the deformations for a training set and then find "eigen-deformations" (see, for example, Hallinan and colleagues 1999, in the context of faces). In other words, the principal components of the deformations, computed on the training set of images, are used as an orthogonal basis of deformations. This basis, if computed from the true population of deformations, should provide the most efficient form of parameterization in the least-square sense. Of course, in order to estimate the principal components in the first place, it is necessary to somehow extract deformations from a large sample, using other bases or parameterizations.

Principal components will not yield a basis allowing for fast-forward and backward transforms. However, if only a small number of components are to be used, substituting the fast-forward and backward transforms with explicit quadrature will not significantly slow down the algorithm. It is also possible to compromise and choose an optimal wavelet packet for the given training sample. This will not be as economical a representation as the principal components basis but will provide a good approximation and will come along with a fast transform algorithm.

In any case, there remains much research to be done into the problem of accurately marking out the components of a face (i.e., detecting detailed instantiation information) despite this being a trivial task for our visual system. The issue of efficient and automatic detection of coarse instantiation information of faces, including pose parameters, in a large scene is discussed in chapters 6 and 8.

5.7.4   Mutual Information Cost Function

In recent years, a new type of data term has been proposed that deals with the situation wherein the pixel intensities for similar structures are not the same (see Viola and Wells 1997; Kim and colleagues 1997). This occurs in medical imaging when two different modalities are used to image the same structure—for example, a PET image and an MRI image of the brain. In this setting, the deformations are typically small, however, the least-square distance between pixel values is entirely inadequate. The proposed solution constructs a bivariate histogram of gray levels—for each pixel, two gray-level values from the two images being matched. The mutual information between the two variables described by the histogram is computed. The algorithm tries to modify the deformation in order minimize the mutual information.

In the algorithm described above we assumed that given the deformation ϕ the image intensities are independent with some distribution $f(\cdot \mid F(\phi(x)))$, where f is Gaussian with mean $F(\phi(x))$ and fixed variance. Whatever distribution is chosen the log-likelihood has the form $\sum_{x \in L} \log f(I(x) \mid F(\phi(x)))$. If f is not known ahead of time, it can be estimated from the empirical distribution of $I(x)$ at all points with the same value of $F(\phi(x))$. If this estimated is plugged in the log-likelihood the result is precisely the mutual information of the empirical bivariate distribution

$(I(x), F(\phi(x))$, $x \in L$. In other words, the mutual information cost function tries to simultaneously estimate the deformation ϕ and the conditional distribution of $I(x)$ given $F(\phi(x))$. If the joint distribution is estimated using a smoothing kernel, the cost function is again differentiable in ϕ (see Hermosillo, Chefd'Hotel and Faugeras 2001).

The problems arising with regard to the two-dimensional models are similar to those mentioned in the discussions regarding the one-dimensional models. Initialization is crucial due to the nonlinear nature of the cost function. This motivates the sparse models described in the next several chapters.

6 Sparse Models: Formulation, Training, and Statistical Properties

In previous chapters, we have described a number of deformable models, all of which require some type of user initialization in terms of pose parameters, such as scale and location. The models are too complex for automatic pose estimation to be efficient. In this chapter, we construct sparse models that can be detected directly, and very quickly, with no user initialization. These models involve relatively small collections of points that typically correspond to landmarks of some type on the object. When these points are identified in the image—namely, the sparse model is detected—an initial state can be determined for any of the algorithms described in previous chapters. In terms of constructing these sparse models, some of the landmarks are easily defined by the user, representing a clearly defined local structure in the image, on any instance of the object. For example, in figure 6.1, we show several landmarks on an axial MRI image of the brain, which are chosen by the user. However, other landmarks may only be found through training on a collection of examples of the object and do not necessarily have a very clear semantic definition.

In both cases, each landmark has a certain characteristic local topography in terms of the image surface. Image 6.2 (left) shows the level curves around the tip of the left ventricle in an axial MRI brain scan. Imagine a binary local feature that is present at the tip of a ventricle for a large proportion of the images of the object. The feature must characterize the local topography of the image in the neighborhood of the landmark. It would be impossible to find such an operator that is on *only* at the tip of the left ventricle, namely, with no false positives. See, for example, the level curves in a neighborhood of a sulcus in figure 6.2 (right). Otherwise put, parts of objects are not clearly identifiable at the local level. It is only after the global object is identified that local information can be disambiguated. It is possible, however, to find a local feature that is on at the tip of the ventricle with very high probability and has a low density of false positives—namely, it is not on in many other places in a typical MRI image.

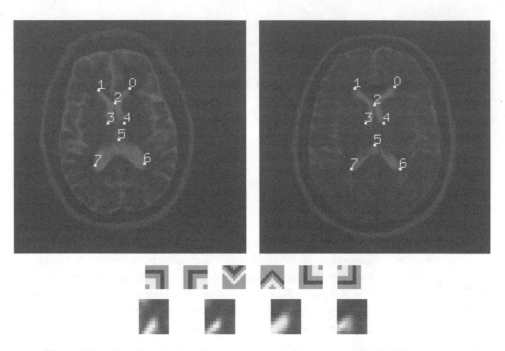

Figure 6.1   (Top) Landmarks chosen on two training images. (Middle) The six comparison arrays used for identifying candidates for the model landmarks. (Bottom) Neighborhoods of tip of upper right ventricle in four axial MRI brain scans, which were identified by the leftmost comparison array.

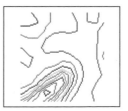

Figure 6.2   (Left) Contour plot of neighborhood of frontal horn. (Right) Contour plot of neighborhood of a sulcus.

Clearly, one local feature associated to one landmark is insufficient to detect the object and its components. As mentioned, there will necessarily be false positives; there is also the possibility of false negatives at the correct location. Furthermore, this one feature does not describe the instantiation of the full object but only a small part. We therefore require a collection of landmarks, each with an associated local feature. A detection consists of finding instances of some or all of these landmarks in the image, which are spatially arranged in a way *consistent with their expected arrangement on the object*. Each of the local features should be invariant within the range of consistent arrangements. For example, if we expect to observe the anatomies in image 6.1 in a range of $\pm 25\%$ scaling, we would expect the local feature, detecting the tip of the left ventricle, to be "on" at the appropriate location at all such scales. These notions are made more precise in the following section, where a statistical model is again formulated in the framework of the discussion of chapter 2.

The question is then, do local features exist, which are stable on the object and of low density on the background, from which to construct such models? Two such families of local features are defined in sections 6.3 and 6.4, which are subsequently used in the detection algorithms of chapters 7 and 8. The second family has a number of free parameters, and hence offers quite a wide range of choices in terms of the complexity and statistics of the features. A detailed study of these statistics as a function of some of these parameters is presented in section 6.5. The main conclusion that emerges from this analysis is that a wide range of possibilities exists to define features that are indeed stable on object and low density on background. Moreover, it is possible to provide reasonable predictions on the density of these features and the number of false detections of the models constructed with these features.

6.1 From Deformable Models to Sparse Models

Sparse models can be motivated as coarse approximations to the more-complex deformable models described in earlier chapters. In the context of random LaTeX images, there is a complete *image synthesis* model; we know precisely the random mechanism producing the images. This is a very rare luxury but helps illustrate some important points. Let $\mathcal{A}$ be the set of admissible linear transformations, and Υ the set of admissible nonlinear deformations. Random elements $A \in \mathcal{A}$ and $\upsilon \in \Upsilon$ are drawn according to some probability and applied to the prototype image I_{proto} generating an image defined by $\upsilon A I_{proto}(z) = I_{proto}(A^{-1}\upsilon^{-1}z)$, for each $z \in G$. Each such image is then placed at a random location in the lattice L. For simplicity, let $\mathcal{A}$, the range of admissible poses, be limited to a range of scales $[1, S]$ for say $S = 2$. Denote by $\mathcal{I}$ the set of all images $\upsilon A I_{proto}$, $\upsilon \in \Upsilon$, $A \in \mathcal{A}$, all presented in the reference grid G. It is, in principle, possible to check for each location $x \in L$, each scale $A \in \mathcal{A}$, and each $\upsilon \in \Upsilon$ whether a deformation under υ of $A I_{proto}$ is present at x. This is equivalent to checking at each subgrid $x + G$ of L, if the data there matches any of the images in the set $\mathcal{I}$, above some prescribed threshold, using some prescribed distance function. The distance function could be defined in terms of the sum of squares of the differences, or the match of the binary feature maps extracted from the images. This is clearly a daunting computation.

A simple way to speed up the above computation at each location is to let the data guide us in finding an optimal deformation in $\Upsilon \mathcal{A}$, using gradient descent or some other optimization technique. However, given the range of scales in $\mathcal{A}$, it is quite unlikely that such a procedure would indeed find the global optimum. We therefore define a more restricted range of scales $\mathcal{A}' = [1, s]$, with, say, $s = 1.25$, and let $\mathcal{I}'$ be the smaller resulting set of images obtained by applying elements of $\Upsilon \mathcal{A}'$ to I_{proto}. Optimization in the reduced set of deformations is more reasonable, and is precisely the approach taken in chapter 5, both for the Gaussian model, which yields a least-squares cost function, and for the Bernoulli model.

The entire range of scales $[1, S]$ can be covered by subsequently subsampling the image at resolutions $S/s, S/(2s), \ldots, S/(ks)$, where $k \doteq \lfloor S/s \rfloor$ and running the same procedure again at all locations. The existence of local minima, namely, the nonconvexity of the associated cost function over the restricted range of poses, is still a significant problem, and even with the advantage gained by optimizing, as opposed to brute-force matching, the entire computation at all locations $x \in L$ and k resolutions is still immense.

Assume a set of n binary local features, $X_i, i = 1, \ldots, n$ can be defined, each of which is always on at a particular location on the object for images in $\mathcal{I}'$ and are quite rare off the object. These features are *invariant* to the smaller range of scales and the deformations in Υ. Specifically, a location z_i on the reference grid is associated to each feature X_i, and if an image from $\mathcal{I}'$ is located at a point $x \in L$ at a particular scale $A \in \mathcal{A}'$ and deformation $\upsilon \in \Upsilon$, then $X_i(x + \upsilon A z_i) = 1$ for all $1 \leq i \leq n$. Now define a set of constraints $\Theta \subset L^n$ on arrangements of these features that is *consistent* with $\Upsilon \mathcal{A}'$, meaning simply that any instantiation of the form $(x + \upsilon A z_1, \ldots, x + \upsilon A z_n)$ is in Θ, for $x \in L, \upsilon \in \Upsilon, A \in \mathcal{A}'$. Otherwise put, the *presence* of an arrangement $\theta \in \Theta$ of these features is an *invariant* property of the images in $\mathcal{I}'$. Now take an image and find all locations of the n local features. If there is an efficient way of finding consistent arrangements from Θ and if the number of such arrangements is low, we have greatly reduced the computational load. The more intensive deformation algorithms need only be applied at these candidate instantiations.

How should the invariant local features be defined? These features need to flag local structures invariant with respect to deformations υA with $\upsilon \in \Upsilon$ and $A \in \mathcal{A}'$.

For example, such a feature would always be on at the top ending of the $\mathcal{E}$ symbol used in chapter 2. The most elementary features, in terms of which we have already defined a cost on deformations, are the coarse oriented edges. These are present in a stable way in such local structures, but are quite frequent in generic images. A group of neighboring edges characteristic of a certain part of the object will typically maintain its relative arrangement as the object deforms smoothly. Thus features defined in terms of a *flexible edge arrangement* will still be invariant to local deformations of the structures of the object. On the other hand, such features are much less frequent in the background, potentially reducing the computation of detections and the number of false positives. If the edges are defined to be invariant to photometric transformations, the edge arrangements inherit this property. This is crucial for real images where the gray-level maps are not as homogeneous as in the synthetic LaTeX scenes.

How to define Θ? Set simple constraints on the locations of the points in θ, either relative to each other or relative to a location x in the image grid, in terms of regions where we expect to find the appropriate features. The features can be anywhere in the respective region for the constraint to be satisfied. This slack in the definition compensates for the fact that we rarely have a precise definition of Υ that would lead to a more specific definition of Θ. There is an explicit or-ing being performed over all locations in the region—indeed, this disjunction is the key to the invariance of the model. This is the advantage of using binary features, invariance naturally translates into an or-ing over certain regions. This property is also exploited in the context of the classification algorithms described in chapter 9.

Finally, in this simplified model we have a straightforward mechanism to deal with occlusion and features that are not pure invariants. It is unrealistic to expect nontrivial features to always be present in the proper part of the object. Instead of looking for *all* local features, look for a *sufficiently large subset* in a consistent arrangement. Thus the sparse models can be viewed as coarse approximations to the more complex ones, with the advantage of explicitly dealing with occlusion and photometric invariance, and leading to efficient detection algorithms.

6.2 Statistical Model

Once more, we formulate a model following the general recipe outlined in chapter 2. Suppose that a collection of binary local features X_i, $i = 1, \ldots, n$ and an associated collection of landmark locations $Z = (z_1, \ldots, z_n)$, are identified for the object class on the reference grid. The collection of locations represents the template for the sparse model. In section 6.3, we explain how these feature-location pairs are identified through training.

6.2.1   The Prior—Admissible Instantiations

Without loss of generality, assume

$$z_c \doteq \frac{1}{n} \sum_{i=1}^{n} z_i = 0$$

We identify a set $\Theta^{(0)}$ of admissible instantiations of the object with center at the origin

$$\theta_c \doteq \frac{1}{n} \sum_{i=1}^{n} \theta_i = 0$$

in particular, $(z_1, \ldots, z_n) \in \Theta^{(0)}$. The set Θ of admissible instantiations in the image lattice L is defined as those elements $\theta = (\theta_1, \ldots, \theta_n)$, for which $\theta_i = x_c + \theta_i'$, $i = 1, \ldots, n$ for some $(\theta_1', \ldots, \theta_n') \in \Theta^{(0)}$—namely, $\theta_c = x_c$. The set Θ consists of all translations of configurations in $\Theta^{(0)}$ and can be identified with the set of pairs $(x_c, \theta') \in L \times \Theta^{(0)}$. This identification is not unique, two pairs can correspond to the same element in Θ.

One form of the set $\Theta^{(0)}$, which is used in chapter 8, has the form

$$\Theta^{(0)} = \{(\theta_1, \ldots, \theta_n) : \theta_i \in Az_i + C, A \in \mathcal{A}\} \tag{6.1}$$

with $\mathcal{A}$ some subset of the invertible 2D linear transformations and with C some neighborhood of the origin. The larger C the looser the constraints on θ, because the points can move independently anywhere within $Az_i + C$. A uniform prior is used on this set. On the other hand, in chapter 7, the set Θ and the prior are defined directly in terms of hard constraints and penalties on the shape of triangles defined by triples of points in Z.

6.2.2   Likelihood and Posterior

The data model is written here for the transformed data $\hat{I}(x) = (X_1(x), \ldots, X_n(x))$ for $x \in L$. We assume that if an object is instantiated at $\theta \in \Theta$, the probability that feature X_i is on at θ_i (i.e., $X_i(\theta_i) = 1$) is at least p_o, for some predetermined probability p_o. As discussed in the previous section, this implies that there must be some interaction between the definition of Θ and the definition of X_i. For example, it is very hard to find local features of interest that are invariant to very large ranges of scaling. Therefore, one seeks to limit the range of scales covered by Θ. The full range of scales at which the object will be detected is obtained by rerunning the *same* algorithm at a small number of lower resolution versions of the original image, as described in section 6.1. In the sequel, assume for simplicity that $P(X_i(\theta_i) = 1 \mid \theta) = p_o$, for all $i = 1, \ldots, n$.

Let p_b denote the probability of detecting a feature X_i at a point x, which is off the object, or even on the object but at the wrong location. Assume that $p_b \ll p_o$ and that p_b is also the same for all local features X_i. We again make an assumption of conditional independence. Given one object is present in the image at instantiation $\theta \in \Theta$, all variables $X_i(x), x \in L, i = 1, \ldots, n$ are independent. Now write the likelihood of the transformed data given an instantiation θ of the object as

$$P(\hat{I}(x), x \in L \mid \theta) = P(X_i(x), x \in L, i = 1, \ldots, n \mid \theta)$$

$$= \prod_{i=1}^{n} \left[p_o^{X_i(\theta_i)} (1 - p_o)^{(1 - X_i(\theta_i))} \prod_{x \neq \theta_i} p_b^{X_i(x)} (1 - p_b)^{(1 - X_i(x))} \right]$$

$$(6.2)$$

The notation $P(\cdot \mid \theta)$ means conditional on an object present at instantiation θ. Let

$$P_0(X_i(x), x \in L; i = 1, \ldots, n) \doteq \prod_{i-1} \prod_{x \in L} p_b^{X_i(x)} (1 - p_b)^{(1 - X_i(x))} \qquad (6.3)$$

denote the probability of the data, given *no* object is in the scene. Define

$$\rho_1 = \log \frac{p_o}{p_b} > 0 \quad \text{and} \quad \rho_2 = \log \frac{1 - p_b}{1 - p_o} > 0$$

Divide 6.2 by 6.3, multiply by the prior, and take logs to obtain the log-posterior, given the data as

$$\log P(\theta \mid \hat{I}(x), x \in L) = \log P(\theta) + n_y(\theta)\rho_1 - (n - n_y(\theta))\rho_2 + C \qquad (6.4)$$

where $n_y(\theta)$ is the number of features for which $X_i(\theta_i) = 1$ and C does not depend on θ.

The posterior is thus formulated as a simple function of the number of "hits," $n_y(\theta)$ at instantiation θ, and the prior $P(\theta)$. It is possible to write a similar form for the posterior in the more general case where $P(X_i(\theta_i) = 1 \mid \theta)$ varies with i. At this point, however, we are constructing a rather crude model, which will quickly identify a small number of candidate instantiations—the only issue of importance is then the order of magnitude of p_o, and hence these probabilities are assumed to be the same.

Compared to the deformable-curve model, which is very similar, here the instantiation θ determines a fixed number of points at which the respective features are evaluated, whereas in the former model, the features were evaluated all along segments that could be of variable length. In the current model, the features are more complex and of lower density. This compensates for the simpler form of the template. In some sense, the current model can be viewed as zero dimensional. Features are evaluated at a discrete set of points, not along line segments or in a 2D domain. In the deformable-curve model, there was a natural way to rotate the model to any angle, because the features depended directly on the angles of the segments. The models described here can in principle be rotated to cover larger ranges of rotations, but this is not as straightforward.

6.2.3   Multiple Objects

When multiple objects may be present, the model becomes more complex, involving a term for each possible number of objects. The unknowns are now both the number of instantiations k and their values $\theta^{(1)}, \ldots, \theta^{(k)}$. The set of unknowns is defined as $\Sigma = \cup_{k=0}^{K} \Theta^k$, where Θ^k is the set of k-tuples of elements of Θ, with K some upper bound on the number of possible objects in the image. There is no particular preference for any one of these states, namely, the number of objects or their location in the scene. We therefore include a uniform prior on Σ. This uniform prior implicitly favors a larger number of detections because the size of Θ^k grows with k. This is consistent with the idea that at this stage we want to avoid missing any of the objects present in the scene, perhaps at the risk of a number of false positives. Ultimately, a more refined and intensive analysis should be used to distinguish real detections from the false positives. Assigning higher prior probability to Θ^k for smaller k would increase the risk of missing real objects.

This uniform prior also imposes no constraints on the relative arrangement of the instances. In some cases, more information may be available and more structure can be introduced into these prior assumptions, but this is beyond the scope of this book. Given k instances at $\theta^{(1)}, \ldots, \theta^{(k)}$, we again assume conditional independence of the features at all pixels, with probability p_o for finding X_i at $\theta_i^{(l)}, l = 1, \ldots, k$ and probability p_b of finding it anywhere else. The above assumptions lead to the log-posterior on $(\theta^{(1)}, \ldots, \theta^{(k)})$ given by

$$\log P\big((\theta^{(1)}, \ldots, \theta^{(k)}) \mid \hat{I}(x), x \in L\big) = \sum_{i=1}^{k} \big[n_y(\theta^{(i)})\rho_1 - (n - n_y(\theta^{(i)}))\rho_2 \big] + C$$

$$(6.5)$$

From this expression it follows that to maximize the posterior we need to find all those $\theta \in \Theta$ for which the term in brackets is positive, namely, find all $\theta \in \Theta$ for which

$$n_y(\theta) > n \frac{\rho_2}{\rho_1 + \rho_2} \doteq \tau_m$$

The number of such θs provides the number of objects present in the image. As we will see below, because the conditional independence model is not entirely accurate, we use training data to find a threshold τ, which is more conservative than τ_m and ensures finding all instances of the object and perhaps some additional false positives. More-detailed processing is then necessary to determine if indeed the object is present at the detected θs or not.

6.2.4   Computation

Two approaches for optimizing the posterior are described in chapters 7 and 8. In the first, we still assume only one object is present in the image. Local features are chosen for a collection of landmarks on the object and their parameters set so that p_o is very close to 1. Unless all features are present (i.e., $n_y = n$), the posterior is 0. A list S_i is generated of all locations of feature X_i in the image. It then remains to find the mode of $P(\theta)$ over all admissible θ such that $\theta_i \in S_i$. This can be done efficiently using dynamic programming when $P(\theta)$ is assumed to have a decomposable form (see chapter 7). In assuming that $p_o = 1$ this method depends on the restrictive assumption that *all* features of the model are found on the object, which is often not the case.

In the second approach, described in chapter 8, a collection of local features of moderate probability, say $p_o = .5$ is identified at a collection of locations in the reference grid. The set Θ is defined as in equation 6.2, and because several objects can be present, following the discussion above, it is necessary to find $\theta \in \Theta$ for which the number of θ_is with $X_i(\theta_i) = 1$ is above some threshold. This is done in two steps, the first of which involves a coarse approximation of $\Theta^{(0)}$ in terms of a product set and detection of candidate centers for the objects. In the second step, at each candidate center θ_c, a scale is estimated and perhaps other pose parameters, and as many points of the model as possible are matched to the data at the estimated pose.

In the remainder of this chapter, we focus on the description of the local features used for the sparse models, methods for training the relevant parameters, and some statistical properties of these features.

6.3   Local Features: Comparison Arrays

There are numerous possibilities for defining local features for image data. The most common filters found in the literature employ a variety of linear filters related to differential operators (see, for example, Malik and Perona 1990; Wiskott and colleagues 1997). It is more difficult to explicitly incorporate geometric and photometric invariance with such filters. It is also more difficult to study the statistical properties of continuous valued variables as opposed to the binary valued features described below. We thus prefer to use binary features involving simple comparisons of pixel intensity differences, with which photometric and geometric invariance are easy to implement. These local features will be more-complex extensions of the ridge features defined for the deformable curve model in section 4.1 and the edge features in the Bernoulli model for deformable images in section 5.4. The increased complexity is needed because the efficiency of the algorithms depends very much on the background probability p_b being small. The density of the features of sections 4.1 and 5.4 in a generic image can be very high.

Define an $m \times m$ array M, of 1s, -1s and 0s. The *sign* of the difference between the intensity at a given pixel x and the intensity at each of the pixels in its $m \times m$ neighborhood $N_m(x)$ is calculated to yield an $m \times m$ array $A(y) = sign(I(x) - I(y))$, $y \in N_m(x)$ of 1s and -1s. A contrast threshold κ can be introduced and any difference of magnitude less than κ is set to 0. If the percentage of matched 1s and -1s between M and A are above prescribed thresholds, the pixel x is considered a candidate for the corresponding landmark. The 0-s region in M contains pixels where the values of A are ignored—this allows for a degree of slack, which is important in obtaining the type of invariance mentioned above. In figure 6.3 are the sixteen 11×11 comparison arrays used in creating the models. White means

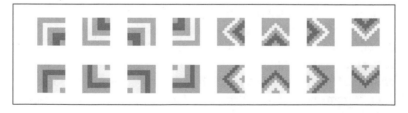

Figure 6.3   Sixteen comparison arrays. White means intensity greater than center value, dark means intensity less than center value, grey means ignored.

intensity greater than center value, dark means intensity less than center value, gray means ignored.

Loosely speaking, these sixteen comparison arrays identify "turns" of level curves of the image (see figure 6.2), pointing in eight different orientations and two gradient flow directions per orientation. These can be viewed as coarse "high curvature" detectors. Recall that we are seeking features with low p_b, and given the frequent occurrence of lines and smooth curves in images, "low curvature" detectors or line detectors would produce a relatively large number of background instances. On the other hand, high curvature points are quite convenient for representing stable local structures of interest on an object.

These operators are robust to rather significant variations in pixel intensities, which are bound to occur between images, as well as to smooth deformations of the local topography of the landmark neighborhood in the template image. They are also robust to a certain range of scales and small rotations. Recall that this was an important requirement on the properties of the operators X_i.

6.3.1   Training

The user points out a collection of landmarks $x_{i,t}$, $i = 1, \ldots, n$ on each of a small number of training images $t = 1, \ldots, T$. In figure 6.1 are two training images of axial MRI scans. Eight points have been marked on similar anatomies, the correspondences are provided by the numbering. For each landmark, we seek the comparison array that, with highest threshold, has no false negatives on the training set. Higher thresholds mean fewer instances of the feature in the background. Note that here we are simultaneously choosing the local feature and estimating the relevant parameters—namely, the thresholds. Let M_j, $j = 1, \ldots, J$, be the collection of arrays, For training image t, let $\tau_{i,t,j,+}$ and $\tau_{i,t,j,-}$ be the number of matches of $A_j(x_{i,t})$ to the positive and negative regions of M_j, respectively. Let $\tau_{i,j,+} = \min_t \tau_{i,t,j,+}$, $\tau_{i,j,-} = \min_t \tau_{i,t,j,-}$, and $\tau_{i,j} = \tau_{i,j,+} + \tau_{i,j,-}$. These are the lowest matches observed with A_j at the points $x_{i,t}$, $t = 1, \ldots, T$. Let $j^* = argmax_j(\tau_{i,j})$, and set the array corresponding to landmark i to be M_{j^*} with thresholds $\tau_{i,j^*,+}$ and $\tau_{i,j^*,-}$. The corresponding model locations z_i, which define the template for the sparse model, are chosen on one of the training images, (for example, the left panel of figure 6.1,) or through some averaging procedure. The result is a list of locations $z_1, \ldots, z_n$, and an associated list of local features $X_1, \ldots, X_n$, defined by comparison arrays, each with two thresholds, $M^{(i)}, \tau_{i,+}, \tau_{i,-}, i = 1, \ldots, n$.

In the example shown in figure 6.1, the first array is used for landmark 0, the second for landmark 1 the third for landmark 2, the fourth for landmark 5, the fifth for landmarks 4 and 7, and the sixth for landmarks 3 and 6. The lower panel of the figure shows a closeup on the tip of the right ventricle in four different images. All were detected by the first array associated to landmark 0. This illustrates the flexibility of this type of local feature to various deformations of the underlying local topography of the image surface. In using comparisons of gray-level intensities, and at times a low minimum contrast threshold, these features detect the same topography at very different contrasts—in other words, photometric invariance is built into the definition. In figure 6.4, we show the locations of all instances of all six features in an MRI image. Compared, for example, to the simple oriented features of chapter 4, shown in figure 4.1, the density is much lower.

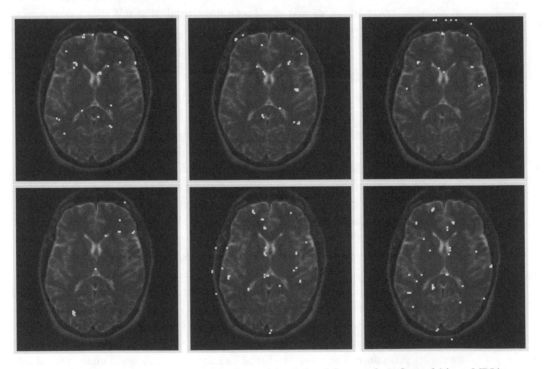

Figure 6.4   Examples of detections of the six local features from figure 6.1 in an MRI image.

6.4 Local Features: Edge Arrangements

We now define a larger and more flexible family of local features, with several free parameters allowing us to control the probabilities p_o and p_b. A systematic analysis of these probabilities is given in section 6.5. These features are also functions of pixel intensity differences.

Start with the edges defined in section 5.4, and in terms of which the Bernoulli data model for deformations was defined. These types of edges are rather frequent in generic images. In figure 6.5, we show all instances of one vertical edge type in two images with faces, which will be processed in chapter 8 (see figure 8.5). Only one edge ($n_e = 1$) is allowed in each 2×2 block.

It is not efficient to base uninitialized detection algorithms directly on the locations of these edges, although it is definitely possible to do so. It proves more efficient to produce features of lower density as functions of the initial edge map. Each feature is defined in terms of a "central edge" of some type e_0, and a number n_r of other edge types $e_1, \ldots, e_{n_r}$, which are constrained to lie in specific subregions $R_1, \ldots, R_{n_r}$, in the neighborhood of the location of the center edge. We refer to the number n_r of additional edges as the *complexity* of the arrangement. In figure 6.6, two examples of such local edge arrangements are shown with $n_r = 2$.

The local feature is detected at a location if the central edge is found at that location and if an instance of each of the n_r edge types is found in the corresponding region. The family of possible subregions is denoted $\mathcal{R}$. The sizes of the subregions are all approximately the same. The subregions can be wedge-shaped, as indicated in figure 6.6, or squares in the neighborhood of the center. Or-ing—allowing

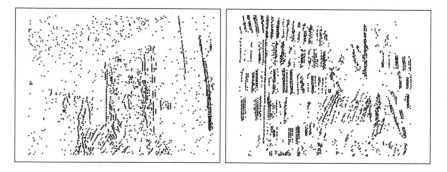

Figure 6.5   Vertical edges detected on two images.

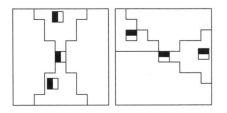

Figure 6.6 Two examples of local edge arrangements with $n_r = 2$ edges in addition to the center one, each allowed to lie anywhere in a wedge shaped region.

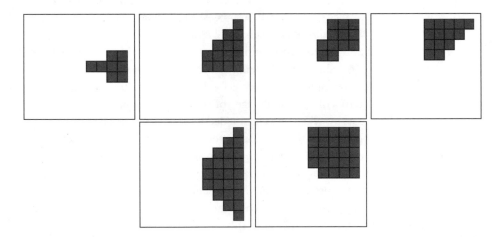

Figure 6.7 (Top) Four of the wedges used to define edge arrangements in the experiments of chapter 8. There are twelve additional wedges obtained by rotating by 90, 180, and 270 degrees. (Bottom) Two of a family of eight larger wedges. The remaining six are obtained by rotating.

the n_r edges to float in their respective subregions—is how geometric invariance is explicitly introduced at this level, as demonstrated in section 6.5 next. The family $\mathcal{R}$ of regions used in the experiments reported in chapter 8 are shown in figure 6.7, alongside a family of larger wedges, which is studied for comparison in section 6.5.

6.4.1 Training

In contrast to the previous section, here we do not assume salient landmarks have been pointed out by the user. The locations of interest are identified as part of the training process. In this case, however, it is necessary to train on *registered* data. Three pose *reference points* p_1, p_2, p_3 are chosen on the reference grid. On each training image $t = 1, \ldots, T$, the user marks three *anchor* points that will be matched to the three pose reference points, determining an affine map A_t from the training image t to the reference grid.

Two-Edge Arrangements

For two-edge arrangements ($n_r = 1$) (i.e., one edge in addition to the center edge), the number of possible arrangements J is on the order of several hundreds. Locations of all arrangement types in each training image t are found and then *registered* to the reference grid. Specifically, a feature j detected at location x adds a count to $F_j(A_t x)$, for each $j = 1, \ldots, J$. Choose a probability threshold $\rho \sim .5$ and an upper bound n on the number of local features. In each disjoint 3×3 box C on the reference grid, find the two-edge arrangement with highest frequency in the training data— that is,

$$F_C = \max_{j=1,\ldots,J} \max_C F_j(z)$$

If the relative frequency $F_C/T > \rho$, the corresponding two-edge arrangement is added to the model together with the location z_C corresponding to the center of the box. All such feature location pairs are identified and if more than n are found, a random sample of n are kept. This yields a list $X_i, z_i, i = 1, \ldots, n$ of two-edge features and associated model locations.

This is the procedure used in chapter 11 to train object representations in the framework of a neural network implementation of these models (see figure 11.4). A similar procedure was used to train the edge templates in section 5.4, except that all locations were kept no matter what the relative frequency.

More Complex Arrangements

When the complexity of the edge arrangements is higher (i.e., $n_r > 1$) the number of possible arrangements is very large, and it is impractical to precompute all locations on all training images. A greedy search is implemented instead, seeking step-wise increments in the complexity of features with high frequency on the object class. Edges are first detected on each training image and their locations are registered to the reference grid using the affine map A_t. Note that we do not register the images themselves but the detected locations of the edges. In each disjoint $c \times c$ box of the reference grid, the two-edge arrangement with highest count is found. All instances of the chosen two-edge arrangement in the box are recorded for each image. Then a loop over all possible additions of one edge/region pair selects the one with highest count in the box, until n_r edge/region pairs are found. The following algorithm provides the details.

Algorithm 6.1: Sparse Model—Training Edge Arrangements

Fix n_r, and $\mathcal{R}$, the family of regions, and choose $\rho < 1$, (typically .5) and let $\mathcal{T}$ denote the training set. Detect the eight edge types in each training image and register the locations using A_t to produce registered edge maps $E_t^{(1)}, \ldots, E_t^{(8)}$ for each $t = 1, \ldots, T$.

1. Set feature counter $I = 0$. Loop over disjoint $c \times c$ (say, $c = 3$ or $c = 5$) boxes on the reference grid. For each such box C:

   (a) For each possible triple (e_0, e_1, R_1), where e_0, e_1 are any possible edge types and $R_1 \in \mathcal{R}$, count the number of training points in $\mathcal{T}$ for which an instance of the triple occurs in C. This means e_0, the central edge, is located at any point $x \in C$ and e_1 is located anywhere in $x + R_1$. Pick the triple with highest count and let $\mathcal{T}_1 \subset \mathcal{T}$ denote the set of data points that have an instance of this triple in C. For each data point $t \in \mathcal{T}_1$, let $W_{t,1} = \{x_{t,m}, m = 1, \ldots, M_{t,1}\}$ denote all locations of the first edge e_0 for which the chosen triple was found. Set $j = 2$.

   (b) Loop over all possible pairs (e_j, R_j) and count how many data points $t \in \mathcal{T}_{j-1}$ have an edge of type e_j anywhere in $x_{t,m} + R_j$ for any one of the locations $x_{t,m} \in W_{t,j-1}$. Find the pair with highest count and let $\mathcal{T}_j \subset \mathcal{T}_{j-1}$ denote the data points that have an instance of this pair. For each data point in $t \in \mathcal{T}_j$, let $W_{t,j} = \{x_{t,m} \in W_{l,j-1} : m = 1, \ldots, M_{t,j}\}$ denote the set of locations of the first edge e_0 for which the additional pair was found.

   (c) $j \leftarrow j + 1$. If $j < n_r$ go to (b).

2. If $|\mathcal{T}_{n_r}|/|\mathcal{T}| > \rho$, record the feature

$$X_I = (e_0, e_1, R_1, \ldots, e_{n_r}, R_{n_r})$$

   at the center z_I of C. For all data points in $\mathcal{T}_{n_r}$ there exists a location $x \in C$ at which an instance of e_0 is present and an instance of e_k is present in $x + R_k$ for each $k = 1, \ldots, n_r$.
   Set $I \leftarrow I + 1$.

3. Move to the next box $c \times c$ and go to 1.

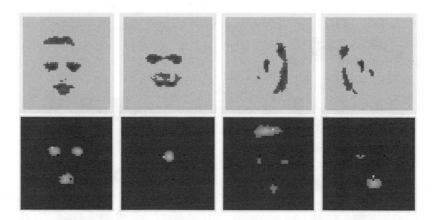

Figure 6.8 (Top) Frequencies of four edge types, the two vertical and two horizontal, after registration. A pixel is on only if 70% of the faces had the corresponding edge in a 5×5 neighborhood of that pixel. (Bottom) Frequencies of four edge arrangements with complexity $n_r = 3$ from the model in figure 6.9. A pixel is on only if 50% of the faces had the corresponding arrangement in a 5×5 neighborhood of that pixel. The reference points are in black, and the model location of the feature in white.

If we initially set out to pick n local features and more have been found, choose a random sample of size n.

In the top row of figure 6.8, we show images representing high-frequency locations of the registered edges for faces. We used 300 faces of the Olivetti database, consisting of 10 views of 30 people. For each of four edge types, the two vertical and two horizontal, a pixel is on if more than .7 of the faces had an edge of that type in the 5×5 neighborhood of that pixel. In the bottom row of the same figure, we show the same information for four edge arrangements from the face representation given in figure 6.9 ($n_r = 3$). Only locations with proportion over .5 are shown. The model location is shown as a white dot and the three reference points in black. Note how the local features are much more specific to particular parts of the face.

In figure 6.9, we show a graphical representation of 20 local features, with $n_r = 3$ at their model locations, which were used as the sparse face model for the face detection experiments shown in chapter 8. The three black dots represent the three reference points and correspond to the location of the two eyes and mouth. In other words, the anchor points identified by the user on each training image were the two eyes and the center of the mouth.

Each local feature is represented by the four edges that define it. The two adjacent rectangles describe the orientation and polarity of the edge. Recall that the edges

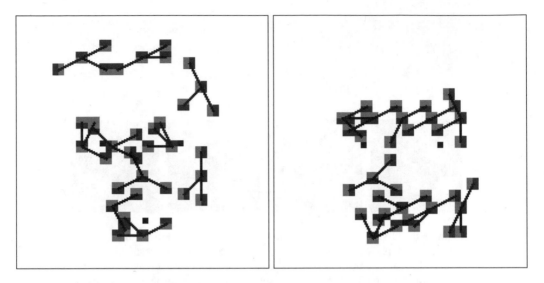

Figure 6.9   The graphs representing local features identified for the sparse face model. Each local feature has a center edge and three other edges around it. The two adjacent rectangles describe the orientation and polarity of each edge.

can have varying locations relative to the center. For example, the upper left-hand feature in the left-hand panel in figure 6.9 has three horizontal edges arranged more or less horizontally and a vertical edge on their left. This appears to capture the curve of the hairline on the left part of the face. The feature directly below that has two horizontal edges with a dark part on the bottom, above two horizontal edges with a dark part on the top. This captures the area around the eye, which is typically darker than its surroundings. These edge groupings not only capture contours but other topographical structures as well. Even a smaller training set of 50 faces (from five people) will yield very similar statistics in terms of the edges and their arrangements. Other representations obtained for other types of objects can be found in chapter 8. Figure 6.10 gives a sense of the density of these features on the same two images used in figure 6.5, which will be processed later on in figure 8.5. Locations of the first feature in the face model above are shown.

Determining the Threshold τ

In principle, if the local features were independent on the object, and their probabilities were given by p_o, a simple calculation using the binomial distribution $B(n, p_o)$

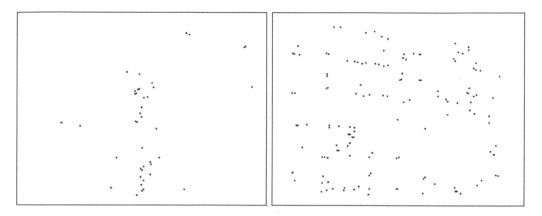

Figure 6.10   For the two images used in figure 6.5 the locations of the first local feature in figure 6.9.

would yield the threshold τ for some chosen false-negative rate r. But due to existing correlations between the features, this analytic threshold is too high and it is better to estimate a threshold from data. Take a sample of unregistered training images for which the range of scales and rotations covers the prescribed range for the detector, determined by $\mathcal{A}$. Choose an acceptable false-negative rate r, say, 5%.

For each training image $I^{(t)}, t = 1, \ldots, T$, let A_t be the affine map taking the three reference points $p_1, p_2, p_3 \in G$ into the three anchor points $x_1^{(t)}, x_2^{(t)}, x_3^{(t)}$, in $I^{(t)}$. Strictly speaking, we should find a value of τ for which $(1 - r)T$ training images have a sequence $i_1, \ldots, i_\tau$ such that an instance of X_{i_j} is found in the region $A_t z_{i_j} + C$ for $j = 1, \ldots, \tau$. Of course, the sequence can be different from image to image. However, there is quite a large degree of uncertainty regarding A_t itself. The three anchor points are provided by the user on each image—at times mistakes are made, and at times the precise location of, say, the center of the eye can be equivocal. We therefore use a looser criterion for determining τ: Find the largest τ for which $(1 - r)T$ of the training images have an admissible instantiation $\theta \in \Theta$, with at least τ indices for which $X_j(\theta_j) = 1$, and the center θ_c is within D pixels from the mean $x_{c,t}$ of the anchor points. The distance D is chosen to be 2–3 pixels.

This choice ensures that we do not discount an image that does have at least τ local features in an admissible instantiation, but these do not necessarily fall in the expected regions according to the affine map A_t.

6.5   Local Feature Statistics

The detection algorithms described in chapters 7 and 8 both rely on the fact that the on-object probabilities of the local features, namely, probabilities at the correct location of the object, are high and invariant with respect to a range of deformations, whereas the density of these same features in the background is low. In terms of the statistical model described in section 6.2, testing whether the object is present or not at a specific instantiation θ is reduced to a simple hypothesis test between two binomial distributions, $B(n, p_o)$ and $B(n, p_b)$, with observations $X_i(\theta_i)$, $i = 1, \ldots, n$. A threshold τ is determined, and if the number of hits is above threshold at a certain instantiation θ, it is declared object—otherwise, it is declared background.

In this section, we study more closely the statistical properties of the edge arrangements on background and on object. The binomial model, which derives from the conditional independence assumption, is an oversimplification; some correlations exist between the features, both on object and on background. However, we will show evidence of very consistent patterns in terms of the dependence of these statistics on the parameter settings. In particular, false-positive densities, although not directly predictable using the conditional independence assumption, can be predicted by fitting some simple linear models.

In studying the statistics of these features, we take the subregion $\mathcal{R}$ as a family of wedges of the 9×9 neighborhood of the origin. We use two sizes: Larger regions with 8–90° wedges, at increments of 45°, and smaller regions with 16–45° wedges at increments of 22.5° (see figure 6.7). For the large regions, there are 24 pixels in each region, whereas for the smaller regions there are between 10 and 14 pixels. The edges are detected in 2×2 blocks, as described in section 6.4. In order to study the dependence of the algorithm on edge density, we take the maximal number of edges n_e, in each 2×2 block to be either one or two. All in all, there are four categories: $n_e = 1, 2$, and large or small wedges, determining the overall density of the local features.

We work with 40 local features identified through training on a face data set. Very similar behavior is observed for features trained for other object types. The forty-edge arrangements were trained using algorithm 6.1, described before. Forty locations on the reference grid were found where an edge arrangement, defined in terms of a central edge and *six* other edges in its neighborhood, was present in at least $\rho = 30\%$ of the registered edge maps of the training set. There is an ordering on the edges in each of these arrangements, determined by the order in which they were identified in the algorithm. It is possible to define *partial* arrangements by taking the first n_r

edges in the ordering for $n_r = 1, \ldots, 6$. Clearly, the partial arrangements will have even higher probability, and will be of higher density on the background. Note that for the given ordering of the edges in an arrangement, as n_r increases, the collection of detections of the local feature is a subset of the previous stage. This allows us to study the density of these arrangements as a function of n_r. We start with the process corresponding to the center edge of the arrangement. At the next step, we keep only those locations where the second edge in the arrangement is found in the appropriate neighborhood, so that we have filtered out the original edge locations. This filtering continues as more edges are added in.

6.5.1   Background Densities

The density of the features on generic images decreases exponentially in n_r—the complexity of the arrangement. The rate of decay depends on the size of the subregions in $\mathcal{R}$ and on the initial edge density, which in our case depends on n_e—the number of edges kept in each disjoint 2×2 block. Forty random background images—including outdoor images from urban and nature scenes, as well as some underwater scenes—were downloaded from the web to obtain these statistics. In addition, nine indoor office images were taken. In figure 6.11, we show the box plots for the log-densities for the four categories as a function of $n_r + 1$ for the outdoor images. The first box corresponds to the density of the edges themselves (i.e., $n_r = 0$). Each of the remaining boxes represents 1600 points—that is, the distribution of densities over forty images for the 40 features at the given level of complexity n_r.

For all four parameter categories, we observe an initial large decrease of the density between $n_r = 0$ to $n_r = 1$. This corresponds to filtering out of edges resulting from random noise, leaving primarily edges that form part of some rudimentary local structure. Subsequently, we observe a linear decay on the log scale of the density as a function of n_r, which may have to do with a gradual *partitioning* of the "space" of local structures.

Of the hundreds of possible arrangements with $n_r = 1$ (two-edge arrangements), defined in terms of a central edge and one additional edge, many can actually be found in real data. Semantically, some could be described as a small segment of a contour within a range of curvatures, some could be labeled as a "slit." For each center edge type e_0, there are $8|\mathcal{R}|$ possible pairs. Many such pairs describe very similar structures due to the slack in the relative locations of the edges. Still, one notes that for each center edge type there is quite a large number (say, S) of mutually exclusive structures determined by the additional edge. Assuming each of these structures is equally likely given the center edge is present, which is obviously an oversimplification, their

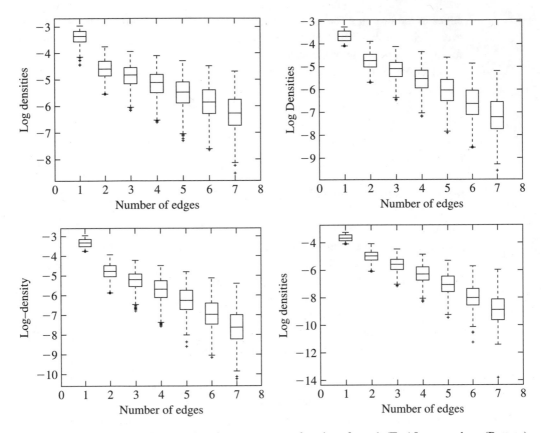

Figure 6.11 Log density of arrangements as function of $n_r + 1$. (Top) Large wedges. (Bottom) Small wedges. (Left) $n_e = 2$. (Right) $n_e = 1$.

probability is at most $1/S$ that of the center edge. This factor corresponds to the first drop in density between $n_r = 0$ and $n_r = 1$.

However, once the first two edges are determined, there is a much smaller number of internally consistent possibilities, representing realistic local structures for the third edge, and hence the slower drop in the density for higher values of n_r. Recall that the features studied here were trained on a real object, so that inconsistent arrangements do not get chosen. Indeed, if the arrangements were defined by randomly choosing the edge types and the regions in $\mathcal{R}$, the density would decay more rapidly.

We fit a linear model where the response variable is the log-density of the edge arrangement (LDA) in an image. There are two predictors: the log-density of the edges (LDE) in the image, and the complexity of the arrangement, $n_r = 1, \ldots, 6$.

Table 6.1 95% confidence intervals for the coefficients of the two predictors: log-density of edges (LDE) and complexity (n_r), and the R^2 coefficient for the regressions

Category	LDE	n_r	R^2
$n_e = 1$, small wedges	[1.21, 1.36]	[−.79, −.76]	.88
$n_e = 2$, small wedges	[1.31, 1.44]	[−.57, −.55]	.87
$n_e = 1$, large wedges	[1.29, 1.41]	[−.50, −.48]	.87
$n_e = 2$, large wedges	[1.16, 1.30]	[−.35, −.33]	.83

Table 6.1 shows 95% confidence intervals for the coefficients of the two predictors, as well as the R^2 coefficient, for each of the four categories. There are 1600 data points for each of these four regressions, consisting of the 40 local features at each of the forty images.

We obtain the following four models for the density DF of the feature as a function of the density DE of the edges and complexity n_r .

$$DF = DE^{1.28} \cdot (.45)^{n_r}$$

$$DF = DE^{1.38} \cdot (.57)^{n_r}$$

$$DF = DE^{1.36} \cdot (.61)^{n_r}$$

$$DF = DE^{1.23} \cdot (.71)^{n_r}$$

There are sizeable overlaps among the confidence intervals for the coefficient of LDE. It appears that the crucial effect comes from the coefficient of n_r—namely, the base of the second exponent. As the regions in the edge arrangement get larger, or as more edges are allowed per block, the rate of exponential decay decreases. The explanation offered above for these rather striking phenomena is quite heuristic. It is hoped that new models on local structures will emerge that provide a more comprehensive explanation.

6.5.2 Statistics on Object

We now turn to the properties of the edge arrangements on object. Specifically, those arrangements that were identified through training on the given object class.

Probability of Features as a Function of Complexity n_r

In figure 6.12, we show box plots of the probabilities of the 40 features on object (in this case, faces) at the correct location, as a function of complexity, for the four

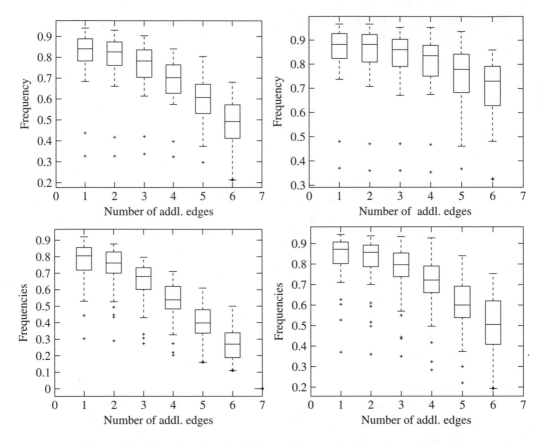

Figure 6.12   Box plots of probabilities on object as function of $n_r + 1$. (Top) Large wedges. (Bottom) Small wedges. (Left) $n_e = 1$. (Right) $n_e = 2$.

categories defined above. For these plots, all faces are at reference pose. The feature is considered present at the model location z if its center is anywhere in a small 5×5 neighborhood $N_5(z)$ of z. The first important property that emerges from these plots is the existence of local features with very high probabilities. This is not only a property of the particular face database used here but of all other examples presented in later chapters. If there is a large degree of variability at the local level, the probabilities will be lower. This variability could be due to nonlinear deformations or to discontinuous changes. For example, some people have glasses and some do not. The more variable the ensemble is *after pose variation is factored out,* the lower the probabilities of the best local features will be, for a fixed set of parameters, and more of these features will be needed to obtain good discrimination from background.

Another property that emerges from the data above is that probabilities of the arrangements, at the correct location in the reference grid, decay very slowly—at most, *linearly* as a function of the complexity n_r. This is in contrast to the exponential decay of the densities on background. A heuristic explanation for this phenomenon is the following. Assume that the object ensemble is obtained from smooth local deformations of a prototype image, sampled uniformly from a set of deformations Υ of size U. No major linear transformations are allowed, so that all deformed instances of the object are more or less at the reference pose. On the template, at a location with some "edge activity," one can identify an arrangement of, say, six edges. The center edge e_0 in the arrangement has an absolute location z in the reference grid. There is a subset Υ_0 of deformations for which there is no edge type e_0 in the 5×5 neighborhood of z. Assuming e_0 is found in $z_0 \in N_5(z)$, for each $k > 0$ there is then a subset Υ_k of Υ of deformations of the template for which the kth edge e_k is not obtained anywhere in $z_0 + R_k$. It is reasonable to assume that the size of these sets $\Upsilon_k, k = 0, \ldots, n_r$ is more or less the same for all k, denoted u, and does not depend on the location z_0 of the first edge. Consequently, the probability of the arrangement consisting of the first n_r edges can be bounded from below by $1 - n_r(u/|U|)$, which is linear in n_r.

This argument holds only if the population is obtained through smooth deformations of a single template. This is rarely the case. However, it is reasonable to assume that the population can be obtained from smooth deformations of a number of prototypes, which are similar in some parts and different in others, so that the argument presented above remains valid in spirit.

Invariance of Features with Respect to Pose

When large-scale deformations are introduced, such as scaling or rotation, we do not expect to find the features at the same location on the reference grid. We now compare the probability that feature X_i is present at location z_i, when the object is at reference scale, to the probability that the feature is present at location sz_i when the object is at scale s. Similarly, with respect to rotation or other global linear transformations. Clearly, the probabilities change drastically with large rotations, because the local features are not rotation invariant in the strict sense. The edges are constrained relative to the center edge in specific regions, and the edges themselves have coarse orientation selectivity. Yet due to the slack in the definition of the edges and their arrangements, we

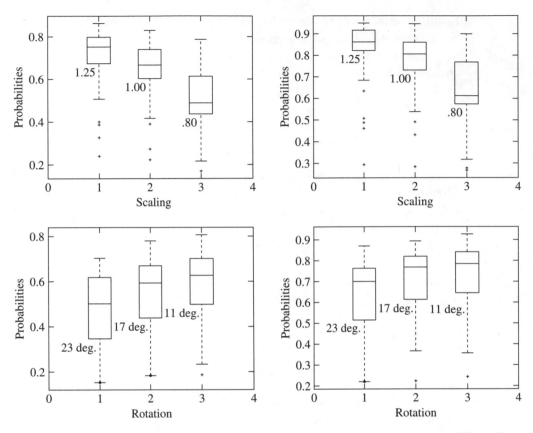

Figure 6.13 Box plots of probabilities for the 40 local features at $n_r = 3$, for different linear transformations using small wedges. (Top) Scaling at 125%, 100%, 80%. (Bottom) Rotation at 23, 17 and 11 degrees. (Left) $n_e = 1$. (Right) $n_e = 2$.

expect a limited degree of rotation invariance. The top panel of figure 6.13 illustrates the stability of the probabilities with respect to upscaling, and downscaling, for the smaller wedges, at $n_r = 3$. The left shows $n_e = 1$, the right $n_e = 2$. The bottom of figure 6.13 illustrates the invariance with respect to rotation. The data was obtained by applying a linear transformation a to the face images, extracting the local features in those transformed images, and finding what proportion of the data had the local feature X_i on, in a small neighborhood of az_i. Observe that the probabilities of the features are indeed robust to a large range of poses. As would be expected for the arrangements defined with larger wedges, the probabilities are even more robust.

6.5.3   False-Positive Rates

The two detection schemes presented in chapters 7 and 8 perform a search for peaks of the posterior. In the two cases, a peak occurs at an instantiation θ only when all or a certain fraction of the features is present. The question arises as to the probability of false positives—that is, the probability of having more than τ features present in an admissible arrangement θ even if there is no object present at that instantiation. We study the false-positive behavior, assuming the set of admissible instantiations $\Theta^{(0)}$ is defined through equation 6.1 with $\mathcal{A}$ covering a range of scales of $\pm25\%$ and rotations of $\pm15°$. For each value of n_r, we use a set of face images to determine a threshold τ, which keeps more than 95% of the faces, as detailed in section 6.4. We then search the forty random background images for configurations of at least τ features at any location and at any of the prescribed linear transformations of $\mathcal{A}$. An efficient way to do this search is detailed in chapter 8—here, we are only interested in the statistics.

As already mentioned, the statistical model described in section 6.2 reduces to a simple test between two binomial distributions, $B(n, p_b)$, and $B(n, p_o)$ for every possible instantiation $\theta \in \Theta$. If the model was accurate, the probability of a false positive at any given pose could be predicted using the tails of the binomial distribution $B(n, p_b)$, or using the normal approximation: $1 - \Phi(\tau - np_b)/(\sqrt{np_b(1 - p_b)})$, where Φ is the cumulative distribution function of the standard normal distribution. Note that the number of possible instantiations in the present context is hundreds of times larger than the number of locations, because at each location one could have on the order of hundreds of scales and rotation combinations. Detected instantiations typically occur in clusters arising from the same object in the image, and the instantiation with the highest number of detected features is chosen to represent this cluster. These considerations make it much harder to predict the density of false positives in terms of a simple probability model. Instead, we provide empirical data on the density of false positives per pixel (i.e., total number of detections divided by the area of the image).

In table 6.2, for each value of n_r, we list the average probability of the 40 features on the training set; the empirical threshold τ, obtained by checking for the highest value for which 95% of the training set of faces is detected (5% false-negative rate); the total false-positive rate where the total number of detections in all forty images is divided by the total area. In addition, we show the 95% confidence interval for the coefficient of the log-density of the local features (per local feature type) in predicting the log-density of false positives in an image, as well as the R^2 coefficient. In figure 6.14,

Table 6.2   False positive rates as function of complexity

n_r	p_o	τ	FP	95% Confidence Interval	R^2
1	.77	25	$3 \cdot 10^{-4}$	[2.28, 3.62]	.82
2	.72	22	$5 \cdot 10^{-5}$	[1.34, 2.69]	.70
3	.64	17	$5 \cdot 10^{-5}$	[1.58, 2.64]	.80
4	.53	11	$2 \cdot 10^{-4}$	[1.88, 2.89]	.84
5	.39	6	$3 \cdot 10^{-4}$	[1.79, 2.6]	0.87
6	.28	3	$8 \cdot 10^{-4}$	[1.50, 1.89]	0.94

Column 1: Complexity of edge arrangements in model. Column 2: Average on-object probability of the arrangements. Column 3: Threshold at 5% false negative. Column 4: False positive density (number of false positives per pixel.) Columns 5, 6: 95% confidence intervals for the regression coefficient of log-density of false positives against log-density of local features in an image. Column 7: R^2 coefficient of the regression.

the scatter plots of the log-density of false positives against the log-density of the local features are shown for $n_r = 1, 3, 5$. The asterisk (*) stands for outdoor images and the "o" for the office images. Some points do not appear because there were no false positives. The estimates using outdoor images provide an upper bound, because there is a much higher density of edges in these. In this experiment, we used the small wedges and $n_e = 1$.

If the features were indeed conditionally independent, as assumed in the statistical modeling, because the probabilities on-object decay linearly with n_r whereas the probabilities on-background decay exponentially, with a larger n_r, a lower false-positive rate could be obtained for some fixed false-negative rate. However, due to correlations between the features on-object, which increase with their complexity, the threshold τ decreases faster than the binomial model would predict and the number of false positives starts to increase.

We see that the properties of this hierarchy of local features is stable and predictable both on-object and on-background. Depending on the task at hand, the computational constraints, and acceptable levels of the two types of error, different feature complexities can be used.

We have described two families of local features—the comparison arrays and the edge arrangements—defined in terms of simple operations involving intensity comparisons and intensity-difference comparisons. We also described two approaches for training the model. In the first, the user selects the points $x_{i,t} i = 1, \ldots, n$ on each of the training images, and it remains only to identify the best local feature and

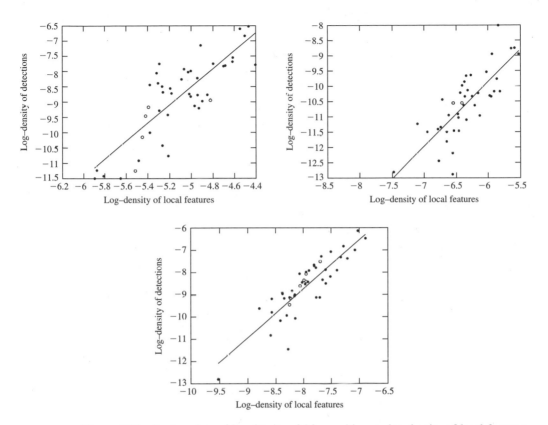

Figure 6.14 Scatter plots of log-density of false positive vs. log-density of local features, $n_r = 1, 3, 5$.

estimate the associated parameters using subimages centered at $x_{i,t}$, $t = 1, \ldots, T$. In the second, the user only selects three anchor points on each training image, which determine an affine map for registration of local feature data to the reference grid. Training involves simultaneously finding the locations of interest $z_1, \ldots, z_n$ and local features for those locations. The anchor points themselves need not be part of the model. In the next two chapters, we describe in detail two methods for finding detections of the sparse models defined in terms of these local features.

7 Detection of Sparse Models: Dynamic Programming

In chapter 6, we described two families of local features that could be used to construct a model for an object. These features exhibit certain invariance properties on the object ensemble and are low density in generic images. The next step is to use knowledge on the variations of the object to constrain the possible arrangements of the instances of the features and to develop an efficient algorithm to detect admissible instantiations. In this chapter, we explore one possible approach, which is relevant when p_o is very close to 1, so that false negatives at the local level are very rare and at most one instance of the object is expected in the image. A more general approach, allowing for partial occlusions and multiple objects in the scene, is studied in chapter 8.

7.1 The Prior Model

The prior is defined so as to favor points $\theta \in \Theta$ with a higher degree of geometric similarity to the model configuration $z_1, \ldots, z_n$. Define a function $\Psi(\theta)$ that measures some form of geometric distance between Z and the instantiation θ. In anticipation of computational issues, we limit ourselves to "triangle"-based functions Ψ of the form

$$\Psi(\theta) = \sum_C \psi_C(\theta_i; i \in C) \tag{7.1}$$

where C is a collection of triples from the set $\{1, \ldots, n\}$. The prior is then simply

$$P(\theta) \propto \exp[-\Psi(\theta)]$$

The functions ψ_C are defined to be invariant to translation and to certain ranges of scale and rotation. They are formulated in terms of the deviation of a candidate triangle $\theta_{i_1}, \theta_{i_2}, \theta_{i_3}$ from the model triangle $z_{i_1}, z_{i_2}, z_{i_3}$. There are two components: hard constraints, which limit the range in which the triangle can vary, and soft constraints, which penalize deviations from the template triangle. The hard constraints used below are very loose and impose a limit of $\pm\pi/2$ on the deviation of each angle of the candidate triangle from the model triangle, and a limitation on the scaling of any of the edges between $1/5$ and 5. The set Θ is defined as those sequences θ that satisfy the collection of hard constraints on θ_C, $C \in \mathcal{C}$.

For a triple $C = \{i_1, i_2, i_3\} \in \mathcal{C}$, the soft constraints have the form

$$\sum_{j=1}^{3} \left((\alpha_{i_j} - a_{i_j}) \bmod 2\pi \right)^2$$

where α_{i_j} is the angle at vertex θ_{i_j} and a_{i_j} is the angle at vertex z_{i_j} in the model triangle. There are many alternatives proposed in the statistical shape literature (see, for example, Bookstein 1991 or Dryden and Mardia 1998). These penalties are translation and scale invariant. As defined above, they are also rotation invariant; however, the local features themselves are not. Because the orientation is usually known, in the present context it is useful to add a rotational constraint on the functions—for example, constraining the absolute angle of an edge to lie within a certain range of the angle of the corresponding edge in the model. Note that because these constraints are translation invariant, there is no particular need to specifically define the set $\Theta^{(0)}$ of admissible instantiations centered at the origin, although the set is implicitly defined through the hard constraint component of the cost function Ψ. Furthermore, because the hard constraints are defined in terms of the same triangles as the soft constraints, we can incorporate them directly into the cost function Ψ by setting $\psi_C(\theta_i; i \in C) = \infty$ if $(\theta_i; i \in C)$ does not satisfy the hard constraints.

7.1.1 Decomposability

When $p_o = 1$, all n local features will appear in an admissible configuration if the object is in the image. The maximum of the posterior is obtained by generating a list S_i of all instances of each local feature X_i, $i = 1, \ldots, n$ in the image. Then for each θ such that $\theta_i \in S_i$, evaluate $P(\theta)$ and find the minimum. Typically, this is not computationally feasible, even if n is on the order of 10 points and the size of S_i is on the order of 50–100. However, when the collection of triples $\mathcal{C}$ has a *decomposable* form, minimization can be efficiently done through dynamic programming.

Decomposability in the present context means that there are $n - 2$ triples defined on the set $I_n = \{1, \ldots, n\}$, and there exists an ordering of the triples $C_1, \ldots, C_{n-2}$ and a reordering $\sigma_i \in C_i$ of the elements in I_n, with the following properties; σ_1 is only a member of C_1. If we remove σ_1 from the list of points and C_1 from the list of triples, then σ_2 belongs only to C_2, and the two other points in C_1 *together* belong to at least one other triple. Eliminate σ_2 and C_2 and so on. At stage $j - 1$, the point σ_{j-1} belongs only to the triple C_{j-1} and after eliminating σ_{j-1} from the list of points and C_{j-1} from the list of triples, σ_j belongs only to C_j, and the two other points in C_{j-1} together belong to the some other triple. This elimination or "peeling" procedure continues until all that is left are $\sigma_{n-2}, \sigma_{n-1}, \sigma_n$, which make up the triple C_{n-2}.

For example, given n indices, the simplest decomposable collection would have the triples $i, i + 1, i + 2$ for $i = 1, \ldots, n - 2$, which has a simple *linear* form. There are other examples where the collection of triples is decomposable but does not have a linear form. The notion of decomposability can be defined in terms of graphs, which have edges between any two indices belonging to the same triple. Thus in figure 7.1, the triples in the collection are those for which all three connecting edges are present in the graph. Decomposability of the graph is equivalent to decomposability of the collection of triples. The numbers in the graphs correspond to the peeling order, and differ for different graphs. The graph on the left of figure 7.1 has the simple linear form. The graph on the right is also decomposable, but is not linear. Decomposability can be easily extended to collections of larger subsets with varying numbers of points (see Bertele and Brioschi 1969 and Rose, Tarjan, and Leuker 1976). However, in the present context, such extensions would lead to massive a slowdown in computation. We therefore limit ourselves to decomposable collections of triples.

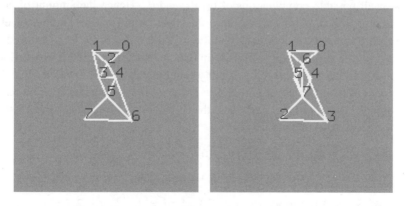

Figure 7.1   Two decomposable collections of triples with the eight model points. Each triangle in the above graphs corresponds to one of the triples. The left hand collection is linear the right hand is not.

7.2   Computation: Dynamic Programming

The description of dynamic programming in this context is very similar to that of chapter 4; however, it is worth repeating due to the somewhat more-complex structure of the function. We assume that the indices and triples in the model are now relabeled according to the "peeling" order described above. The state space S_i associated to each index $i = 1, \ldots, n$ is the list of locations $\theta_{i,j}$, $j = 1, \ldots, J_i$ for which $X_i(\theta_{i,j}) = 1$. Dynamic programming proceeds as follows. Because 1 is the vertex in C_1, which is not in any other triple (the first to be eliminated), we can write

$$
\begin{aligned}
\Psi(\theta_1, \ldots, \theta_n) &= \sum_{i=1}^{n-2} \psi_{C_i}(\theta_k; k \in C_i) \\
&= \psi_{C_1}(\theta_k; k \in C_1) + \sum_{i=2}^{n-2} \psi_{C_i}(\theta_k; k \in C_i) \\
&\overset{\text{def}}{=} \psi_{C_1}(\theta_k; k \in C_1) + \Lambda(\theta_2, \ldots, \theta_n)
\end{aligned}
\tag{7.2}
$$

where $\theta_i \in S_i$, $i = 1, \ldots, n$. Assume $C_1 = \{1, a, b\}$. For any fixed pair $\theta_a \in S_a$, $\theta_b \in S_b$ of candidate points for landmarks a and b, let $\theta_1^*[\theta_a, \theta_b]$ be the choice of $\theta_1 \in S_1$, which minimizes $\psi_{C_1}(\theta_1, \theta_a, \theta_b)$. Because $\Lambda(\cdot)$ does not depend on θ_1, it is easy to see that the optimal instantiation $(\theta_1^*, \ldots, \theta_n^*)$ satisfies $\theta_1^* = \theta_1^*[\theta_a^*, \theta_b^*]$. Note that finding $\theta_1^*[\theta_a, \theta_b]$ for all possible pairs $\theta_a \in S_a$, $\theta_b \in S_b$ requires evaluating $\psi_{C_1}(\theta_1, \theta_a, \theta_b)$ for all possible combinations of θ_1, θ_a, and θ_b. Hence the amount of computation is proportional to m^3, where m is an upper bound on the number of elements in each of the sets S_i. For each pair (θ_a, θ_b) the index $\theta_1^*[\theta_a, \theta_b]$ is stored as well as $\psi_{C_1}(\theta_1^*[\theta_a, \theta_b], \theta_a, \theta_b)$, so that the amount of storage required is proportional to m^2.

According to the decomposability requirements, there exists a triple C_{u_1}, which contains both vertices a and b. The index u_1 is not necessarily the next one in the ordering, *except* in the case where the collection of triples has a linear structure. Let $C_{u_1} = \{a, b, c\}$. Define

$$
\begin{aligned}
\hat{\psi}_{C_{u_1}}(\theta_k; k \in C_{u_1}) &= \hat{\psi}_{C_{u_1}}(\theta_a, \theta_b, \theta_c) \\
&= \psi_{C_{u_1}}(\theta_a, \theta_b, \theta_c) + \psi_{C_1}(\theta_1^*[\theta_a, \theta_b], \theta_a, \theta_b) \\
\hat{\psi}_{C_i}(\theta_k; k \in C_i) &= \psi_{C_i}(\theta_k; k \in C_i) \quad \text{for } i = 2, \ldots, n-2, i \neq u_1
\end{aligned}
$$

and

$$\Phi(\theta_2, \ldots, \theta_n) = \sum_{i=2}^{n-2} \hat{\psi}_{C_i}(\theta_k; k \in C_i)$$

Note that $\psi_{C_1}(\theta_1^*[\theta_a, \theta_b], \theta_a, \theta_b)$ is a function of θ_a and θ_b only, and hence $\hat{\psi}_{C_{u_1}}(\cdot)$ is a function of $(\theta_k, k \in C_{u_1})$. It is easily seen that $\Phi(\theta_2^*, \ldots, \theta_n^*) = \Psi(\theta_1^*, \ldots, \theta_n^*)$ and $(\theta_2^*, \ldots, \theta_n^*)$ is the minimizer of the new function $\Phi(\cdot)$. The original problem is thus reduced to a similar one with one vertex *eliminated*. The new function is still a sum of local functions on a decomposable collection of triples of indices.

By *eliminating* the vertices one at a time in increasing order of the labels, the problem can be solved when only the last 3 vertices—$n - 2, n - 1, n$—are left. When $\theta_{n-2}^*, \theta_{n-1}^*, \theta_n^*$ are determined, we can go backward and determine $\theta_{n-3}^*, \ldots, \theta_1^*$ sequentially. At step j set θ_j^* as $\theta_j^*[\theta_k^*, \theta_l^*]$ (which is already stored) where k, l are the other two elements of C_j. The indices k, l are necessarily greater than j so that θ_k^* and θ_l^* have already been determined. Because the amount of computations needed to eliminate one vertex is proportional to m^3, the total amount of computations is proportional to nm^3. We summarize this procedure in the following algorithm.

Algorithm 7.1: Sparse Model Detection—Dynamic Programming

- *trip* − $n \times 3$ list of triples. *trip*(i, j)—jth vertex in ith triple.
  Points ordered by peeling order: *trip*$(i, 1) = i$.

- *locs*—vector of n arrays:
  locations of the n local features in the image.
  locs$[i](k, 0)$, *locs*$[i](k, 1)$—coordinates of kth instance of ith feature.
  num$[i]$—number of instances of feature i.

- function *par*(n_1, n_2, n_3)—return index m if $m < n_3$ and m belongs to a triple with n_1 and n_2,
  if no such m exists return -1.

- *rec*$[i], i = 1, \ldots, n$—arrays of dimensions *num*$[n_2] \times$ *num*$[n_3] \times 2$:
  $n_2 = trip(i, 2), n_3 = trip(i, 3)$.
  rec$[i](l, k, 1)$—optimal instance of i for the lth instance of feature n_2,
      and kth instance of feature n_3.
  rec$[i](l, k, 2)$—stores the value (initialized to 0).

- for $n_1 = 1 : n - 2$
  $n_2 = trip(n_1, 2), n_3 = trip(n_1, 3)$

Find index of triples that have already been peeled based on any of the edges of the current triple,

$m_2 = par(n_1, n_2, n_1), m_3 = par(n_1, n_3, n_1), m_4 = par(n_2, n_3, n_1)$

$(m_2, m_3, m_4 < n_1)$

for $l = 1 : num[n_2]$

for $k = 1 : num[n_3]$

    currmin $= 0$.

    for $j = 1 : num[n_1]$

        $a = rec[m_2](j, k, 2), b = rec[m_3](j, l, 2), c = rec[m_4](l, k, 2)$

        $v = \psi_{n_1}(j, k, l) + a + b + c.$ (ψ_{n_1}—cost function of triple n_1.)

        if $(v < currmin)$ *currj* $= j, currmin = v$.

    end

$rec[n_1](l, k, 1) = currj, rec[n_1](l, k, 2) = currmin.$

- *opt*—vector of length n. Initialize to -1. Will contain optimal configuration.
- $VAL = \min_{k,l} rec[n - 2](k, l, 2)$, $opt(n - 1) = k_{min}$, $opt(n) = l_{min}$.
- for $n_1 = n - 2 : 1$

    $n_2 = trip(n_1, 2), n_3 = trip(n_1, 3)$

    $m_2 = opt(n_2), m_3 = opt(n_3)$

    $opt(n_1) = rec[n_1](m_2, m_33, 1)$.

end

In figure 7.2, we show the six steps of the dynamic programming algorithm for matching the linear model of figure 7.1. At each step, we recover the optimal match corresponding to the subgraph covered up to that step. It is interesting to observe that due to the translation and scale invariance of the triangle cost functions, the initial optimal matches are far removed from the actual structures we are seeking to detect. Only after a sufficient amount of information is integrated does the optimal match settle down at the correct location. The structure of interest is typically close to the center of the image, however, this information is *not* used in the algorithm. The structure would be detected anywhere and at a large range of scales.

In figure 7.3, we show matches of the two models shown in figure 7.1 to several axial MRI images. In figure 7.4, we show some failed matches of the linear model. Most often, failed matches will contain a large subset of correct matches but one or two that are wrong. This is due on one hand to the very loose hard constraints introduced in the cost functions shown here. A more judicious estimation of the variability of each of the triangles in the model could probably avoid these partial mismatches. On

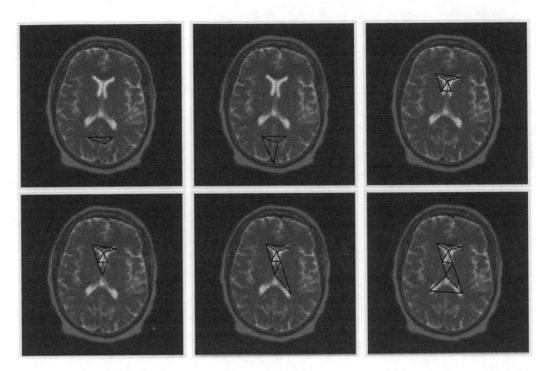

Figure 7.2 Six steps of dynamic programming for the graph shown in figure 7.1. At each step we show the optimal configuration for the subgraph which has already been peeled.

the other hand, false negatives do occur at the local feature level, and necessarily lead to a wrong detection.

7.2.1   Coarse-to-Fine Computation

The efficiency of the computation of the model instantiation depends critically on the decomposability property of the collection of functions and the low density of the features in the background. Ideally, however, one would like to evaluate a candidate instantiation in terms of the cost of *all* possible triangles in the model that correspond to the full graph on the n model points. The decomposable collection can be viewed as a *coarse* model that is easily matched. A more sophisticated implementation of dynamic programming can yield not only the top match but the top M matches—see, for example, Rabiner and Juang (1993) in the case of the linear

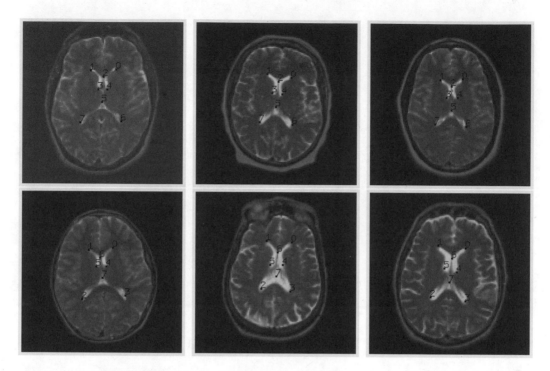

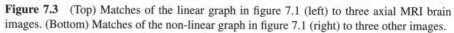

Figure 7.3   (Top) Matches of the linear graph in figure 7.1 (left) to three axial MRI brain images. (Bottom) Matches of the non-linear graph in figure 7.1 (right) to three other images.

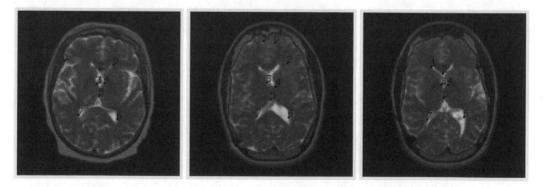

Figure 7.4   Three partial mismatches of the linear graph model.

graph. One can also run several different graphs (as shown in figure 7.1) to obtain different candidate instantiations. The role of the coarse model is then to provide a small number of candidates likely to have low cost for the full function. At each of these it would be very easy to evaluate the full cost function and determine the optimal match in terms of this more-complete model. Estimating an upper threshold of this cost in terms of a training sample of object images could provide a way of ruling out false matches in images that do not contain the object. We continue to pursue this notion of a coarse-to-fine implementation of the detection problem in chapter 8.

7.3 Detecting Pose

When the main source of variability in object instantiation is described in terms of affine transformations (i.e., pose) with perhaps a small degree of nonlinear variability, it is possible to avoid dynamic programming. Given a list of features and a list of model locations on the reference grid ($X_i, z_i, i = 1, \ldots, n$), one searches for triples of features in the image. A triple $\theta_{i_1}, \theta_{i_2}, \theta_{i_3}$ of instances of features i_1, i_2, i_3 in the image determines a unique affine map a taking θ_{i_j} to z_{i_j} for $j = 1, \ldots, 3$. This map provides a prediction for the location for all other features, $\theta_i = az_i$, and if there is an instance of feature i in a small neighborhood of θ_i for each $i = 1, \ldots, n$, then an instantiation of the object has been found. One can even allow some omissions, as long as some given fraction of the features is found in the expected location az_i. Once omissions are permitted, it is necessary to carry out a systematic search over all possible triples i_1, i_2, i_3 in the model until a triple of instances $\theta_{i_1}, \theta_{i_2}, \theta_{i_3}$ is found, providing an affine map a.

In this type of search, we assume that the affine map provided by any triple of detected features is reliable in predicting the locations of the others. This would not work, for example, with the ventricle structures in the MRI brain scans, due to the wide variability in the scale of the substructures. For example, in figure 7.3, the scale of the two "arms" defined by the top ventricle varies in a range of approximately 2 : 1, whereas the entire central ventricle structure is more or less the same size across images. Using the affine map determined by the two tips of the upper ventricles and the cusp in between could result in wrong predictions for the locations of the other features. On the other hand, this type of scheme can be relatively successful for objects such as faces (as suggested in Amit and Geman 1997; Burl, Weber, and Perona 1998 and is closely related to the alignment method in Ullman 1996).

The loop through all possible triples can be computationally intensive, and even on relatively rigid objects one particular triple of detected features can yield rather erroneous estimates of the correct pose. A more systematic and efficient computational approach to detection of instantiations with missing features is described in chapter 8.

7.4   Bibliographical Notes and Discussion

There is a vast literature on graph matching using a variety of other techniques. These techniques are more general than dynamic programming in that they are not constrained to special decomposable graphical structures. In Haralick and Shapiro (1992), the term used is *inexact consistent-labeling* and several algorithms are described using heuristics to overcome the immense combinatorial burden. In Grimson (1990) the same problem is called *searching correspondence space,* and again, a number of algorithms are suggested mainly in the context of rigid objects. These themes are revisited in Ullman (1996). Recently, methods that produce a "soft" assignment of model points to data points has been studied (see Gold and Rangarajan 1996; Rangarajan, Chui, and Bookstein 1997). However, all these methods are necessarily slow due to the inherent complexity of the general graph-matching problem. They are usually applied to hand-picked collections of points. They are rarely applied to images where there is a substantial amount of clutter, which significantly increases the number of detected features.

The idea of using dynamic programming to find optimal feature arrangements was proposed in Fischler and Elschlager (1973), although there is no specific recipe for defining local features. The computational procedure described in this chapter is essentially the same. More details on the application of this approach to matching deformable structures in MRI brain scans can be found Amit (1997).

We have started exploring the use of more complex local features of relatively low density in the background. Fortunately, it is possible to identify such features that are at the same time highly probable at certain locations on the object. The resulting models are sparse and, given the appropriate structure, can be computed very efficiently. The dynamic programming on decomposable graphs for the MRI images takes no more than 100 milliseconds on the Pentium III 700 MHz for each step. This grows linearly with the number of vertices in the graph.

The use of dynamic programming has already been introduced in chapter 4. And in principle, the dynamic programming algorithm described here is the same. However, there is a major difference in terms of the definition of the state space at each step.

In the model described in chapter 4, the state space at step k is the region S_k. These regions can be taken of moderate size, on the order of hundreds, due to the initialization provided by the user. In the models described in this chapter, we seek to avoid user initialization. This means that in principle, every point in the image is in the state space for each step of the dynamic programming. Clearly this is computationally impossible. The solution comes in the form of the low-density local features. Indeed, one could still imagine that the entire image is the state space, however, we add a cost to the match of a point in the model to a point in the image, which is infinite if the latter does not pass the test associated to the local feature. The proper way to compute the optimal match is then to find the points that pass the test associated to each local feature, and those subsequently become the state space for the corresponding step in the dynamic programming.

8 Detection of Sparse Models: Counting

The decomposable graphs presented in chapter 7 have been partially successful in automatic anatomy detection in medical imaging. They rely heavily on finding instances of all the local features at the correct location on the object and are sensitive to occlusion or other sorts of noise. Moreover, when searching for objects at a large range of scales in large images, dynamic programming becomes very slow. Finally, if several instances of an object can be present in the image, dynamic programming becomes significantly more complicated.

The solution involves a coarser model. After detecting all instances of the local features in the image, instead of directly trying to find arrangements satisfying the complex geometrical constraints, try to find arrangements satisfying a simpler set of constraints that is consistent with the original one. Then check if the more complex constraints are satisfied. The idea is illustrated in figure 8.1. The original model involves constraints on relations between pairs or larger subsets of the points. Various admissible configurations are presented in the top three panels. Now replace this with a simple model that only constrains the locations of the features relative to a central point, independently of each other, as illustrated in the bottom panel of figure 8.1. A point in the image becomes a candidate "center" if a sufficient number of the features are found in their corresponding regions.

At each such candidate center, search through the instantiations in $\Theta^{(0)}$ and pick the one for which the most features are found at their expected location. If this number is below a threshold, rule out the candidate center. For those candidate centers that remain, the locations of the features that were found together with the *expected* locations of those that were not found provide an instantiation of the model.

Here again we have a coarse-to-fine procedure. First we use a model with a much coarser set of constraints to find candidate centers. At this stage, we expect to hit all correct locations together with a number of false positives. Then a more detailed

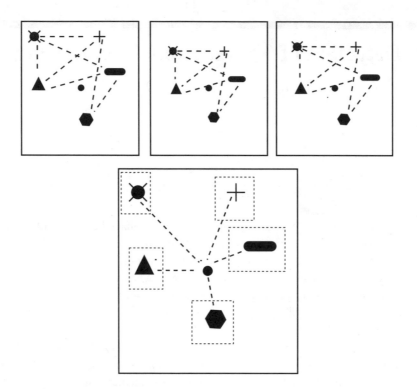

Figure 8.1   (Top) Three feature arrangements consistent with a complex set of constraints. (Bottom) Coarse model. Features can be found anywhere in their respective regions relative to a center point.

instantiation is computed, both in order to filter out false positives from the previous stage and to provide the full description of the detection. Subsequently, an even more refined process can be implemented such as one of the deformable models described in earlier chapters with the detected instantiation serving as an initial point.

In order to detect the object at a wide range of scales (say, 4 : 1), reprocess the image using the exact same algorithm at a number of smaller resolutions. For example, if the original range of scales of the detection scheme is $\pm 25\%$, subsample the object at scales 0.75, 0.56, 0.42, 0.32, 0.24, and rerun the detection algorithm at each new resolution. Thus the model is given for the smallest range of scales at which the object is detected. The method described here is very efficient and takes around .5 second for processing a standard 240×320 image, at all resolutions, on a Pentium III, 700 MHz.

8.1 Detecting Candidate Centers

Here, we will use the instantiation sct Θ defined by equation 6.1 and take a uniform prior on Θ. The on-object probability p_o is assumed less than 1, although much larger than p_b. Maximizing equation 6.5 involves finding values of θ for which $n_y(\theta)$ is greater than some threshold τ. Specifically, find pairs (x_c, θ) with $x_c \in L$ and $\theta \in \Theta^{(0)}$ such that

(D) There exist indices $i_1, \ldots, i_\tau$ for which $X_{i_j}(x_c + \theta_{i_j}) = 1$ for $j = 1, \ldots, \tau$.

There are several ways to find such instantiations, all of which involve counting the number of features of a specific type present at a specific location in the image.

The brute-force approach involves looping through all $x_c \in L$, $\theta \in \Theta^{(0)}$, counting how many indices satisfy $X_i(x_c + \theta_i) = 1$, and recording those with a count greater than τ. This is clearly a massive loop over all locations in the image, and for each location, a large number of instantiations. An alternative is the Hough transform (Hough 1962 and Grimson 1990), which consists of a reordering of the loops.

Create an array H indexed by all elements in Θ. Find all instances $x_{i,j}, j = 1, \ldots, J_i$ of each of the local features X_i, $i = 1, \ldots, n$ in the image.

1. For each $i = 1, \ldots, n$,

   For each $j = 1, \ldots, J_i$, loop through elements Θ. For each θ such that $x_{i,j} = \theta_i$ add 1 to the entry corresponding to θ in H.

2. Find all entries in H with value greater than τ.

If the local features are of low density in generic images, it is computationally more efficient to index into admissible configurations through the locations of the features, rather than carrying out the brute-force loop. This algorithm is feasible provided there is an efficient way to loop over elements in Θ, or some analytic indexing mechanism to find those elements in Θ for which $x_{i,j} = \theta_i$.

A more efficient way to solve this detection problem is to pursue a coarse-to-fine procedure. Find a product set $\Theta_p^{(0)} \subset L^n$, which contains $\Theta^{(0)}$. By product set, we mean a set of the form $\{\theta : \theta_i \in B_i, \ i = 1, \ldots, n\}$ where $B_i \subset L$. If, for example,

$\Theta^{(0)}$ is defined through a set of transformations Υ, then take $\Theta_p^{(0)} = \prod_{i=1}^n B_i$ with

$$B_i = \Upsilon z_i = \{ v z_i, v \in \Upsilon \}, \quad i = 1, \ldots, n \tag{8.1}$$

With the larger set of instantiations $\Theta_p^{(0)}$, detect *candidate centers*—namely, points x_c satisfying

(DP) There exists some $\theta \in \Theta_p^{(0)}$ and τ indices $i_1, \ldots, i_\tau$ for which $X_{i_j}(x_c + \theta_{i_j}) = 1$.

Any location x_c, for which there exists $\theta \in \Theta^{(0)}$ such that the pair (x_c, θ) satisfies condition (D) above, will *necessarily* be identified as a candidate center satisfying condition (DP), simply because $\Theta^{(0)} \subset \Theta_p^{(0)}$. In all experiments below, we use $\Theta^{(0)}$, defined in equation 6.1, with $\mathcal{A} = \Upsilon$ some subset of linear maps covering a range of scales of $\pm 25\%$. Thus $B_i = \mathcal{A} z_i$.

In a brute-force search for candidate centers, each location $x \in L$ would be visited, counting how many of the regions $x + B_i$ contain an instance of the corresponding feature X_i—that is, $\max_{y \in x + B_i} X_i(x) = 1$. In some cases, one can search over a coarse subgrid of the image grid L and the brute-force method becomes efficient. (See, for example, the work in Fleuret 2000 and **?**.) In our context, it will be more efficient to reverse the loops and use the Hough transform, which in this case is easy to implement, because $\Theta_p^{(0)}$ is a product set.

Algorithm 8.1: Sparse Model—Counting Detector, Step I

1. For $i = 1, \ldots, n$, find all instances of X_i, at $x_{i,j}$, $j = 1, \ldots, J_i$.

2. Initialize to 0 an array C the size of the image.

3. For $i = 1, \ldots, n$, do

(a) Initialize to 0 an array D the size of the image.

(b) For $j = 1, \ldots, J_i$
Set $D(y) = 1$ for all $y \in x_{i,j} - B_i$.

(c) Set $C(x) = C(x) + D(x)$, $x \in L$.

4. Find those locations x in C for which $C(x) \geq \tau$.

The idea behind this loop is illustrated in figure 8.2 in terms of the coarse model shown in figure 8.1. Each instance of feature X_i detected at location x, "votes" for a region $x - B_i$ of candidate centers. Here, $n = 5$ and $\tau = 3$. In the upper-right-hand corner, a location has received three votes and becomes a candidate center.

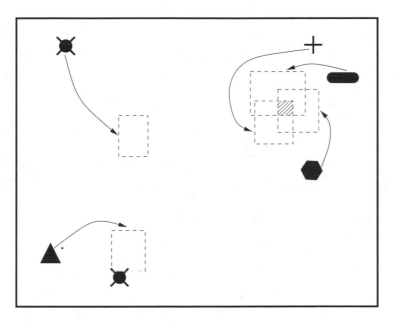

Figure 8.2 An illustration of the voting procedure of the Hough transform.

The calculation done in item 1 is efficient and only requires lookups in small subregions of the lattice determined by the subregions defining the local features. The calculations in item 2 are very efficient because the loops are only over locations of local features, which are rare, and over the regions $x_{i,j} - B_i$. The size of these regions depends on the distance of the point z_i from the origin and the size of the set $\mathcal{A}$. As indicated, we restrict the range of scales covered by $\mathcal{A}$ to $\pm 25\%$ and $\pm 15°$ rotation. The size of the reference grid is approximately 30×30, so that typically the regions B_i are on the order of several tens to one hundred pixels.

In figure 8.3, we show four of the twenty stages of the implementation of the Hough transform for step I of the counting detector, with the face model shown in figure 6.9. In the first two stages, we show an image with the locations of the corresponding local features (denoted as "+") and the distribution of the counts recorded in the array C used in item 3(c) before. For the other two stages, we show only the distribution of counts. At each of these stages, it is possible to make out the shape of the corresponding region B_i. Note how the distribution of counts gets more and more peaked at the face. (The image being processed here is shown, with the results of the entire counting algorithm, in figure 8.6 on the right.)

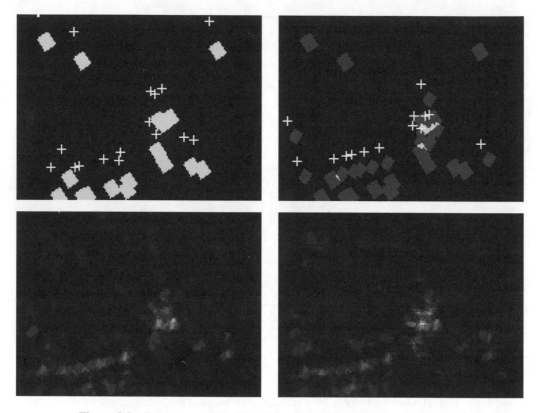

Figure 8.3   Four stages of the Hough transform. (Top) First two local features. Locations marked as "+" and count maps (0-black, 1-gray, 2-white). (Bottom) Count maps after detection of two other local features later on in the process. Candidate centers for faces emerge as bright regions.

8.2   Computing Pose and Instantiation Parameters

At each candidate center, x_c, identified by the first step of the counting detector, we need to recover information regarding the instantiation. First we estimate pose parameters such as scale and rotation. The most straightforward method, used in the examples below, involves a brute-force search through the range of allowable linear maps. Add a small range of translation to the set of allowable linear maps $\mathcal{A}$. Let C be a small 3×3 or 5×5 neighborhood of the origin. Let $\tau_a = \tau$, the threshold used in condition (D).

Algorithm 8.2: Sparse Model—Counting Algorithm, Step II

1. At candidate center x_c, for each $a \in \mathcal{A}$.

2. Loop over $i = 1, \ldots, n$. If there is an instance of X_i at some point x in the region $x_c + az_i + C_i$, add one to a counter N_a. Also record the location of x in a list, $X_a(i) = x$.

3. Let $a^* = argmax_{a \in \mathcal{A}} N_a$, be the map with highest count. If $N_{a^*} < \tau_a$ the location x_c is discarded. Otherwise, the detection is assigned the affine map a defined through $a(z) = x_c + a^* z$.

Steps I and II together represent the full counting algorithm. The main computational cost is in implementing step I because it involves image-wide detection of the local features. Among the few locations that it detects, it is very fast to implement step II to obtain the instantiation.

8.2.1   Edge-Based Model for Step II

Step II is described in terms of the features used in the original object model. It yields locations satisfying condition (D). But in practice, the features used for this step do not have to be the same features used for the first step. One of the important properties of the more complex features, employed in the initial detection step, is their low density in the background. This is essential for computational efficiency and to keep a tab on the number of false positives. However, once a location x_c is selected, these issues are irrelevant. Indeed, in step II, one can use the simpler edge features that have already been extracted in the process of finding the edge arrangements. These are stored and used for step II.

Training of the edge-based model used for this step would proceed as described in section 6.4. There are much larger numbers of high probability edges on the reference grid than edge arrangements.

8.2.2   Determining Thresholds

Now there are two thresholds to determine, τ for step I, and τ_a for step II. We thus use the following modification of the threshold training procedure given in section 6.4.

- Find the largest value of τ for which at least $(1 - r)T$ of the training images has a candidate center, resulting from step I, within D pixels of $x_{c,t}$—the mean of the three anchor points for image t.

- Find the largest value of τ_a for which at least $(1 - r)T$ of the training images has at least one candidate center resulting from steps I (using τ determined above) and II, within D pixels of $x_{c,t}$.

8.2.3   From Pose to Instantiation

The outcome of this stage is a list of affine maps $a_k, k = 1, \ldots, K$ of the reference grid into the image, corresponding to detected instantiations of the object. These are represented through a *detection triangle* $a_k z_1, a_k z_2, a_k z_3$. In addition, for each such map, there is a list X_{a_k} of the locations of those model points that were detected in the correct regions: $a_k z_i + C$. For those model points z_i that were not detected, it is possible to "extrapolate" their location by taking $X_{a_k}(i) = a_k z_i$. In this way, we recover an entire instantiation element $\theta \in \Theta$ for each detection. Note that this instantiation is not simply given by $a_k z_1, \ldots, a_k z_n$. For those features that were found in step II, their original location in the region $a_k z_i + C$ is recorded. The larger the neighborhood C, the more flexibility there is in terms of the final instantiation, at the price of more false positives.

8.2.4   Clustering

The local features occur in clusters. Because they are only used for the crude initial detection of candidate locations, they can be clustered without significant loss of information. Typically, we find all features of the same type in disjoint 5×5 blocks and replace them by one such feature at the mean location.

Further efficiency can be gained if instead of recording the local features on the original lattice and then clustering they are directly recorded on a coarse sublattice and the Hough transform is performed using a coarse version of the B_i sets on the coarser lattice. Candidate centers are then properly injected into the original lattice where the full instantiation information is then recovered in step II.

Detected instantiations will also occur in clusters. Given that only one instance of the object is present in a certain region, it is necessary to pick one detection from the cluster. This can be done in a variety of ways. In the examples below, the detections are clustered according to the distance between the detection triangles. In each cluster, the map a with highest count N_a of detected features, is chosen.

8.2.5   Invariance

The detection scheme described here covers the range of poses determined by the set $\mathcal{A}$, as well as a range of nonlinear deformations, which is difficult to quantify. It is also quite robust to nonsmooth variations, such as occlusion of part of the object and changes in internal structures. The examples below will illustrate these points. The invariance to the range of poses in $\mathcal{A}$ is explicitly obtained through the definition of the sets B_i defined in equation 8.1, as well as in the implementation of step II. Invariance to other deformations and degradations comes from two sources. The first is again the large degree of slack introduced in the counting detector. The decoupling of the constraints resulting from the use of the product set $\Theta_p^{(0)}$ allows for rather large nonlinear deformations. In addition, the fact that in both step I and II a detection survives if the number of counts is above some threshold allows for certain parts of the object to change quite drastically or be entirely occluded.

8.3   Density of Candidate Centers and False Positives

In section 6.5, we studied the false-positive density of the sparse models, disregarding the means by which these models are detected. Some additional statistics are relevant at this point that bear upon the computation time and shed some more light on the false-positive density. Recall that originally the model simply involved a configuration of local features of predetermined complexity n_r. However, now we have split the detection into two steps. The first detects a coarser model and the second recovers the pose and instantiation parameters using the basic edges.

The density of the candidate centers detected by step I will now be higher than the density of false positives presented in table 6.2—see, for example, column 3 of table 8.1. In the former, an instance of the feature could be anywhere in the 5×5 neighborhood of the expected feature location $a z_i$, just to accommodate small local variations. However, now an instance can be anywhere in the region B_{z_i}, which is

Table 8.1 τ and τ_a, candidate location and false-positive rates for false-negative rates under 5%

n_r	τ 5% FN	Candidate Centers	τ_a 5% FN	FP I + II
1	29	$9 \cdot 10^{-4}$	58	$8 \cdot 10^{-5}$
2	25	$2 \cdot 10^{-4}$	58	$3 \cdot 10^{-5}$
3	21	$5 \cdot 10^{-5}$	53	$3 \cdot 10^{-5}$
4	15	$8 \cdot 10^{-5}$	58	$2 \cdot 10^{-5}$
5	8	$2 \cdot 10^{-4}$	58	$5 \cdot 10^{-5}$
6	5	$3 \cdot 10^{-4}$	57	$7 \cdot 10^{-5}$

much larger and may contain close to 100 pixels. Still, for the various values of n_r, the number of candidate centers in a 240×320 image varies between several tens to several hundreds. As long as the number is on the order of tens, subsequent computations at these candidate centers do not amount to a large fraction of the computing time. However, as this number grows, step II starts dominating in terms of computation time. It is then necessary to devise more efficient algorithms for step II. We emphasize that the statistics shown here are obtained from outdoor images, which have a very large density of edges. On indoor scenes, the numbers are much lower.

In this context, we see why a model solely based on edge features would be problematic. Edge densities range between .03 to .06 edges per pixel, for each edge type. Even for a restricted set of admissible transformations $\mathcal{A}$, the minimal size of the B neighborhoods would be on the order of 30–40 pixels. But then the expected number of edges of any one type in any of the regions becomes very close to 1 if not greater. This implies that the number of false positives is on the order of the number of pixels in the image and nothing has been gained in this step.

Taking into account step II of the algorithm, which is based on edge features, the density of false positives turns out to be even lower than that recorded in table 6.2. This is shown in table 8.1. The thresholds τ and τ_a were estimated with the procedure outlined above for each value of n_r. The values of τ are larger here than in table 6.2 because the constraints in step I are now defined in terms of $\Theta_p^{(0)}$, which is much larger than $\Theta^{(0)}$. These thresholds are determined with a small set of hundred faces, which were not used for creating the model. For different values of n_r, the final false-positive rates are quite similar due to the fact that the same edge-based model is used in step II. However, the density of candidate centers detected in step I varies quite significantly. This has an important effect on the the final computation time, in terms of the time required to compute step II.

8.4   Further Analysis of a Detection

After an instantiation θ is detected, a map from the reference grid into the image can be defined. This map could be the affine map a or complex map obtained through some form of interpolation of the correspondence between z_i and θ_i for $i = 1, \ldots, n$. The best known method involves thin plate splines (see Bookstein 1991); a much more computationally intensive alternative is proposed in Joshi (1997), where the interpolated map is guaranteed to be a homeomorphism; a more efficient computation of such homeomorphisms can be found in Camion and Younes (2001).

In the examples below, we restrict ourselves to the affine map. The region of interest (ROI) aG, is obtained by applying the map a to each point of the reference grid. The data $\hat{I}(x)$, $x \in aG$ can be registered back to the reference grid to produce

$$\hat{I}_a(z) = \hat{I}(az), z \in G \tag{8.2}$$

and can then be further analyzed using any of the deformable models described in earlier chapters. These can serve not only to provide a more detailed instantiation but also to filter out false detections by keeping only those detections that yield a fit of the template below some cost level, determined using training data.

8.4.1 Detection as Classification

The detection scheme provides a classification at each possible instantiation θ between the two classes, *object* and *nonobject*. Note that in the first two steps of the algorithm there was hardly any use of nonobject or background images, in terms of training. The reason is that the background image population is so large and diverse that a very large sample would be needed to yield reliable estimates for a global classifier between object and nonobject images. Large data sets of many thousands of images have been used for this purpose in Rowley, Baluja, and Kanade (1998) and Sung and Poggio (1998). The sparse-object models described here can be trained successfully with several tens of examples. The only information regarding background in the counting algorithm involves the densities of the local features, studied in chapter 6. Only a crude estimate of these is needed simply to ensure the feasibility of the first step of the algorithm. However, once a detector is produced, the population of *false positives* is much more homogeneous and constrained.

Using the original training sample of the object, together with a sample of false positives, a classifier can be trained. Run the detector on all the images of the object in the training set and register the pixel intensities, or the edge data, or the edge arrangement data, from the ROI defined by the detection, to the reference grid, as specified in equation 8.2. The same is done on images containing no object, each of which may yield a number of registered detections, to produce a population of false positives. This data is then used to train classifiers of the type described in chapter 9. In figure 8.4, we show a sample of ROIs of false positives for the face detector. The reference grid has been reduced to a 16×16 lattice immediately surrounding the area around the eyes and mouth. Below, in the middle panel, we show the histogram maps of four edge types (two vertical and two horizontal) on this population, compared to the maps for the face population shown in the bottom panel. The similarity is quite striking, indicating that this false-positive population is quite restricted. The

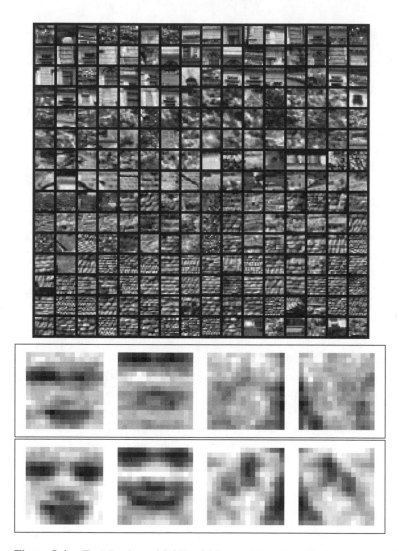

Figure 8.4   (Top) Registered ROI's of false positives from the face detector. (Middle) Edge maps for this population. (Bottom) Edge maps for face population. Reference grid is reduced to a 16 × 16 lattice covering the immediate region around the eyes and mouth.

edge histograms for randomly selected 16×16 images in the background population are *uniform*. And still for the human eye there is no question that most of the false positives are *not* faces.

8.5 Examples

In this section we illustrate some aspects of the counting detector for a variety of objects: faces, randomly perturbed LaTeX symbols in cluttered scenes, the axial MRI scans, and an example of a 3D object at a limited range of viewpoints. In addition to detections of the sparse model, we show examples of how these detections can provide automatic initialization for the deformable models described in chapters 3, 4, and 5. Specifically, we will use the maps a, estimated in step II, to initialize the templates. Recall that the sparse model represents the smallest range of scales at which the object is detected, and the algorithm is applied at six different resolutions to cover a range of scales of $4:1$.

The edge arrangements in the examples are defined with the 16 smaller wedges shown in the top row of figure 6.7. The complexity of the arrangements is 3 (i.e. $n_r = 3$), and apart from the MRI example, we always pick $n = 20$ arrangements for the model with lower bound $\rho = .5$ (see algorithm 6.1).

8.5.1 Faces

The face model shown in figure 6.9 was trained from 300 face images of the Olivetti data set. Much smaller data sets yield very similar results. The original images were downscaled to 44×36. The centers of the two eyes and the mouth were manually marked on each image and used as the three anchor points. The mean locations of each of these three landmarks are used for the three reference points p_1, p_2, p_3 on the reference grid, as defined in section 6.4. At this scale, the mean distance between the center of the eyes is 14 pixels and the distance between the center of the mouth and the middle point between the two eyes is also 14 pixels. Edges are extracted on each downscaled image, after which their locations are registered to the reference grid using the affine map taking the anchor points to the reference points. The edge statistics are graphically represented in figure 6.8, and in terms of these, an edge model for step II was derived with 110 edge-type/location pairs. The 20 edge arrangements of complexity $n_r = 3$ obtained from training are shown in figure 6.9. A model using $n_r = 1$ is shown in chapter 11. The range $\mathcal{A}$ of linear maps at which we expect to

Figure 8.5   (Top) Detections from step I. (Middle) Detections from step II. (Bottom) Detections remaining after final classifier. Detection triangles—mapping of the reference points into the image by a.

detect a face at a given resolution covers $\pm 25\%$ scaling and $\pm 15°$ of rotation. The smallest scale at which a face is detected is approximately 10 pixels between the two eyes. Faces at much larger scales are detected by subsampling the image and rerunning the detection algorithm.

The results of step I of the detection algorithm using this model, and processing six resolutions covering a range of scales of $4:1$, are shown in the top row of figures 8.5 and 8.6. In the middle row are shown all detected affine maps obtained from step II.

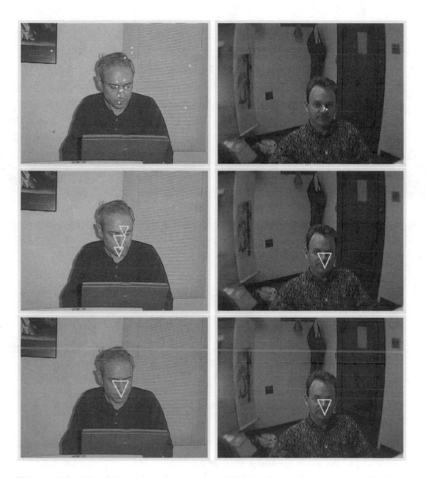

Figure 8.6   (Top) Detections from step I. (Middle) Detections from step II. (Bottom) Detections remaining after final classifier. Detection triangles—mapping of the reference points into the image by a.

The affine maps are represented using the detection triangle showing the locations of the two eyes and mouth.

A final classifier was produced for face versus nonface using randomized classification trees (see chapter 9). These trees were trained using the registered edge data of the face training set against registered edge data from false detections obtained on a collection of random images, as shown in figure 8.4. The results are shown on the bottom row of figures 8.5 and 8.6. Some additional detections are shown in figure 8.7.

Figure 8.7   Some additional examples of face detections: steps I and II.

The training set for this classifier is quite small—300 face images of 30 different people (10 per person) and a similar number of false detections. This is therefore the least stable component of the algorithm and increases the number of false negatives.

Deformable Models Initialized at Detections of Sparse Model

In figure 8.8, we show a close-up on the four faces of figures 8.5 and 8.6 and the locations of the points in the instantiation obtained from step II. The white dots show edge features detected at the estimated pose and the black dots show the extrapolated features that were not detected. If the features in the model are labeled according to the components of the face to which they belong, we obtain an estimate not only of where the centers of the two eyes and mouth are but other parts of the face as well. For example, the location of other parts of the eyes, or part of the nose, the hairline, and so on.

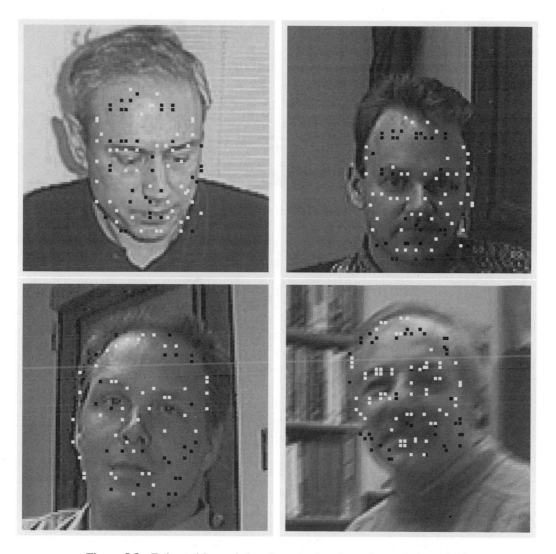

Figure 8.8 Estimated instantiation θ on the four faces detected above. White dots show detected edge features, black dots show extrapolated features.

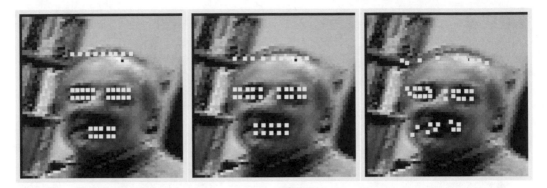

Figure 8.9   Pose detected on right hand image in figure 8.5 initializes Bernoulli model for deformable images.

One can also initialize a deformable image algorithm at the detected pose. Due to the high variability in lighting and illumination of faces, we implement the Bernoulli data model from section 5.4. This data model, being based on probabilities of edges that are very robust to illumination changes, inherits some of these properties. On the left in figure 8.9, we show the location of a set of points chosen on the reference grid mapped into the image by the detected pose. In the middle, we show the outcome of a global search on a range of scale and location parameters for updating the pose. On the right is the outcome of the deformable-image algorithm using a small number of basis coefficients. Note how the outlines of the eyes have been adjusted as well as the hairline, which in the initial instantiation was outside the face. The first example of this procedure was shown in figure 5.4, together with the edge maps and the edge data used to drive the algorithm.

8.5.2   Randomized LATEX Symbols

Displays with randomized deformations of LATEX symbols are useful for investigating properties of the sparse models. The background has objects with many similarities to the one being detected, making the problem of particular interest. We use 32 randomly perturbed versions of the prototype, as shown in figure 8.10, for training. The random perturbations involve random rotation of up to $15°$, and $\pm 25\%$ scaling independently in each coordinate. The 20 local features identified in the training step are given in the bottom panel of figure 8.10. The reference grid is approximately 30×30.

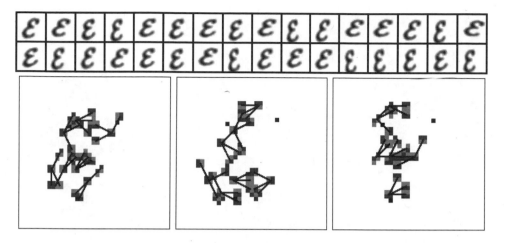

Figure 8.10   (Top) Thirty-two randomly perturbed $\mathcal{E}$'s used for training. (Bottom) The 20 features of the model represented on the reference grid. The three reference points are shown in black.

Here it is possible to produce a detector from the prototype alone by simply picking some existing arrangement of edges extracted from the prototype in each region of the reference grid. Such a procedure may pick an edge or a particular arrangement that is very unstable and only present in the particular image of the prototype. This is avoided by producing a small randomly perturbed training set as above, in which case unstable arrangements are eliminated.

Some detections in randomly generated scenes containing a large number of randomly deformed LATEX symbols are shown in figure 8.11. Again, these are obtained from six different resolutions. There are at most three instances of an $\mathcal{E}$ in each image. The top panels show the outcome of steps I and II, and in the bottom panels, the outcome of running the classifier of object versus false positives, based on registered edges. In the bottom panels, only the triangle vertices are shown to enhance the view of the underlying symbols. The use of a classifier among different object classes, detected by the same model, is discussed in chapter 10. In the top row of figure 8.12 is an example of a deformable contour initialized with the scale and location of the detection, then the final detection of the deformable contour algorithm. In the bottom row, we show a similar experiment with the deformable curve algorithm.

Very similar results are obtained for any of the symbols in the database. However, certain symbols are more "generic" in their shape and share many features with a

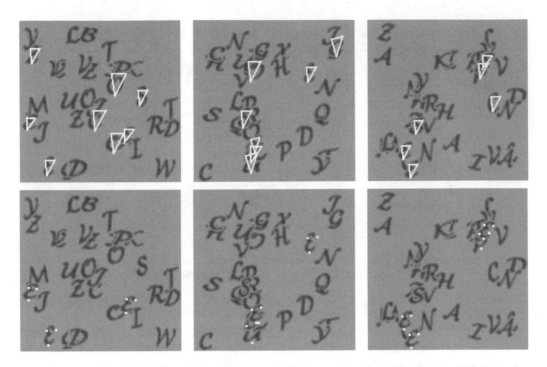

Figure 8.11   (Top) Three examples of detections of the $\mathcal{E}$ model, steps I and II. Detection triangles are shown. (Bottom) Results after applying the classifier of object vs. false positives. Triangles shown as three points for better viewing.

substantial number of other symbols. The best example being the digit 0, which has much in common with many round symbols. The representations trained for these symbols usually produce more false positives. Although a drawback from the point of view of accurate detection, we turn this vice into a virtue in chapter 10, where we discuss ways to integrate detection and recognition.

The random LaTeX displays are artificial and do not represent all the complexities of real scenes. However, in many respects these scenes force us to deal with some important issues such as clutter, confusing classes, and detection at a variety of poses. The background clutter in these images contains many components and parts of the detected object itself. This reinforces the point that detection cannot rely on individual local features and forces us to think about detecting configurations. The existence of objects very similar to the one we want to detect forces us to deal with recognition as well as detection. It seems there is still much to be explored in this controlled synthetic context.

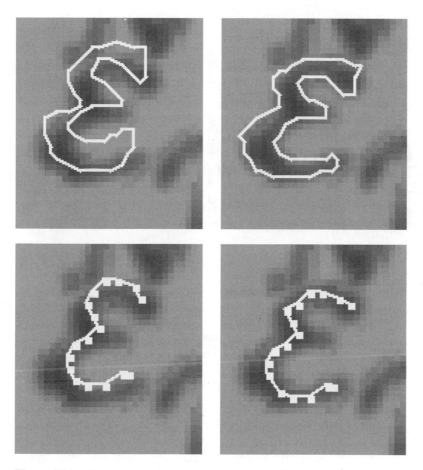

Figure 8.12   (Top row) A deformable contour algorithm initialized by a detection in the middle panel of figure 8.11. On the left is the initial contour. On the right the final contour. (Bottom row) The result of the deformable curve algorithm initialized the same way.

8.5.3   3D Object—Range of Viewing Angles

Detecting a rigid 3D object from multiple views is a complex problem. Some of the original work in the field attempted to construct 3D models and match them to data. Many of these models are described in Grimson (1990) and Haralick and Shapiro (1992). We take the *view-based* approach in which significantly different views of the object are to be considered as different 2D objects that are linked together symbolically. Much as if in the LATEX scene we set out to detect a *subset* of symbols

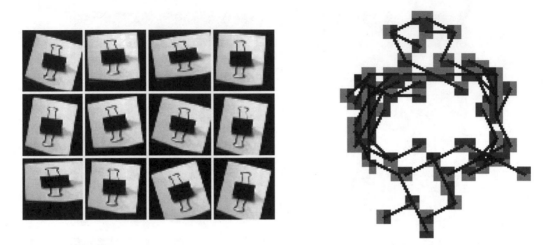

Figure 8.13   A sample of the synthetically generated training images for the clip, and the 20 features identified in training.

as opposed to a particular one. Thus detection involves a sequence of searches for each of these possible objects or views.

Here we focus on developing a sparse model to detect an object from a limited range of views. The problem then reduces to the detection of a *nonrigid* two-dimensional object and can be addressed with the tools we have developed. The object model is trained as the LaTeX symbols using only one prototype image, which is deformed 32 times with random affine transformations. A sample of these deformed images is shown in figure 8.13, together with the model, which is constructed of 20 local features of complexity $n_r = 3$ on a reference grid of approximately 40×40. Note that the local features describe a rectangle of certain aspect ratio to which are attached, on the top and the bottom, two additional wirelike rectangular structures.

The outcomes of the counting detector are shown on images in figure 8.14. No final classifier has been implemented. The algorithm is run at the six resolutions. The detections appear to be invariant to changes in viewing angle around the vertical axis, clutter, occlusion, variable lighting, and articulation of the handles, despite the fact that no such examples were shown in training. Here we see the advantage of treating a rigid object in the same way as deformable objects. In the discussion section and in chapter 10, we offer some preliminary ideas on the concept of detecting 3D objects as unions of their 2D views. How can this be integrated into a more general scheme of object detection and recognition and how to avoid the combinatoric explosion of representing multiple objects at multiple views?

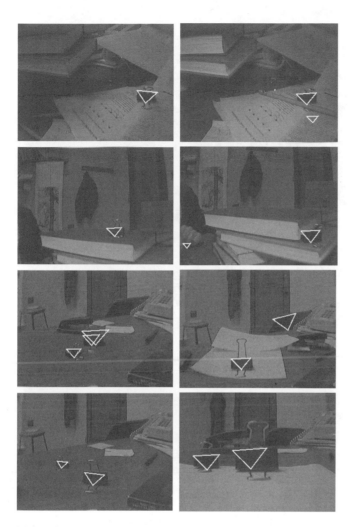

Figure 8.14   Eight examples of detections of steps I and II combined.

8.5.4   MRI Images

The MRI images are trained on 18 examples of more or less the same axial slice. The reference grid in this case is larger because we have attempted to create a model for the entire structure and reducing to a small 40×40 grid destroys many of the important components. Thus the reference grid is 128×128, and 100 features are identified. These are shown in figure 8.15. In this case, the same features are used

Figure 8.15   The model obtained for axial MRI images.

for step II as well. This experiment demonstrates the applicability of the counting detector for highly deformable objects.

In figure 8.16 we show the outcome of steps I and II in terms of the estimated instantiation. Note how the multiplicity of features introduces a large degree of flexibility. Even if parts of the internal structure are missing or significantly deformed, the detection succeeds. We show only the close-ups on the ventricle region for those images that actually contained such structures. On those parts that are present or are not severely deformed, the detected instantiation has local features found in the data. For the rest, we show the extrapolated location of the undetected edge features. In order to illustrate the correspondence between the detected features, a number is attached to each point.

Subsequent to detection, a deformable-contour algorithm is implemented, initialized at the expected location of the anterior ventricles, determined automatically relative to the detected instantiation. The initial contour has a shape similar to the

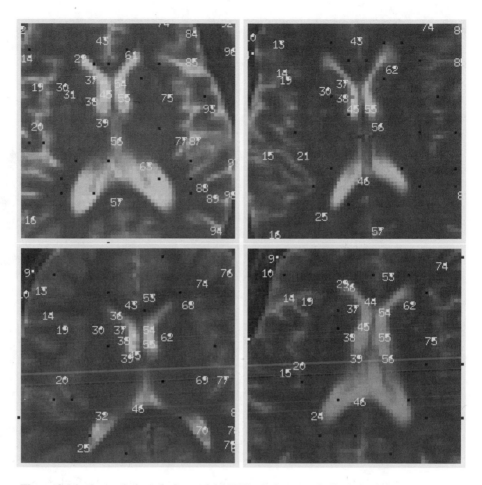

Figure 8.16 Instantiations in four axial MRI brain images. Ordinal numbers are shown for detected features. A black dot denotes an undetected feature at location az_i.

outline of these ventricles (figure 8.17). Four points have been marked on the contour to show the correspondences derived from the contour match. A more efficient approach, which has not been implemented here, would initialize the elastic contour using the local features detected in step II, which are known to lie on the outline of the anterior ventricles. The important fact to remember here is that the entire process is completely automatic, no user initialization is required.

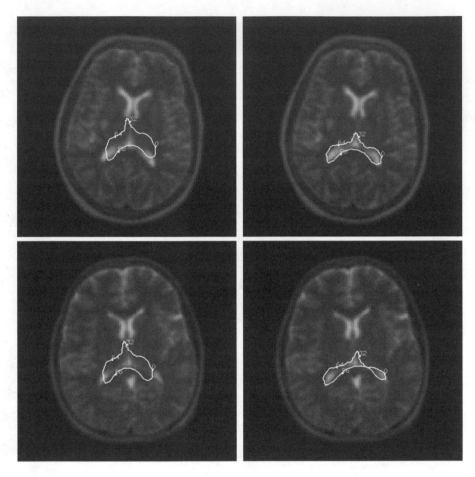

Figure 8.17   Two examples of a deformable contour initialized at the location of the anterior ventricles and the final state after running the elastic deformation algorithm.

8.6   Bibliographical Notes and Discussion

The material in this chapter is based on Amit, Geman, and Jedynak (1998), Amit and Geman (1999), and Amit (2000), where it is shown how the counting algorithm can be implemented in a neural network architecture. The network can detect any model evoked in memory using a priming mechanism. This architecture is described in chapter 11.

8.6.1   Object Detection with Arrangements of Local Features

The idea of using local feature arrangements for object detection both for faces and other objects can also be found in Burl, Leung, and Perona (1995), Cootes and Taylor (1996), Wiskott and colleagues (1997), Burl, Weber, and Perona (1998), Van Rullen and colleagues (1998), and most recently in Viola and Jones (2001). In these approaches, the features, or certain relevant parameters, are also identified through training. However, the models presented here make use of a hierarchy of binary features with hardwired invariances and employ a very simple form of spatial arrangement for the object representation. This leads to an efficient implementation of the detection algorithm. The representations described in the other papers make use of various types of linear filters with a rather large support. The invariance properties of the filters are not clear, neither with respect to photometric transformations nor with respect to deformations. In the models described in Burl, Leung, and Perona (1995) and Van Rullen and colleagues (1998), only a small number of features are used, which appear to be more complex than the ones suggested here and, for faces, are typically concentrated around the eyes and mouth. One problem with overdedicating resources to only a small number of locations is the issue of noise and occlusion, which may eliminate some locations. Again, in the context of faces, if the goal is to detect faces on a large range of scales from 50–60 pixels between the eyes down to 10–14 pixels between the eyes, local information can be quite ambiguous.

In the work by Viola and Jones (2001) an interesting collection of binary features is defined by comparing mean intensities in rather large rectangular regions. These appear very robust to illumination changes and are computed extremely fast. Using cumulative sums of the image intensities computed once at the start, the sum of the values in a given rectangle can be obtained with a simple operation of the cumulative sums at each of the corners.

8.6.2   Cutting the Invariance Pie

The Hough transform has been extensively used in object detection (see Ballard 1981; Grimson 1990; Rojer and Schwartz 1992). However, in contrast to most previous implementations, the local features used here are more complex, and are *identified through training*. On the other hand, in many of the implementations of the Hough transform referred to in Grimson (1990), there is an attempt to obtain full rotation invariance in one shot. Our implementation is intentionally *not* fully rotation invariant. It allows the use of much richer features and hence rarer in the background, reducing false positives and computation time.

This brings up the recurrent question of how to cut up the "invariance pie," which came up in the discussion section of chapter 5. Should the detection of a face be done at once for all rotations, including upside-down faces? Or should we define ranges of pose parameters for which detection is done with one procedure, but using different procedures for different ranges, or the same procedure at rotated versions of the image? Should features be photometric invariant or should different detection models deal with different lighting conditions? For example, none of the models used in this chapter can detect the object if the polarity is flipped and the object becomes lighter than the background. The edge features on which the entire model is based are sensitive to the direction of the gradient modulo 2π. To detect the objects at both polarities one can either incorporate polarity invariance by taking oriented edges modulo π; detect even faces, which are half darker and half lighter than the background at the price of more false positives; or run the face detector twice with the edge polarities flipped.

8.6.3   View-Based Detection of 3D Objects

This issue also comes up regarding the detection of 3D objects. The use of full 3D models, as suggested in Marr and Nishihara (1978) and found in much of the work described in Grimson (1990), is an extreme approach that claims the model should be invariant to all viewing angles. On the other hand, the view-based approach recently being proposed in Ullman (1996), Tarr and Bülthoff (1998), and Riesenhuber and Poggio (2000), requires only invariance within a range of viewing angles that represent smooth changes in the image of the object, as we have done for the clip or for chess pieces in chapter 10. This implies that even rigid 3D objects should be modeled as deformable objects, because their 2D views are not rigid at all. Moreover, working with sparse models for nonrigid objects allows us to cover quite a wide range of viewing angles with one detector. Working in this context makes the understanding of 2D nonrigid object detection and recognition even more important, because all the analysis has been reduced to the two-dimensional domain.

On the other hand, significant changes in viewing angle that completely change the resulting image—for example, viewing the clip from the side or from the front—lead to separate models. Indeed, significantly different views can be considered as *different 2D objects.*

8.6.4   Parts

In Biederman (1995) there is a strong emphasis on the role of generic 3D parts, called *geons,* as the building blocks for 3D object representations. These objects, which consist of blocks, cylinders, and other simple geometric structures, are detected in a view-based manner, but the idea is that not too many views are required to model them, and that the entire library of 3D objects can then be modeled quite simply in terms of rather coarse relationships between the geons. We have not experimented with this idea, but in terms of the models used in this chapter, it implies introducing an intermediate level between the local features and the object models. Sparse models using local features would be constructed for the geons, and the complex object models would be constructed in terms of very coarse geometric relationships between the geons. If the geon detectors have very low false-positive rates, such as the "clip" detector, then there is no need for refined definition of the relationships between the geons, because very few spurious elements will be detected. We return to related ideas in chapter 10.

8.6.5   Hierarchy of Detection Models

Comparing the various models described in this manuscript in terms of the set Z of points defining the template, we see that the smallest set was used in the sparse models, whereas the largest sets were used for the deformable-image models. In between lie the deformable-contour and deformable-curve models. But the size of the template in the sparse models is really a matter of choice. The number of stable local features can be rather large—in particular, if the probability threshold ρ used in training is lowered. Indeed, taking more and more local features and representing them as in figure 6.9, we would get a very dense configuration of edges (see, for example, face models shown in chapter 11).

In most detection experiments in this chapter, we limited ourselves to 20 local features. However, in training for edge arrangements on faces, for example, close to 100 were found, with above-threshold probability. There may be two reasons not to use all 100 local features. The first is that the main computational burden of the algorithm for $n_r = 3$ is in step I—in particular, the calculation of the locations of all the local features. The second is that some of these features may be highly correlated on background. Ignoring the computational cost and assuming that the correlations are not strong, it would be preferable to use more local features from the point of view of false-positive and false-negative probabilities.

Following a detection, one could smoothly deform the model to best fit the transformed data—namely, the local features extracted from the image. This is precisely what is done by the Bernoulli model for deformable images. In other words, feature-based image deformation is a natural algorithmic sequel to the feature-based detection using sparse models. It is a refinement of the detection process. On the other hand, the "dense" Bernoulli model can be viewed as the "true" model, which is difficult to compute if pose is not predetermined. This is obtained using a sparse subset that enables efficient detection of coarse instantiation information providing an initialization to the smooth deformable model, which fine tunes the instantiation in terms of the full model. The one-dimensional models can be viewed as intermediate approximations that identify continuous curves given the initial matching of the sparse set of local features. So rather than a collection of different models, we can embed all these models as successive approximations to a "dense" two-dimensional model.

A related but different approach to coarse-to-fine modeling and computation is presented in Fleuret and Geman (2001). Pose space is recursively partitioned and a detector is trained for each cell of pose space, using examples with poses randomly sampled from the cell (in contrast to the approach here, where training is performed at a reference pose). There is then a systematic method of exploring the image—first in terms of detecting the object at one of the coarse poses and subsequently narrowing down to more refined poses.

The use of only eight edge types to define the local arrangements is quite limited. This family of elementary features should be extended to include texture information and color and motion information when available. Texture discontinuities may define important transitions that are not well captured using the simple edge detectors. However, once an appropriate set of elementary features is defined, the same mechanism can be used to construct the more complex local features, and finally the global models. The models described in the experiments above were all trained with the same parameters. Some small choices had to be made regarding the size of the reference grid and locations of the reference points, but no particular information we might have had regarding the object is used. Other parameters produce similar results, perhaps at some computational cost. In this sense, we have here a generic method of producing object models from very primitive elementary features, using very small training sets.

9 Object Recognition

Recognition refers to the classification of an object or shape present in an image. Classification is meaningful only when the image under investigation contains a single object. Thus it must be preceded by some procedure whereby a subimage of the entire scene is selected, in which it is hoped only one object is present. This is still quite vague, because the subimage could, for example, contain only one whole object, but parts of many others. These may not necessarily pass as objects, however, they are part of the subimage and need to be ignored in the classification. In other words, one would want to identify on-object pixels, and use only those to classify. This is precisely the segmentation problem discussed in the Introduction. Some preliminary ideas for *segmentation* based on a top-down flow of information, as opposed to a purely bottom-up approach, are explored in chapter 10. There, detection is used to identify instantiations of *coarse* models, which detect *object clusters* with elements from several object classes, and following detection, a classification among these classes is performed.

In this chapter, we proceed as though some mechanism is able to identify a region of interest (ROI) in the large image, which contains an object and not much else. The goal is to classify which object is present. We can even assume that the region is registered to a fixed-size reference grid. Either a bounding rectangle is provided and the ratio between the largest dimension (width or height) and the dimension of the reference grid determines a scaling, or a pose has been estimated, determining a region of interest in the image, which is mapped onto the reference grid.

We work in the context of characters and symbols because it is easy to produce data and study various aspects of the classifiers. The two examples used in this chapter are the LaTeX database, which we have already encountered, and some handwritten digit databases. In the first case, it is possible to control the degree of variability in each class and study the behavior of the classifiers in different situations. Moreover,

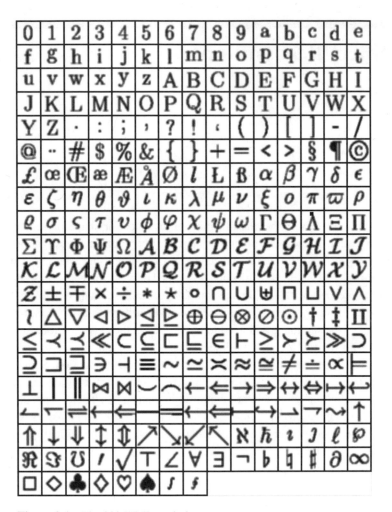

Figure 9.1   The 293 LATEX symbols.

it is interesting to study how classifiers behave in the presence of hundreds of classes. Ultimately, one would hope to be able to recognize among the thousands of objects the human is familiar with (see Biederman 1995).

Figure 9.1 shows the 293 prototypes, and figure 9.2 shows 20 samples of one deformed symbol, as well as some examples of deformations of a random collection of other symbols. The handwritten digit databases are used as a reality check to see how well one can perform on real data. We use the NIST (National Institute of

Figure 9.2   (Top) Deformed images of one symbol. (Bottom) One deformed sample from a collection of symbols.

Standards and Technology) special database (Garris and Wilkinson 1976) and parts of the USPS database produced and distributed by CEDAR, SUNY Buffalo. One could also experiment with recognizing views of 3D objects placed against homogeneous backgrounds, but then there is hardly any difference from recognizing shapes and characters, where more abundant databases are available. Object recognition in more complex gray-level images is explored in chapter 10.

It is important to note that the particular domain of optical character recognition (OCR) has many interesting dedicated solutions, some of the most successful being LeCun and colleagues (1998) and Simard and colleagues (2000), which are discussed in the last section. Extensive reviews can also be found in Nagy (2000) and Plamondon and Srihari (2000). Although we will be working with binary character data, we want to be able to extend the methods to objects in gray-level images. For that reason, we will also experiment with the photometric invariant binary features introduced in earlier sections, which have proved to be powerful for detection in gray-level images.

In the preceding chapters, we have seen that objects and shapes can be detected in terms of sparse models defined as flexible arrangements of local image features. The simplest model encountered corresponds to the first step of the counting detector and has the form of a *star* type arrangement, where the features are constrained to lie in regions defined relative to a center (see figure 8.1). In this chapter, we consider the problem of classification among several shapes using similar ingredients. Arrangements of local features are used to discriminate among objects. Geometric and photometric invariance are explicitly incorporated in the flexibility introduced in the arrangements, as well as in the definition of the local features.

Two alternatives to defining the local features are explored. The first employs a form of local image coding that is adapted to the particular family of images being analyzed—in this case binary images. The alternative to such dedicated local features is to employ the same edges and edge arrangements used for detection in the previous chapters. These are generic and not adapted to a particular data set, but have proven to have the desired invariance properties. As we will see, the results with the two families of features are comparable. Two approaches to describing the local feature arrangements are explored.

- **Absolute.** An arrangement is a list of feature/region pairs denoting which features are expected to be found in which region of the reference grid. The larger the regions the more invariant is the arrangement to various linear and nonlinear deformations, but then the arrangement is less discriminating. Because information is expressed in terms of absolute regions in the reference grid, preregistration to the reference grid is assumed here.

- **Relational.** Arrangements are described in terms of coarse constraints on the *relative angles* between pairs of features. There are no fixed regions or locations in the definition of these arrangements. The information is not coded in terms of absolute locations. This means that there is no need for preregistration of the image to the reference grid. This approach will allow us to classify images that are of different dimensions. The arrangements are similar to those employed in the graphical-template algorithm in chapter 7 and in the object-detection algorithm in chapter 8.

9.1   Classification Trees

Most literature on classification methods assumes that a fixed-size predictor vector, X_f, $f \in \mathcal{F}$, is precomputed for each data point. The main focus is then which type of classifier to employ, how to train, and how to predict test error. A large variety of classifiers have been proposed over the years, the most popular ones being Fisher's linear discriminant analysis and variations thereof, discussed in Duda and Hart (1973) and Ripley (1994); feed-forward neural networks, extensively covered in Ripley (1994) and Bishop (1995); support vector machines (see Vapnik 1995); and binary classification trees (see Breiman and colleagues 1984).

In this chapter, recognition will be achieved using binary classification trees, which are especially well suited for tapping into the information provided by the feature arrangements—particularly the relational arrangements. A binary query is associated to each node in the tree. The query at the top node is applied to a data point. If the answer is "yes," the data point moves to the right-hand child node, if it is "no," the data point moves on to the left-hand child node. At the new node, the associated query is applied. Again, according to whether the answer was positive or negative, the data point proceeds right or left. When the point reaches a terminal node, it reads out a label associated to that node. The queries attached to the nodes are found during training. The goal is to split the training data at a node so that the distribution on class in the children nodes will be as peaked as possible.

As we will see, it is crucial to produce *multiple* classification trees from the same training set. Relying on one classifier is unstable, even with rather large training sets. Using a randomization procedure, classification trees are produced that are significantly different from each other. They classify the data from "different points of view." Combining the output of such collections of classifiers yields drastic reductions in error rates. Randomization also allows us to grow a tree trained on tens of thousands of images in a few seconds. Typically, other classifiers take much more time to train. Moreover, there are very few parameters to set in growing the tree and it appears that the results are not too sensitive to the setting of these parameters.

Recognition with trees is also fast. A data point simply proceeds down the tree and at each node, the appropriate query is applied. The number of operations is thus determined by the depth of the tree. This is typically no more than 10 on average with the large data sets employed here. We start by describing how a classification tree is grown.

9.1.1   Training

Let $\mathcal{L}$ be the training data set with data from K classes. For an element $\omega \in \mathcal{L}$, let $1 \leq Y(\omega) \leq K$ denote the class label and let $X(\omega) = \{X_f\}_{f \in \mathcal{F}}$ be the vector of predictors, assumed to be binary. Let $\mathcal{L}_t$ be the data at node t, let $\hat{P}_t$ be the empirical distribution determined by the data points at node t (i.e., the uniform distribution on $\mathcal{L}_t$) and let F_t be some subset of the full set of predictors $\mathcal{F}$. For each $f \in F_t$, calculate the conditional entropy on class given X_f—that is,

$$
\begin{aligned}
C(f) = {}& H_t(Y \mid X_f) \\
= {}& -\hat{P}_t(X_f = 1) \sum \hat{P}_t(Y = c \mid X_f = 1) \log \hat{P}_t(Y = c \mid X_f = 1) \\
& -\hat{P}_t(X_f = 0) \sum \hat{P}_t(Y = c \mid X_f = 0) \log \hat{P}_t(Y = c \mid X_f = 0)
\end{aligned} \tag{9.1}
$$

This is a special case of the conditional entropy defined in equation 4.19, because X_f is binary.

The function $C(f)$ is a measure of the "purity" of the split induced by X_f. The aim is to produce children nodes where the data is more concentrated around one class or a small number of classes. Other purity measures have been used to determine node purity and are described in Breiman and colleagues (1984). The overall performance is typically not affected by choice of purity measure. Pick f_t, which minimizes $C(f)$, over $f \in F_t$. The associated predictor X_{f_t} most reduces the entropy or uncertainty regarding class, and f_t becomes the query associated to node t in the tree.

All training data points in $\mathcal{L}_t$ for which $X_{f_t} = 1$ proceed to the yes node t_y and form the set $\mathcal{L}_{t_y}$ and all those for which $X_{f_t} = 0$ proceed to the no node t_n and form the set $\mathcal{L}_{t_n}$. Note that f_t is chosen based on the training data at node t, which determines $\hat{P}_t$. All these data points have answered the same way to all queries along the path from the root node to t. Thus using $\hat{P}_t$ is equivalent to using the original empirical distribution at the root node, but conditioning on the sequence of answers to the queries along the path.

The set of predictors F_t inspected at node t depends on the context. In all applications reported here, it is a random subset of $\mathcal{F}$. The nodes of the tree are split depth first starting from the root node. Various criteria can be used to stop the splitting—for example, a lower bound on the number of data points at a node, or on the number of data points in the top two classes, or on the entropy on class. Also, if none of the candidate predictors further reduces entropy, the node is not split and becomes a terminal node.

Once the tree T is grown, at each *terminal* node t we denote the conditional distribution on class given that node by $P(Y = c \mid t)$. This distribution is estimated using the training data through

$$\mu_T(c) \doteq \hat{P}(Y = c \mid t) = \frac{|\mathcal{L}_t^{(c)}|}{|\mathcal{L}_t|}$$

where $\mathcal{L}_t^{(c)}$ is the set of training points of class c at node t. These estimates are not necessarily reliable, and depend on the number of training data points that reached the node. Finally, the terminal node t is labeled by the mode of μ—that is,

$$\hat{Y}_t = argmax_{1 \leq c \leq K} \mu_t(c)$$

9.1.2   Testing and Error

A test data point ω can now be "dropped" down the tree. At each node t, the point goes left or right according to whether the value of $X_{f_t}(\omega) = 0$ or 1. The data point reaches some terminal node denoted $T(\omega)$, and is classified according to the label $\hat{Y}_{T(\omega)}$ attached to that node.

It is possible to grow the tree until pure nodes are reached, meaning that the error rate on the training set is 0. This of course does not imply a 0 error rate on the test set, because the estimated "pure" conditional distributions in the terminal nodes are unreliable. More-reliable estimates are obtained with shallower trees where more training data is present in each terminal node. Then the error rate on the training set is nonzero—however, the difference between training error rate and testing error rate may be smaller. There have been many attempts to deal with this payoff by growing pure trees and then pruning them backward (see Breiman and colleagues 1984). This more-refined processing becomes unnecessary when multiple trees are grown.

Note that if the depth of the tree is say, 10, a data point dropped down the tree has been classified with only 10 predictors having been evaluated. In our case, there may be thousands of predictors, and obviously a very small number has been used to classify the data point. One way to access this large pool of predictors is to grow very deep trees, but even with data sets of several tens of thousands, one runs out of data quite quickly. Only very few terminal nodes will be of depth greater than, say, 20. The alternative is to grow multiple trees instead of only one and then somehow combine the information.

9.1.3   Unsupervised Trees

There are situations where data is provided without labels, and we seek to find clusters of similar shapes, which can subsequently be labeled. This is called unsupervised learning, also known as clustering or vector quantization. (For a broad range of methods see Duda and Hart 1973; Gersho and Gray 1992; Ripley 1994; and Bishop 1995.) Here we describe one way to achieve this using binary trees.

Because no labels are provided, all data points with exactly the same values of *all* the predictors are a "class." Thus there are $2^{|\mathcal{F}|}$ classes, where $|\mathcal{F}|$ denotes the number of predictors, and the class variable Y and the predictor vector X uniquely determine each other. Recall that at node t we denote by $\hat{P}_t$ the empirical distribution on the data at that node, and H_t is the entropy with respect to that distribution. Using the same cost function introduced in equation 9.1 for the case of labeled data, and the relation between conditional entropy and joint entropy of equation 4.20, we write

$$H_t(Y \mid X_f) = H_t(Y, X_f) - H_t(X_f)$$
$$= H_t(Y) - H_t(X_f) \tag{9.2}$$

The second equality follows from the fact that Y completely determines X and in particular X_f, so that the joint entropy of Y and X_f is the same as the entropy of Y. Because $H_t(Y)$ does not depend on f,

$$argmin_f H_t(Y \mid X_f) = argmax_f H_t(X_f) \tag{9.3}$$

Because X_f is binary, setting $p_f = \hat{P}_t(X_f = 1)$ we have

$$H_t(X_f) = -p_f \log p_f - (1 - p_f) \log(1 - p_f)$$

The function $-p \log p - (1 - p) \log(1 - p)$ is concave and maximized at the value $1/2$, so that the maximization in 9.3 reduces to searching for that predictor f that is closest to splitting the data at the node *in half,* or

$$C(f) = |\hat{P}_t(X_f = 1) - 1/2|$$

A stopping criterion based on depth or number of data in a node can be used.

Such trees provide some form of partitioning of the population of images. Typically, images falling into the same terminal node will be similar in shape because they have in common the answers to the sequence of queries on the path from the root of the tree to the terminal node. Furthermore, if class labels are assigned to some collection of images, possibly different images from those used to produce the unsupervised tree, it is possible to drop these down the tree and obtain class distributions at the terminal nodes. The tree can then be used as a classification tree.

9.1.4   Multiple Trees

Randomization

In the description of the basic tree-growing protocol, we already mentioned the possibility of choosing the set F_t randomly from all possible predictors $\mathcal{F}$. This could be a rather small subset—indeed, in the experiments reported below we sometimes sample several tens from a collection of hundreds of thousands of possible predictors. This randomization allows us to generate different trees from the same training data set. A data point dropped down two such trees will have had different predictors evaluated along the paths from root to terminal nodes.

There are two ingredients in randomization. The most important is choosing the sets F_t of candidate predictors at each node as a random sample from the collection of all possible predictors. The second is estimating the optimal predictor using a random sample of the data points at each node. The sizes of these two random samples are parameters that need to be set. In most experiments below, both are on the order of a few hundred or less.

Aggregation

After N trees $T_1, \ldots, T_N$ have been produced, the optimal way to aggregate the information is to maximize the posterior given the N random variables defined by the trees. Namely, classify a test point ω as

$$\hat{Y}(\omega) = argmax_{1 \leq c \leq K} P(Y = c \mid T_1(\omega), \ldots, T_N(\omega))$$

where $T_n(\omega)$ is the terminal node reached by ω in tree T_n. This posterior is impossible to estimate for much the same reason it was impossible to grow a very deep tree. There is not enough data.

However, if the random variables T_n, defined by the trees, were *conditionally independent* given Y—that is,

$$P(T_1 = \tau_1, \ldots, T_N = \tau_N \mid Y = c) = \prod_{n=1}^{N} P(T_i = \tau_i \mid Y = c)$$

the posterior on class given the N trees could be given analytically in terms of the individual posteriors. Specifically, given a sample point ω, let $\tau_i = T_i(\omega)$, $i = 1, \ldots, N$. If the prior on class is uniform, $P(Y = c) = 1/K$, then using Bayes's rule twice, and the fact that the trees are conditionally independent, we have

$$P(Y = c \mid T_1 = \tau_1, \ldots, T_N = \tau_N) = P(T_1 = \tau_1, \ldots, T_N = \tau_N \mid Y = c) \cdot \frac{C_1}{K}$$

$$= C_2 \prod_{n=1}^{N} P(T_n = \tau_n \mid Y = c)$$

$$= C_3 \prod_{n=1}^{N} P(Y = c \mid T_n = \tau_n) P(T_n = \tau_n)$$

$$= C_4 \prod_{n=1}^{N} P(Y = c \mid T_n = \tau_n)$$

where C_1, C_2, C_3, C_4 do not depend on the class c. Thus maximizing the posterior, given the output of all the trees, is equivalent to maximizing

$$\sum_{n=1}^{N} \log P(Y = c \mid T_n = \tau_n)$$

over $c = 1, \ldots, K$. Using estimates of these conditional probabilities, the classifier would be

$$\hat{Y}(\omega) = argmax_c \sum_{n=1}^{N} \log \mu_{T_n(\omega)}$$

This assumption of conditional independence is of course very strong and unrealistic. Also, using logarithms may be somewhat unstable. The simplest alternative is to directly average the terminal distributions—namely, to classify by maximizing

$$\hat{Y}_A(\omega) = argmax_{1 \leq c \leq K} A_N(c, \omega)$$

where

$$A_N(c, \omega) = \frac{1}{N} \sum_{n=1}^{N} \mu_{T_n(\omega)}(c), \quad c = 1, \ldots, K \tag{9.4}$$

We call $A^{(N)}$ the aggregate distribution and $\hat{Y}_A$ the *aggregate classifier*. As will be shown below, aggregating multiple trees leads to drastic decreases in error rates relative to the best achievable individual tree in the context of shape recognition. It provides very robust classification even with quite small data sets and is quite insensitive to parameter settings. In section 9.5, we provide some additional pointers as to why this aggregation produces significant improvements.

Boosting

Thus far, we have described a mechanism for generating different trees using randomization. Each tree is produced disregarding all the others according to the same protocol, determined by the number of random queries sampled at each node, and the stopping criterion on splitting nodes. Another related approach to producing multiple trees is known as *boosting,* as described in Freund and Shapire (1997) and in Schapire, Freund, Bartlett, and Lee (1998), where the trees or more generally the classifiers are produced with some dependence on the previously generated classifiers. The idea is that more effort should be dedicated to the "hard" examples, namely, those examples in the training set that have been misclassified by the trees already grown. This is done by using a weight vector on the training data, with the weight on a data point increasing every time it is misclassified and decreasing if it is correctly classified.

In the simplest two-class case, this is done by setting an initial uniform weight vector W_1 on the training set $\mathcal{L}$. A tree T_1 is grown with the training data using some chosen protocol. The training error $e_1 = \hat{P}(Y \neq \hat{Y}_{T_1})$ of the tree is obtained, where we recall that $\hat{P}$ is the empirical distribution and $\hat{Y}_t$ is the class label attached to the node t. The misclassified points in the training set have their weight increased by a factor of $(1 - e_1)/e_1$. The weights on the training set are then renormalized to produce the new weight vector W_2. After $n - 1$ trees $T_1, \ldots, T_{n-1}$ have been produced and given an updated weight vector W_n, a new tree T_n is grown with the weighted training sample. *All probabilities and entropies are calculated using the empirical distribution $\hat{P}_{W_n}$ determined by the current weights on the individual training points.* In particular, the training error e_n of T_n is evaluated in terms of the weighted training data. The weights on the misclassified points are again multiplied by $(1 - e_n)/e_n$, and the entire weight vector normalized to produce W_{n+1}.

After N trees are produced, they are aggregated either as described in equation 9.4 or as proposed in Schapire, Freund, Bartlett, and Lee (1998) by a weighted vote between the N classifications Y_{T_n}, namely,

$$\hat{Y}_B(\omega) = argmax_{1 \leq c \leq K} A_N^B(\omega, c)$$

where

$$A_N^B(\omega, c) = \sum_{n=1}^{N} \beta_n 1_{Y_{[T_n(\omega)=c]}}$$

and

$$\beta_n = \log\left(\frac{1 - e_n}{e_n}\right) \tag{9.5}$$

In Friedman, Hastie, and Tibshirani (2000), it is shown that the somewhat mysterious protocol of boosting, together with the particular weighting in equation 9.5, corresponds to a step-wise gradient descent on a cost function formulated in terms of an exponential moment of the aggregate classifier, which is evaluated on the training set. Under quite general conditions, this gradient-descent procedure is guaranteed to decrease the value of the cost function very rapidly toward zero, on the *training set*. However, typically on *test* sets this same cost function diverges very quickly. So the success of boosting cannot be attributed to the particular cost function being used. Indeed, many variations, including the one used in the experiments below, produce very good results. The main reason for this success lies in the fact that boosting is producing weakly dependent trees, perhaps even more so than the randomization protocol, as discussed in section 9.5 at the end of this chapter.

The original boosting protocol encounters problems when $e_n \le .5$, namely, when the error of classifier T_n is higher than .5. This is by no means uncommon in multiclass problems. We therefore substitute a reweighting of the form $1/e_n$. The protocol no longer has the appealing interpretation of a gradient descent on a simple cost function. However, it performs just as well and produces stable results. All experiments reported here with boosting employ this reweighting scheme. Furthermore, we use the aggregation scheme of equation 9.4 as opposed to that of equation 9.5, so that the trees are all equally weighted.

9.2   Object Recognition with Trees

We now return to the original problem of object recognition. The crucial question is which predictors to use in producing the tree, or any other classifier. The most naive approach would simply use the gray-level intensities at each pixel on the reference grid, which is the original form of the data. However, we have seen throughout previous chapters that this would not accommodate the geometric and photometric variabilities inherent in the problem. The gray-level intensities are therefore again transformed into collections of binary features—robust to *local* geometric variations and to photometric transformations. Such binary features can then be *spread,* (the or-ing operation) in various ways to obtain flexible representations invariant to *global* geometric variations.

9.2.1 Local Features

Two types of binary local features have been used in the experiments. The first is adapted to the particular image population being analyzed, and the second is generic.

Microimage Codes

In the particular setting of binary images, we define local features that are adapted to the training data. These ideas can in principle be extended to gray-level images, however, in this more complex context it is not clear how to accommodate photometric invariance as well as invariance to local deformations. This is definitely a direction requiring more research.

Start with a sample S of small, 4×4 subimages, henceforth called microimages, of the training data, keeping only those that are not constant, namely, those that are neither all black nor all white. Produce an unsupervised tree of depth d with this data, using the methodology described in section 9.1.3. There are only 16 predictors corresponding to the pixel value $(1/0)$ at any of the 16 locations in the 4×4 microimage, thus there are at most 2^{16} "classes" in this data. Such a tree provides a partition or quantization of the population of binary microimages. Each terminal node of the tree contains approximately the same number of microimages. The path from the root to a terminal node determines a subset of the form $\{s \in S : s_{i_0} = a_1, \ldots, s_{i_4} = a_4\}$ where $i_0, \ldots, i_4$ are the locations (on the 4×4 grid) used at the nodes along the path and $a_1, \ldots, a_4$ are 0 or 1 according to whether the path goes left (no) or right (yes) at a node. Not surprisingly, the most common microimage in the deeper nodes of the tree actually represents some form of oriented edge.

Any local 4×4 microimage is now classified by dropping it down the tree and determining which terminal node it belongs to. The microimage is labeled not only by the terminal node, but also by the intermediate nodes along the path to the terminal node. Thus if the tree is of depth 5, the microimage is given 5 labels. The labels corresponding to depth 1 nodes are assigned to about half the data. They are very crude characterizations of the microimage and are very common. The labels further

Figure 9.3   Locations of features corresponding to depth 1, 2, and 3 along one path of the code tree.

down along the path to the terminal node represent finer and finer characterizations. In figure 9.3, we show the locations of features corresponding to depths 1, 2, and 3 along one path of the code tree. We perform a clustering on the locations of the features so that only one instance of each local feature type is present in each 5×5 region. Due to this clustering, the locations of depth k are not precisely a subset of the locations for depth $k - 1$.

In the experiments, we find that all levels of detail are necessary, not only the finest one. The coarser nodes are more invariant to local deformations, the finer nodes convey more information on the local binary configuration.

In figure 9.4, we show 3 levels of this tree and the most common configuration found at each of the eight depth-3 nodes. Observe that the tree partitions among microimages corresponding to edges of different orientations. This is achieved in a purely data-driven manner. The most common images in deeper nodes typically correspond to boundaries with a slight curve or bend, and may be viewed as a conjunction of two edges.

Generic Local Features Produced from Edges

From the quantization described above, we see that oriented edges are reasonable representations of clusters of microimages, as are finer features, represented by local edge arrangements, of which we have made extensive use in previous chapters. As an "engineered" alternative to the features defined above, we use the following 264 local features: 8 edges corresponding to the 8 basic orientations defined in section 5.4 and $256 = 8 \times 8 \times 4$ two-edge arrangements defined in chapter 6. We use the larger wedges shown in figure 6.7 corresponding to the angles $0, \pi/4, \pi/2, 3\pi/4$.

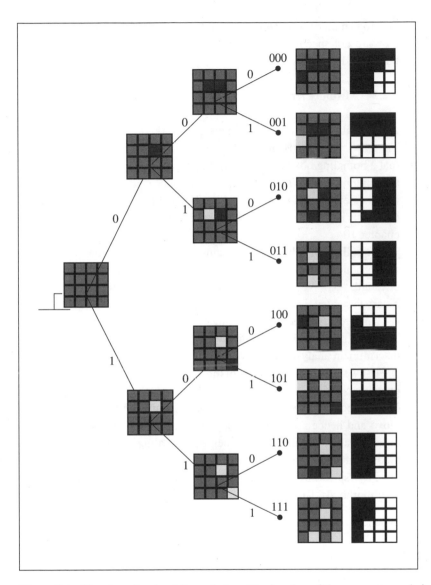

Figure 9.4 First three levels of the code tree. The location of the query at a node is shown in the children nodes as white if the value is "1", and as black if the value is "0". The most common configurations at the eight depth three nodes are shown.

Due to symmetry, other angles are not needed. The advantage of these features is that they are not specifically tailored to any particular data set and can be used in both binary and gray-level images.

9.2.2 Absolute Arrangements

Assume all images have been registered to a fixed reference grid G (say, 32×32). The LaTeX database is created this way in the first place. In other cases, one assumes that a bounding box has been identified for the symbol or a pose has been estimated, allowing us to register the data to the reference grid. The dependence of the classifier on this step is crucial and should not be taken lightly. It implies that some form of detection is necessary prior to classification. We continue to explore this issue in chapter 10.

The collection of binary local features $X_1, \ldots, X_N$ is now applied at all locations in G to produce a fixed dimensional binary predictor vector $X_\alpha(z)$, $\alpha = 1, \ldots, N$, $z \in G$, of length $|G| \cdot N$. The gray-level intensities have been replaced by an N-vector of binary variables. The set $\mathcal{F}$ is the collection of all pairs $f = (\alpha, z)$, $\alpha = 1, \ldots, N$, $z \in G$. This predictor vector, after being calculated for each image in the training set, can be fed into *any* standard classifier: feed-forward neural nets, classification trees, linear discriminant analysis, and so on.

First we should note that any of these classifiers would produce a very sensitive and unstable classifier—the reason being that under the smallest variations of an instance of a symbol of some class, the locations of quite a number of the local features will move and hence completely change the corresponding predictor vector. Invariance to local variations and a certain degree of scaling and translation must be explicitly incorporated into the predictors. With binary features, this is easily and naturally done by "spreading" (or-ing) the output of the original local feature detectors to $s \times s$ neighborhoods. Define

$$X_\alpha^s(z) = \max_{y \in N_s(z)} X_\alpha(y) \tag{9.6}$$

where $N_s(z)$ is an $s \times s$ neighborhood of z, namely, $X_\alpha^s(z) = 1$ if $X_\alpha(y) = 1$ *anywhere* in the $s \times s$ neighborhood of x. This is an explicit disjunction or or-ing that is directly incorporated into the data and any resulting classifier will inherit a certain degree of invariance. In our context, spreading on rather large 15×15 regions yields optimal results. It should be kept in mind that while or-ing increases the stability of the classifier, it decreases the discriminating power of each of the coordinates of the predictor vector.

Multiple randomized classification trees are trained using these predictors and aggregated as described above. Results obtained on the LAT_EX and NIST databases are reported in section 9.4 where they are also compared to results with the relational arrangements described in the following section.

9.3   Relational Arrangements

In this section, we describe a more complex approach to the object classification problem. We no longer assume that the object has been registered to a reference location and scale. This means that absolute locations of features are meaningless and we can only use information regarding the relative spatial arrangement of local features; for example, information on the angles of the vectors connecting pairs of local features. Once a relational arrangement is defined, the associated query asks whether or not such an arrangement is present *anywhere in the image*. The arrangement is also defined in an entirely scale-invariant manner—it can be present at any scale. In the sequel, we will define these arrangements more precisely, define a partial ordering on the set of arrangements, and explain how the associated queries can be incorporated into classification trees. As will become apparent, it is not clear how such "queries" can be systematically employed in the context of other types of classifiers.

In figure 9.5, we show a collection of symbols in all of which a particular relational arrangement has been found, described in terms of a graph with edges between pairs of

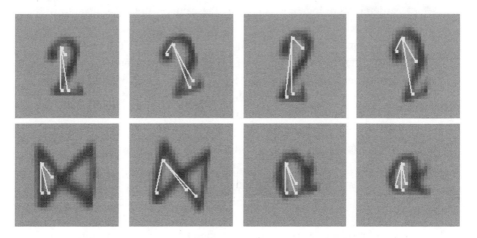

Figure 9.5   Eight images from a depth 5 node in a classification tree with the associated arrangement. Two of the queries on the path to this node were answered no.

features between which a relation has been defined. Note the variations on the angles and distances between the nodes of the graph. There are no distance constraints in the relations defined between the features. All these images reached some internal node of a classification tree grown with relational arrangements as described below. The conditional distribution on the 293 LATEX classes given the presence of this arrangement is far more concentrated than the original uniform distribution. The entropy is 5.74 down from the entropy on the uniform distribution on 293 class, which is 8.19. Despite the large degree of flexibility introduced in the definition of the arrangement, it carries a significant amount of information on the shape in the image.

9.3.1   Relations Between Local Features

Define wedges $W_k, k = 1, \ldots, K_w$ centered at the origin spanning the angle $2(k-1)\pi/K_w$ to $2(k+1)\pi/K_w$. If feature X_α is present at location x and feature $X_{\alpha'}$ at location y, we say that they satisfy relation R_k if $y \in x + W_k$. Typically, we use $K_w = 16$ so that there are 16 possible binary relations between any two features.

A relational arrangement is a labeled graph with vertices $V = \{1, \ldots, d\}$ and directed edges defined as some subset of $V \times V$. Each vertex $i \in V$ is assigned a label $1 \leq \alpha(i) \leq n$, which corresponds to one of the local features. Each edge $(i, j) \in E$ is assigned a label $1 \leq \beta(i, j) \leq K_w$. The arrangement is present in the image if there exists an ordered set of locations $x_1, \ldots, x_d$ such that a feature of type $\alpha(i)$ is present at x_i, for each $i \in V$, and $x_j \in x_i + W_{\beta(i,j)}$, for each $(i, j) \in E$. Each arrangement defines a binary variable on images: either it is present or it is not. Note that any ordered set of locations satisfying these conditions is an instance of this arrangement. Because the relations are defined very loosely and only constrain the relative angles, a relational arrangement can have a quite a number of possible instances.

We denote by $\mathcal{A}$ the set of all possible arrangements. Note that the local edge arrangements defined in chapter 6 are special cases of relational arrangements, where all relations are with respect to the first vertex, with an additional constraint on the distance between the local features in the relation.

9.3.2   Growing Trees with Relational Arrangements

The arrangements are defined in terms of graphs, thus providing a natural partial ordering, under which a graph precedes any of its extensions. The partial ordering corresponds to a hierarchy of structure. Small arrangements with few local features produce coarse splits of shape space. As the arrangements increase in size, they convey more information about the images that contain them. However, fewer images contain these arrangements. One straightforward way to exploit this hierarchy is to build a classification tree, using the collection of arrangements as candidates for the queries, with the complexity of the queries increasing with the depth of the node.

Define a *minimal extension* of an arrangement $A \in \mathcal{A}$ to mean the addition of exactly one local feature and one relation binding the new local feature to an existing one. Let $\mathcal{B} \subset \mathcal{A}$ denote the set of arrangements involving only two local features and one relation. Now build a tree using the protocol described in section 9.1.1. At the root node r, F_r is a random sample from $\mathcal{B}$. Denote the chosen query A_r. Those data points that do not have an instance of the arrangement proceed to the "no" child node r_n, where again we search through $\mathcal{B}$. Those data points that do have an instance of A_r proceed to the "yes" child node r_y and have one or more instances of A_r, which we call the *pending arrangement,* at r_y and denote it by P_{r_y}.

At the node r_y, the set F_{r_y} of candidate queries is a random sample of minimal extensions of the pending arrangement P_{r_y}. If we select A_{r_y} as the query for node r_y, this will be an arrangement with three local features and two relations. The "no" child node of r_y inherits the same pending arrangement P_{r_y}. The "yes" child node r_{yy} has the pending arrangement $P_{r_{yy}} = A_{r_y}$.

More generally, at any given node t, the pending arrangement P_t is the same as at the parent node p if t is the "no" child ($t = p_n$). At $t = p_y$ we have $P_t = A_p$, which again is a minimal extension of P_p. F_t is always a random sample of minimal extensions of P_t. There is no pending arrangement at a "no" node t, for which all ancestors are also "no" nodes, and the set F_t is again a random sample of $\mathcal{B}$.

The number of possible arrangements in $\mathcal{A}$ is essentially infinite. Using only minimal extensions greatly reduces the number of candidate queries at a node. It is also very easy to check if the minimal extension exists for each instance of the pending graph. Still, there are very large numbers of possible minimal extensions at every stage. In this context, randomization not only serves to create different trees, it also reduces the number of queries that need to be checked.

An illustration of the effects of these queries on splitting the data can be seen in figures 9.5 and 9.6. Figure 9.5 shows a collection of images that reached a depth-5 node, with one instance of the pending arrangement. The first row of figure 9.6 shows images that reached that same node and continued to the "yes" child. The additional feature was found in these images in the proper angle relative to an existing feature in one of the instances of the pending arrangement. The 2s in figure 9.5 did not have such a feature and went to the "no" child node. One more split of the depth-6 node is also shown in the second row of figure 9.6. The αs have gone to the "no" node and the $\bowtie$s to the "yes" node.

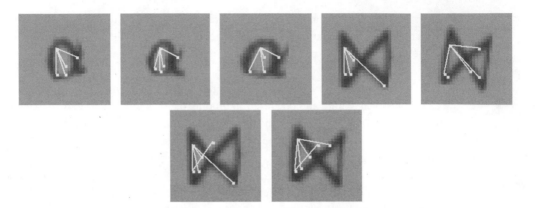

Figure 9.6   Examples of node splitting. All five images in the top row lie in the same node and have a pending arrangement with four vertices. All these images were in the node represented in figure 9.5. The two's shown in that figure went to the "no" node. One more step of the splitting separates the αs from the $\bowtie$s by asking for the presence of an additional feature.

Figure 9.7   The pending arrangement at the terminal node in five different trees for a single instance of a 2.

Training is more complex than for standard classification trees described earlier. At each node, a list must be assigned to each data point consisting of all instances of the pending arrangement, including the coordinates of each participating feature. If a data point passes to the "yes" child, then only those instances that can be incremented with the new relation are maintained and updated; the rest are deleted. The more data points, the more bookkeeping. There is an inherent asymmetry in the tree, in that the pending arrangement at terminal nodes with many "no" answers on the path from the root will be small. However, in many terminal nodes, as shown in figure 9.7, the arrangement describes a complex structure, and dropping the data down the tree automatically identifies the instantiations of this structure in the image. In this sense, the relational trees can be viewed as a classification *combined* with a sparse model instantiation.

The importance of using multiple randomized trees is illustrated in figure 9.7, where we show the arrangement found on a single instance of a 2 in the terminal node it reached in five different trees. The five trees are using different aspects and properties of the shape to classify this data point. A more robust classification is then possible when the information from all trees is pooled together. Because the arrangements are defined in an entirely scale- and translation-invariant manner, the resulting trees are very robust to scaling and translation. Indeed, the incoming data does not need to be registered in any way, as will be illustrated in the experiments below.

9.4   Experiments

We experiment with the LATEX database and portions of the National Institute of Standards and Technology (NIST) database (Garris and Wilkinson 1976), which consists of approximately 223,000 binary images of isolated digits written by more than 2000 writers. We use 100,000 for training and 50,000 for testing. For this database we use microimage codes dedicated to binary images. On the LATEX database, the generic features are used.

In all trees reported below, the nodes are split as long as there are at least m data points in the second-largest class. The default value we use is $m = 3$, but in some experiments, m can reach up to several hundreds. The parameter Q represents the number of random queries sampled at each node while training the tree—this can range anywhere from several tens to hundreds of thousands. For absolute arrangements, the parameter s denotes the degree of "spread" (a detected feature is spread to the $s \times s$ neighborhood of the original location) and ranges from 3 to 15. For relational arrangements, the parameter K_w determines the number of wedges used and their width. At all nodes with more than 200 training points, we take a random sample of 200 to determine the best query from among the Q randomly sampled queries; otherwise, we use all training data at the node. Unless otherwise specified, 100 trees are produced in each experiment.

9.4.1   NIST

The NIST data is initially preprocessed as follows. The original images are binary. Each image is blurred with a Gaussian filter of standard deviation 1 pixel. If the dimensions of the image are less than 32, the bounding rectangle of the digit is identified and is placed in the center of a 32×32 grid. If the largest dimension d of

Table 9.1   NIST: Different protocols

Tree Protocol	Absolute $Q = 20$ $s = 15$	Absolute $Q = 100$ $s = 15$	Absolute $Q = 200$ $s = 15$	Relational $Q = 20$ $K_w = 8$	Relational $Q = 100$ $K_w = 24$
Aggregate rate	98.7%	99.03%	98.9%	98.5%	98.8%
Individual rate	90%	93%	94.2%	77.2%	86.7%

100,000 training data and 50,000 test. Q, number of random queries sampled at a node; s, size of "spread" parameter for trees with absolute arrangements; K_w, number of wedges in relative arrangements (width of wedge is $2\pi / K_w$); $m = 3$, number of data points in second largest class at a node to stop splitting. Row 1: aggregate classification rate with 100 trees. Row 2: average classification rate of the individual trees.

the image is greater than 32, the image is downscaled by a ratio of $32/d$ and is again centered in a 32×32 grid. Then the image is rebinarized using a threshold of .25, assuming the pixel values are in the range $(0, 1)$. It is necessary to binarize the image to detect the microimage codes.

The results in table 9.1 show the effect of producing multiple classification trees. (The aggregate classification rate as a function of the number of trees for one of the experiments is shown in figure 9.9.) Note how very similar aggregate classification rates are obtained with very different classification rates on the individual trees. The best result obtained on one tree using no randomization at all was 95.8%, thus the aggregation of multiple randomized trees plays a very important role in reaching above 99% classification rates. With absolute arrangements, similar results are obtained using a coarser grid for the features. Features are extracted on the original image; however, their coordinates are rounded off to the nearest multiple of 2 or 4. The number of predictors is then reduced by a factor of 4 and 16, respectively. The s parameter is adjusted accordingly to $s = 7$ and $s = 2$, respectively. In both settings, the classification rates obtained were 98.8%. In figure 9.8, we show the first 100 of the 500 misclassified NIST digits.

The trees generalize well to other data sets. For example, the relational arrangement trees were applied to a data set of 5,000 handwritten digits obtained from the USPS database produced and distributed by CEDAR, SUNY Buffalo. The classification rate was 97.3%. The conditions under which the postal digits are written are very different. In writing zip codes on an envelope, no bounding box is provided, so that their sizes and slants exhibit a larger variability than that of the NIST database. Several other comparisons are interesting for this database. In table 9.2, we show classification rates as a function of the size of the training set—all other parameters fixed. In table 9.3, we compare results on the small 5,000 sample training set as a function of the stopping

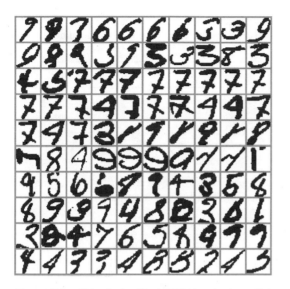

Figure 9.8   100 misclassified NIST handwritten digits.

Table 9.2   NIST: Classification rates of the aggregate classifier and the individual trees as a function of the training sample size—absolute arrangements ($m = 3$, $s = 15$, $Q = 20$)

Sample Size	5,000	10,000	50,000	100,000
Aggregate rate	97.3%	97.9%	98.6%	98.7%
Individual rate	80.23%	83.3%	88.6%	90%

rule, which affects the depth of the trees. As the value of m decreases the trees get deeper. In many instances of the use of classification trees, deeper trees may exhibit lower classification rates due to overfitting. This does not seem to occur in this case, probably due to the large degree of spreading. For $m = 1$ we obtain pure trees, namely, trees for which there is only one class of training data present at each terminal node. These appear to perform best.

Boosting

We implement the boosting protocol with the reweighting factor of $1/e_n$ and aggregate the trees according to equation 9.4. The terminal distributions μ_{T_n} are in this case estimated during training with the weighted training data. It appears that

Table 9.3   NIST: Absolute arrangements—classification rates of the aggregate classifier and the individual trees with 5000 training data, as a function of the stopping criterion ($m = 3$, $s = 15$, $Q = 20$)

Stopping Criterion	$m = 20$	$m = 10$	$m = 3$	$m = 1$
Aggregate rate	96.0%	96.5%	97.2%	97.6%
Individual rate	72.8%	76.8%	80.2%	80.4%
Average depth	6.1	6.93	8.49	9.86

Table 9.4   NIST: Absolute arrangements—classification rates of the aggregate classifier with and without boosting as a function of the stopping criterion

Stopping Criterion	$m = 20$	$m = 10$	$m = 3$	$m = 1$
Randomized aggregate rate	96.0%	96.5%	97.2%	97.6%
Boosting aggregate rate	96.8%	96.5%	95.2%	*

5000 training data are used. Boosting is not applicable for pure trees since the training error rate is 0 ($Q = 20$, $s = 15$).

when deep trees are used, so that the training classification rate is very high, boosting overfits the training data and performs worse than simple randomization (table 9.4). However, for shallower trees, boosting enables the aggregate classifier to "overcome" some limitations of the individual classifiers. If certain data points of different classes are hard to separate without querying a large portion of their respective strokes, shallow trees risk having them end up in the same terminal nodes, especially because the trees are aiming at improving the purity of the nodes over the entire training set. Boosting will cause the weights of such data points to increase significantly. Their relative weight in determining the purity of a node increases and subsequent trees in the boosting procedure may be able to separate these hard examples.

For the larger data set, we observe the same properties of boosting. Using the parameters yielding the best performance with 100,000 training data for the randomized protocol produces a rather low classification rate with boosting. However, table 9.5 shows randomized boosting outperforms simple randomization with shallower trees with $m = 100$, (average depth of 9.76 vs. 12). In figure 9.9, we show the aggregate classification rate as a function of the number of trees. The curves for other experiments look very similar.

Table 9.5   NIST: Absolute arrangements—classification rates of the aggregate classifier with boosting for various protocols with boosting and 100000 training data

Protocol	$m = 100$ $Q = 1000$	$m = 100$ $Q = 20$	$m = 50$ $Q = 20$	$m = 20$ $Q = 20$
Boosting aggregate rate	99.29%	99.09%	99.07%	98.8%
Individual rate	74.7%	62.4%	69.3%	76.4%
Average depth	9.8	9.8	10.8	12.0

The best result of 99.29% was achieved with boosting: $m = 100$ and $Q = 1000$.

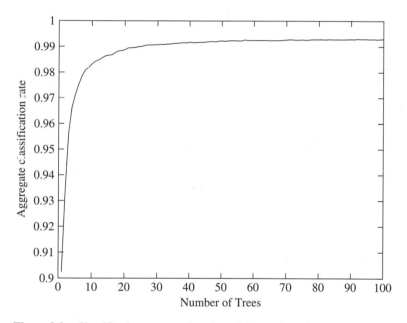

Figure 9.9   Classification rate as a function of the number of trees.

The "Hard" NIST Data Set

One additional portion of the NIST data set, containing approximately 50,000 samples, was produced by high school students as opposed to employees of NIST. This data set is more challenging—the variability in shape and size appears to be greater. Using the best trees reported above on this more difficult set, we achieve a very low classification rate of 95.2; with a combination of 30,000 samples from the original set and 30,000 from the hard set, we reach 98.75% on a mixed test set of 10,000 images. The best results on this combination of the data sets is reported in LeCun and colleagues (1998) and discussed below.

9.4.2   LaTeX

Similar results emerge from experiments with the LaTeX database. Here, however, there are only 32 training samples per image and the number of classes is 293. We use 50 samples per class for testing. Quite a large variability is introduced in the images with the synthesized deformations. Table 9.6 illustrates the importance of spreading, showing that the optimal spreading box is around 15, which is *half* the image size. From this table, we also see the drastic improvement in performance enabled by aggregation. Here we use absolute arrangements with the 264 generic features of edges and edge arrangements.

An interesting comparison in table 9.7 shows the effect of the number of randomly sampled questions on performance. No randomization is done in the data points used to select the split at each node—that is, all data points are used to choose the optimal split. The optimal number appears to be at $Q = 20$. Although the individual trees produced with higher values of Q have a higher classification rate, the aggregate rate decreases due to the fact that the trees become more similar. The optimal performance

Table 9.6   LaTeX: Comparison of results for different values of the spread parameter s

Spread Parameter	$s = 3$	$s = 7$	$s = 15$	$s = 23$	$s = 31$
Aggregate rate	82.9%	94.7%	96.1%	94.9%	90%
Individual rate	10%	28%	39%	40%	38%

Absolute arrangements are used with the 264 generic features and $Q = 20$.

Table 9.7   LaTeX: Comparison of results for different values of Q

Number of Questions	$Q = 20$	$Q = 500$	$Q = 1000$	$Q = 10000$
Aggregate rate	96.1%	96.08%	95.9%	93.6%
Individual rate	41.5%	58.9%	60.86%	64.99%
Boosting aggregate rate	96.9%	97.2%	97.2%	96.6%
Individual rate	32%	51%	52%	56%

Top two rows: randomized trees. *All* data points at a node were used to select the optimal query. Absolute arrangements, $m = 3$, $s = 15$. Bottom two rows: with boosting.

is achieved with randomization both in the queries and in the sample used to choose the optimal split. When using $Q = 200$ and a random sample of 200 of the entire training sample at a node (when the size is larger than 200), the classification rate achieved is 96.7%, with a mean classification rate per tree of 52%. A different pattern emerges for boosting. Here, there is improvement with the number of random queries used, and the best rate achieved is 97.2%, with $Q = 500$. This difference is discussed in section 9.5.

Clutter

The performance of the relational arrangements under various protocols is shown in table 9.8. On the whole, it seems that the absolute arrangements perform slightly better than relative arrangements. However, this is in an idealized setting, where the object is well centered in the image.

It is therefore of interest to study the effect of clutter on the classifier. The clutter is produced by taking c additional random symbols, extracting a random 6×6 window, and adding it to the image at random locations. Examples of cluttered images are shown in figure 9.10, with $c = 2$ in the top row and $c = 4$ in the bottom row. After clutter is added, the bounding box of the data is recomputed and used for centering the image. This mimics the effect of clutter on the image-registration procedure. The relational arrangements are by definition entirely translation invariant. With absolute arrangements, despite the spreading, there is some sensitivity to moderate shifts.

The performance with absolute arrangements degrades faster than that with relational arrangements, as shown in table 9.9. It appears that this is not only due to shifting, but also due to higher sensitivity to erroneous noisy features that are present in the background. However, the drop in performance is too large in both cases, implying something is missing in these classification schemes. Some consolation can be found if instead of taking the mode of A_N, we check if the correct class is among the top 5 classes. After all, we start out with 293 classes, and reducing to a choice among 5 is still useful. The results are shown in table 9.9 in parentheses.

Table 9.8   LaTeX: Different protocols with relational arrangements

Number of Questions	$Q = 200$ $K_w = 8$	$Q = 200$ $K_w = 16$	$Q = 1000$ $K_w = 16$	$Q = 20$ $K_w = 16$
Randomized aggregate rate	94.5%	95%	95.5%	92%
Individual rate	37%	35%	41%	19%

Figure 9.10 LATEX symbols with clutter. (Top) Two clutter elements. (Bottom) Four clutter elements.

Table 9.9 LATEX: Performance results in the presence of clutter for relational arrangements and absolute arrangements

	Relational $Q = 200$ $K_w = 16$	Absolute $Q = 200$ $s = 15$
$c = 0$	95% (99.6%)	96.6% (99.8%)
$c = 2$	78.4% (91.4%)	62.5% (80.4%)
$c = 4$	57.8% (73.8%)	44.7% (63.8%)

The values in parentheses denote the percentage of test points which had the correct class among the top 5.

Possibly the final discrimination between these 5 candidates should be done using some more-detailed analysis in terms of a deformable model. We have already seen that the deformable curve models are very robust to clutter. We could try to fit each of these five models and choose the one with the highest value of the cost function given in equation 4.12. Trying all 293 models would be computationally very intensive, but trying 5 is reasonable. Moreover, it may not be necessary to try them at each classified data point, only for those where there is evidence of ambiguity.

9.5   Why Multiple Trees Work

In section 9.1, we motivated the aggregation of multiple trees with an ideal situation where the trees T_n, considered as random variables, are conditionally independent given the class label. Intuitively, this is related to the observation made later that different trees classify the data using different aspects of the data, or different points of view. If we *know* the label of a data point ω, then observing $T_n(\omega)$, say, in terms of the terminal distribution $\mu_{T_n(\omega)}$, will not help us predict the terminal distribution at the terminal node $T_m(\omega)$ encountered by ω in another tree. This is because the two trees are using different aspects of shape to classify ω, and therefore the confusions, reflected in the terminal distribution, will probably be different. This is only a conditional property. If we *do not know* the class label of ω ahead of time, than the mode class in $T_n(\omega)$ would serve as a good prediction for the mode class in $T_m(\omega)$. Otherwise put, these trees are in no way *unconditionally independent*.

The trees are never really conditionally independent. Rather, one observes that the conditional covariances between these trees, computed in terms of the terminal distributions μ_{T_n}, are much smaller than the conditional variances. Let ν denote a bound on the conditional variances, and let γ denote some bound on *all* the conditional covariances. We denote the conditional variance given $Y = c$ as $Var_c()$, and the conditional covariance as $Covar_c()$. The conditional variance of the aggregate $A_N(d)$ is expanded as follows.

$$Var_c(A_N(d)) = \frac{1}{N^2} \sum_{n=1}^{N} Var_c \mu_{T_n}(d) + \frac{1}{N(N-1)} \sum_{n \neq m} Covar_c(\mu_{T_n}(d), \mu_{T_m}(d))$$

$$< \nu/N + \gamma, \quad \text{for } d = 1, \dots, K \qquad (9.7)$$

Thus when the number of trees is large, the conditional variance of the aggregate is dominated by γ.

For each class c, write the conditional mean of the aggregate as

$$\theta_c^{(N)}(d) = E_c(A_N(d)) = \frac{1}{N} \sum_{n=1}^{N} E_c(\mu_{T_n}(d)), \quad d = 1, \dots K$$

If the individual trees have reasonable classification rates, then the mean weight on class c, given $Y = c$ will be larger than the mean weight on all other classes—that is,

$$\theta_c^{(N)}(c) - \theta_c^{(N)}(d) > M^{(N)} > 0, \quad \text{for all } d \neq c$$

for some constant $M^{(N)}$.

If $M^{(N)}$ is significantly larger than the standard deviation of each of the variables $A_N(d)$ for $d = 1, \ldots, K$, restricted to class c (i.e., if $M^{(N)} \gg \sqrt{\gamma}$), then $A_N(c)$, with high probability, will be larger than $A_N(d)$ for all $d \neq c$ and hence the probability of error is small. We see that the key to low error rates with multiple trees is having γ small relative to $M^{(N)}$. By contrast, the key to low error rates with one tree is having ν small relative to $M^{(1)}$, which is approximately the same as $M^{(N)}$ because it is an average of means. However, in all LaTeX experiments, ν is 10–20 times larger than γ.

The expectations and variances used in this discussion are never known—at best they can be estimated from training data. It is, however, interesting to observe that there is a high correlation between the quantities γ and M *estimated from training data* and the ultimate error rates on *test data*. We implemented 19 different protocols for the NIST database with absolute arrangements, with 5,000 training data (500 per class), varying the stopping rule and the number of random questions sampled, with and without boosting. The log of the *test* error rate $\log(e)$ is then regressed on $\log(\gamma)$ and $\log(M)$. Here, instead of upper bounds we redefine γ and M as follows.

$$\gamma = \frac{1}{K} \sum_{c=1}^{K} \sum_{d=1}^{K} Var_c(A_N(d))$$

$$M = \frac{1}{K} \sum_{c=1}^{K} (\theta_c(c) - argmax_{d \neq c}\theta_c(d))$$

These quantities are all estimated from *training data*.

We obtain $R^2 = .92$ and the regression equation is $\log(e) = .32 - 1.8\log(M) + 1.3\log(\gamma)$. The scatter plot of log error versus predicted log error is given in figure 9.11. Although the information in γ and M is not sufficient for precise prediction of the test error, it is quite suitable for deciding which protocol is preferable once the regression estimates are obtained. This decision can be made on the basis of *training data alone*.

Predicting the test error rate directly from the training error rate would be far less stable—particularly for protocols such as boosting, which typically quickly achieve close to 0 error rate on the training data, or protocols growing pure trees, which by definition have 0 error rate on the data.

Note that the test classification rates for the different protocols ranged between 73% and 98%. The variable M ranged between .02 and .85, whereas γ ranged between .001 and .04. The best performance, 98%, was achieved at $M = .58$ and $\gamma = .034$. These values also gave the highest *predicted* classification rate of 97.7%.

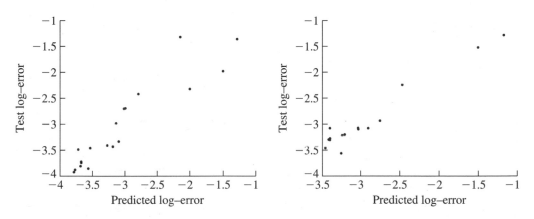

Figure 9.11   Scatter plot of log-error vs. predicted log-error for a variety of protocols. (Left) NIST dataset. (Right) LaTeX dataset.

A similar regression using LaTeX experiments yields $R^2 = 97.2$. It is clear from these regressions that the error rate depends on a ratio γ^a / M^b. Indeed, in some cases M can be higher but the error rate is also higher because γ is high as well.

Both randomization and boosting are somehow achieving low values of γ relative to M. For randomization, we already discussed the intuition behind this. Different trees, using an enormous pool of features and queries, are accessing the data from different points of view. There is no danger of overfitting because the trees are trained in total disregard of each other.

By contrast, in boosting, the reduction of γ is achieved through the reweighting of the training points that are misclassified. In concentrating on these points, the algorithm is actually trying to produce a *negative* conditional covariance between the new classifier and the current aggregate. This general effect can be achieved with a variety of protocols and has very little to do with the specific protocol involved in the original derivation of the boosting algorithm. However, boosting still depends on estimates provided by the training set and risks overfitting, as seen in the deeper trees reported in table 9.4. On the other hand, on the NIST database with the large training set of 10,000 data points per class, when randomization is used in conjunction with boosting and a conservative stopping rule, the best results are achieved. On the LaTeX database, the best results are also achieved with boosting using somewhat larger numbers of randomized queries.

9.6   Bibliographical Notes and Discussion

The work in this chapter is based on Amit and Geman (1997) and Amit, Geman, and Wilder (1997), where only relational arrangements were studied. Some of the ideas on shape quantization explored in Amit and Geman (1997) led to the development of the sparse models described in chapter 8. On the other hand, the very large disjunctions used in step I of the counting algorithm motivated the current experiments with absolute arrangements, where very large values of the spread parameter s is used.

In studying shape recognition, we have touched on two research areas. The first is general classification theory, otherwise known as pattern recognition or machine learning. This covers general issues such as types of classifiers, aggregation methods, estimation of test errors, and so on. The literature on this subject is described in detail in books such as Ripley (1994), Bishop (1995), and the classic book on pattern recognition by Duda and Hart (1973). The main reference for classification trees in the statistics literature is Breiman and colleagues (1984) and in the computer science literature, it is Quinlan (1986). The idea of growing multiple classifiers and aggregating them is more recent and can be found in Kwok and Carter (1990), Breiman (1994, 1998), and Schapire, Freund, Bartlett, and Lee (1998). A more detailed analysis of multiple classifiers from the point of view of the discussion in section 9.5 can be found in Amit and Blanchard (2001).

The second area of research is more specific to computer vision and involves identifying what are the appropriate predictors to be used in the shape and object classifiers; what functions of the data will have appropriate invariance properties on one hand, and discriminatory power on the other. Descriptions of different types of local features can be found in books on computer vision such as Haralick and Shapiro (1992), and many proposals for local features can be found in recent work such as Malik and Perona (1990) and Wiskott and colleagues (1997). Any form of binary feature can be incorporated in the methodology described in this chapter. The binary aspect is crucial for the "spreading" operation in the context of absolute arrangements, or for the definition of the relational arrangements. In principle, features with continuous outputs could be quantized, each quantile serving as one form of binary feature. Alternatively, continuous outputs can be maximized over a neighborhood, as a generalization of or-ing; this has been proposed in Riesenhuber and Poggio (1999).

Much work has also gone into identifying functions of the data that are invariant to geometric transformations—in particular, various functions on distances and angles between specific points that are entirely invariant to certain groups of linear transformations. An extensive treatment of such methods can be found in Reiss (1993).

These methods are based on prior localization of very particular landmarks on the object and do not address the stochastic aspect of images, which precludes such precise localization based only on local information. One could view the use of multiple flexible arrangements of robust local features as an attempt to adapt such ideas to a more realistic view of the data. However, this adaptation means losing full invariance. The shape recognition methods described above, as with the detection algorithms described in earlier chapters, are not fully rotation invariant, nor are they fully invariant to other linear deformations.

Another interesting approach to the classification of characters, which attempts to deal explicitly with invariance to linear and nonlinear deformations, is described in Hastie and Simard (1998), and Simard and colleagues (2000). The idea is to implement nearest-neighbor classification, or approximations to nearest neighbors using a deformation-invariant distance. The distance is essentially based on the linearized two-dimensional template matching described in chapter 5. The distance between a sample image and a training example from a given class is measured after the optimal deformation between the two is computed. A very low-dimensional space of deformations is used. It is very computationally demanding to do this with respect to large numbers of training examples, so the authors describe a method for creating smaller numbers of prototypes for each class, essentially centroids of the training data of each class, computed using the deformation distance. The method still relies on preprocessing the data into fixed-size images and uniform gray-scale ranges.

The most successful handwritten character recognition reported to date can be found in LeCun and colleagues (1998). The classification tools used are multilayer feed-forward neural networks based on the raw pixel intensity input. Although the authors emphasize the fact that very little is done in terms of design of features and that everything is left to the training procedure, the actual architecture and constraints imposed on the network are of primary importance and interest. Due to the enforcing of translation invariance of the network weights at certain layers, and blurring and subsampling in other layers, the network ends up producing a sequence of feature detectors that are then in some sense "or-ed" to allow for local invariances. The layers involving translation-invariant weights are called *convolution nets*. If instead of classification trees we had used a feed-forward network based on conjunctions of edges, the resulting network would be qualitatively very similar to the one reported in LeCun and colleagues (1998). The difference would that we would have hand designed the input-level weights defining the input convolution network, as well as the weights defining the second-layer convolution network. We revisit this issue in chapter 11, where we design a biologically plausible network for detection and recognition. The classification rate reported in LeCun and colleagues (1998) is 99.3%;

this is done by training on a mixed set of 30,000 from the "easy" set and 30,000 from the "hard" set, and testing on a mixed set of 10,000. An additional aspect of the work described in LeCun and colleagues (1998) is the parsing of character strings—namely, zip codes. We will discuss that aspect in chapter 10.

Two aspects are clearly missing from the experiments described above, which could easily be incorporated in the same framework, both of which may also help with the sensitivity to clutter encountered earlier. The first is the use of features from more than one resolution. It is possible to extract edges from the data both at the original resolution and at lower resolutions and use them all in growing the trees. The second aspect, which has been explored in the literature, is the use of "parts" (see Shapiro 1980; Brooks 1981; and Haralick and Shapiro 1992 for an extensive review). Usually, parts are given a very clear semantic meaning such as *loop* or *crossing* or *ending,* or a generalized cylinder in 3D. One expects to find a loop in an 8, but not in a 4. However, the description of a loop would need to be very flexible if it were to "hit" all possible 8s, and then probably loops would be found in many other places where they are not expected, including in some 4s. However, if we view loops just as another generic object being detected, as described in chapter 8, then it becomes a feature detected at certain locations. It would have certain statistics on the different classes that would affect its use in the classification trees. It is a more global feature than the ones used up to now and perhaps bears more discriminating power. We will see some pointers to this in the next chapter. Fully incorporating features that are more global and involve a prior detection process into classification appears to be a promising research direction.

10 Scene Analysis: Merging Detection and Recognition

The object-detection algorithms described in earlier chapters are dedicated to finding instances of a particular predefined object in a scene. On the other hand, the input to the classification trees in chapter 9 was an image in which the object is more or less centered and not much else is present. What should be done when faced with a scene containing several tens from a collection of hundreds or thousands of objects? If for each object we had a very accurate detector with extremely low false-positive and false-negative rates, we could in principle run each such model and obtain a labeling of all the objects in the image. However, this would undoubtedly be a very inefficient approach.

As discussed in the Introduction, the prevailing paradigm for analyzing complex scenes assumes an initial "bottom-up" stage of segmentation that does not employ any prior information on the object class or classes. This stage provides candidate regions of objects in the scene that should, in principle, include the object and not much more. The regions would subsequently be fed into a classifier.

We will explore a different approach in which the initial processing stage always involves detection of a sparse model. However, the detector is now designed to detect more than one particular class—it is a detector for a *cluster* of objects, which may contain subsets of some classes and the entire population of other classes. The detection provides an estimate of pose with which data in a region of interest in the image can be registered to the reference grid. This registered data is then classified into one of the several classes in the object cluster. Even though the detector we use is less specific, it still selects only a small number of candidate poses for further processing, determined by the shape information encoded in the model. The advantage over bottom-up processing is that even if parts of the object boundaries are ambiguous (e.g., the object is partially covered by another and segmentation merges the two into one region, or a lighting effect creates an artificial boundary inside the object), the detector can still identify an approximate pose for the target object and thus provide reasonable input into the classifier. Another advantage is the following: The detection algorithm uses complex features such as edge arrangements, which are rare in the background. If these are the local features being registered to the reference grid and used to classify, there is much less clutter in the neighborhood of the object.

In the next section, we illustrate these ideas in the context of detection and recognition among three different chess pieces in a real image. Following that, we explore detection and recognition in scenes produced with symbols, both artificial LaTeX scenes and zip codes. Finally, in section 10.3 we discuss possible strategies for creating object clusters in a more systematic way.

10.1   Classification of Chess Pieces in Gray-Level Images

We study a very limited problem of detecting and recognizing among three different chess pieces: a knight, a rook, and a queen, all black. The difference between the queen, the bishop, and the king at the resolution of images we acquired was too small to obtain reasonable discrimination. One prototype image is acquired on a flat background for each of the three objects, as shown in figure 10.1.

Each of the prototypes is perturbed with a sequence of 100 random affine maps to produce a database for training a sparse model and a set of classification trees. In terms of the production of the training set, this is the very same procedure used for the LaTeX data in the previous chapter and for the clip detector: One prototype is used to produce a small sample for training. Samples of each are shown in figure 10.2. The

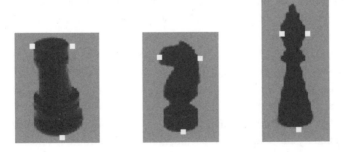

Figure 10.1   The prototype image of three chess pieces. Overlaid on the prototype are the three pose reference points used to register the object to the reference grid.

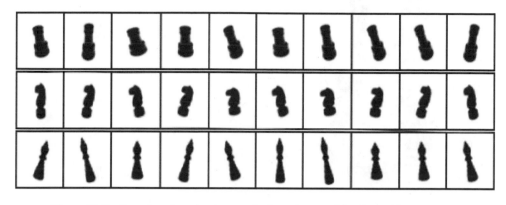

Figure 10.2   Samples of randomly perturbed prototypes of the three objects.

coordinates of the three pose reference points chosen on the prototypes are mapped according to the random affine map to produce three anchor points for each of the perturbed images.

Edges are extracted from each of the 300 perturbed images, 100 per class, and reregistered to the reference grid. This data is then used to train a sparse model for the *union* of the three classes. We use features with three edges, a center edge and two additional edges ($n_r = 2$), requiring each feature to be present in at least 50% of the data. These features will be used for classification as well, so we take as many as are found (i.e., one for each 3×3 region in the reference grid), yielding 30 features. The threshold τ, for the number of hits to declare a detection, was set to 17 by finding the largest value with no false negatives on the training data. The local features obtained in the model are shown in figure 10.3.

The model we observe is some combination of common elements we would obtain from producing separate models for the three different pieces. In figure 10.4, we show several detections of this model on training data from the three classes. Note in figure 10.4 that due to the low threshold, a given instance of an object may be hit with several detections, yielding several different poses. We need to keep this in mind when training the classification trees.

The detector is run on the training data of the three classes. For every training image, we register the feature data to the reference grid, for *each* detection obtained in terms of the detected pose, using equation 8.2. In this case, the data consist of all instances of the 30 features used for the detection. Thus if a detection hits the upper part of the shape, the registered data concentrates on the lower part of the reference grid, and vice versa if the lower part of the shape is hit. This is illustrated in figure 10.5,

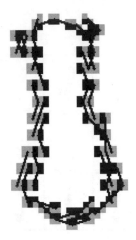

Figure 10.3 The 42 model features obtained for the combined class of rooks, knights and queens.

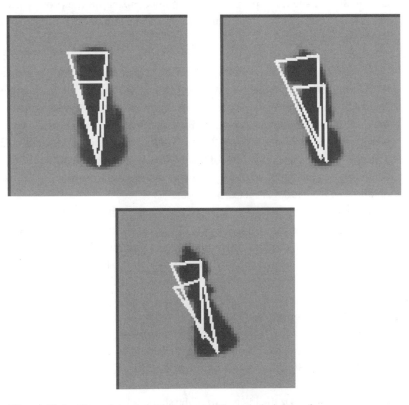

Figure 10.4 Hits of the detector on a sample rook, knight and queen.

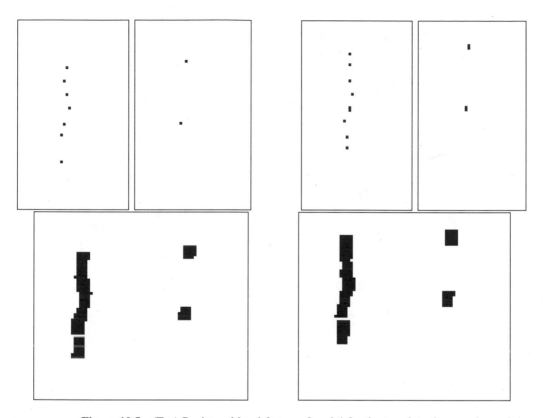

Figure 10.5   (Top) Registered local features 0 and 4 for the two detections on the rook in figure 10.4. (Bottom) The data after spreading the features in 5 × 5 neighborhoods prior to classification.

where the registered locations of 2 of the 30 features are shown for the detections on the rook in figure 10.4. Note that we have constrained the reference grid to a 60 × 30 window around the three reference points. This allows us to limit the clutter to the close neighborhood of the detection. The labeled and registered local feature maps obtained from training data are used to produce fifty randomized decision trees using absolute arrangements and a spreading parameter $s = 5$.

In figure 10.6, we show a detection and classification on an image with a rook. The rook is placed on a wood texture that responds to the edge detectors in many locations. Despite the fact that to our eyes the rook appears perfectly well separated from the background, in terms of the initial edge input to the algorithm, there is significant clutter in the neighborhood of the object. The left-hand column of figure 10.6 shows

Figure 10.6   (Left column) Locations of horizontal and vertical edges of two polarities in the image. (Right column) Top: Classified detection. Locations of local features 0, 4, 12 of the sparse model in the image.

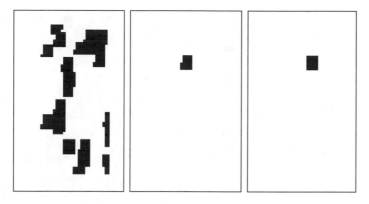

Figure 10.7   Registered local features 0, 4, and 12 on the reference grid from around the detection shown in figure 10.6.

the locations of horizontal and vertical edges of the two polarities. The lower three panels of the right-hand column show the locations of three of the edge arrangements in the model. The density is significantly lower. It is possible to employ other complex local features for classification; however, from the computational point of view, it is very convenient to use features that have already been detected.

In figure 10.7, we show registered local features (0, 4, 12) from the region of interest (ROI) around the detection. Despite the fact that these features are less frequent, they still produce noise in the background that can potentially confuse the classifier. Constraining the reference grid to a narrow window around the three pose reference points helps but cannot entirely solve the problem (see, for example, the registered data for feature 0). Moreover, constraining the window too far will lead to a loss of important information for classification. In figures 10.8 and 10.9 we show some additional examples of classified detections, including some misclassifications.

First note that classification is invariant to a range of variations in scale, rotation, and other transformations occurring due to the change of the position of the object relative to the camera. The reasons for the misclassifications are usually quite apparent. For example, in many cases, if some long dark vertical object is standing behind the rook it will be misclassified as a queen, which has no horizontal structure at the top. If a dark structure is present near the upper left-hand part of the rook, it will be misclassified as a knight. In addition, there are false positives that do not correspond to any of the three pieces. The human eye is rarely fooled by such problems. This is probably due to two factors. At the low level, the visual system probably employs a richer and more powerful collection of local features not solely based on edges. At the high

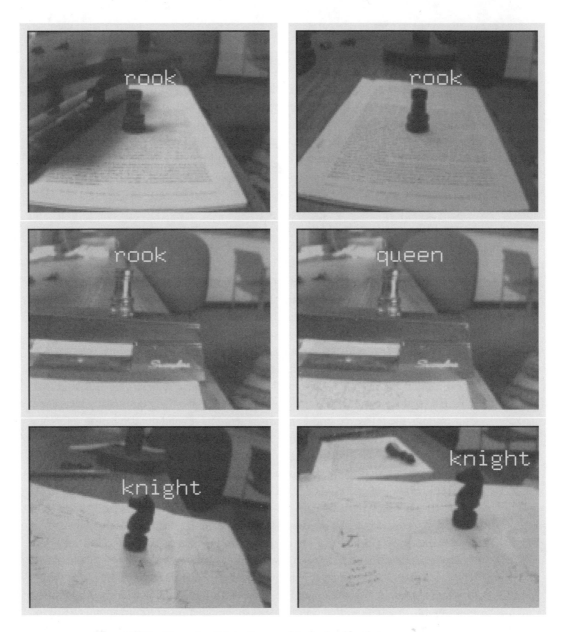

Figure 10.8   Example of detections and their classification.

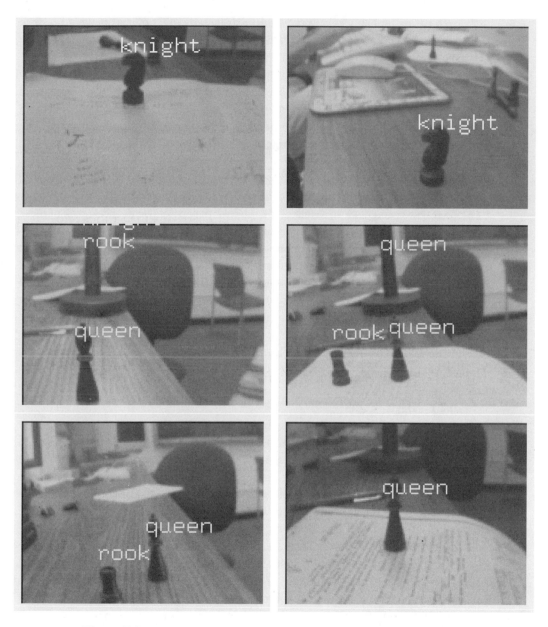

Figure 10.9   Example of detections and their classification.

level, we are probably able to *simultaneously* classify other objects in the immediate neighborhood of the piece and thereby provide more convincing explanations of the data.

Further analysis of the output of the classifier is always possible. One of the deformable models for the identified class can be fit to the data in the region of interest in order to obtain more detailed instantiation information. Furthermore, an upper bound on the fit of each model to examples of the correct class can be estimated from training data. Any fit above this bound is rejected. We have not implemented such a step in the current experiments.

This form of processing can also be used to solve ambiguities. Note that the output of the multiple classification trees consists of a weight on each of the classes. If other classes have weight close to that of the mode, it may be of use to check each of these candidates in terms of a more detailed model.

Some degree of rotation invariance in detection and classification is apparent, but these are limited, and the algorithm will fail with significant rotations in the plane of view or rotations around the vertical axis of a piece, such as the knight, which is not rotationally symmetric. In the present context, the opposite orientation of the knight would have to be treated as a separate object in the collection.

10.2   Detecting and Classifying Characters

10.2.1   LaTeX Scenes

In this section, we report similar experiments with 62 LaTeX symbols (10 digits, 26 uppercase and 26 lowercase letters) and handwritten zip codes. The only difference with the previous section is that we use a sparse model trained on a particular class, in this case the symbol "0," as opposed to the entire collection of classes. The motivation here is that training with the union of all the classes would result in a very nonspecific model with numerous false positives. There is not much in common in terms of the shapes of all 62 symbols. One alternative is to train for one class and then resolve the ambiguities due to false positives using a classifier. The sparse model for the "0" is trained with 32 random samples of the "0" class. From this sample, 32 local edge arrangements were found of complexity $n_r = 3$. The threshold $\tau = 24$ is needed to keep all training samples of the "0." This detector is then run on examples from all 62 classes (32 of each) with a threshold $.8 * \tau = 19$. This is quite a loose threshold, permitting quite a number of detections on other classes. Detections are registered to

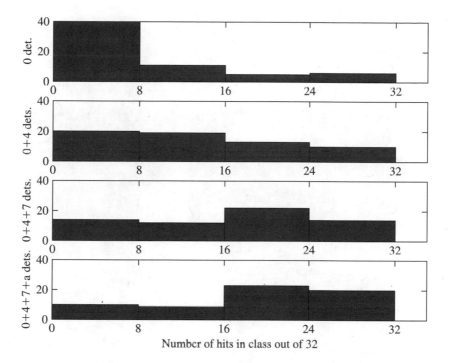

Figure 10.10   The histograms show the distribution over the 62 classes of the number of samples (out of 32) hit by the corresponding union of detectors. For example with the "0" detector alone only six classes are hit at above 28 samples out of the 32. With all four detectors 20 classes are hit at above 28 samples out of the 32.

the reference grid, and multiple classification trees are trained, using the local features from the "0" model. In the first histogram in figure 10.10, we show the distribution over the 62 classes of the number of training examples (out of 32) hit by the "0" detector.

In figure 10.11, we show results on some artificial LaTeX scenes. The entire procedure of detection and classification on images with approximately 30 symbols takes on the order of 250 milliseconds on the Pentium III 700 MHz. There are more detections present than shown in the image. Detections are clustered according to the procedure outlined in chapter 8. However, now, to represent the cluster, we no longer choose the detection with the largest number of detected local features, rather, the choice depends on the output of the classifier. Recall that classification is performed with 50 randomized trees, which are aggregated as in equation 9.4. Each

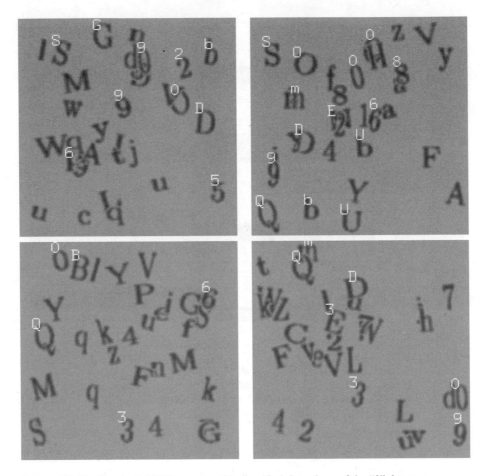

Figure 10.11   Synthetic LaTeX scenes with classified detections of the "0" detector.

detection in the cluster is classified according to the mode of the aggregate. We choose the detection with highest weight at the mode. This, in some sense, is the detection in the cluster that is classified with the most "confidence." Because every detection is classified prior to clustering, there is more information available that is not used in the present context—for example, the actual weights on the different classes provided by the aggregates, or the class labels assigned to other detections in the cluster. All these could help disambiguate confusions and reduce the number of errors.

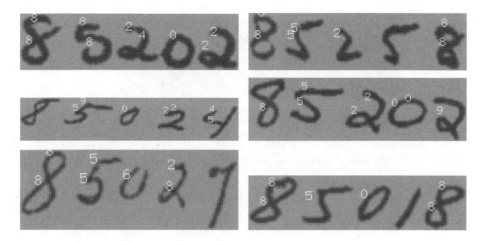

Figure 10.12   Detection and classification on zip codes.

10.2.2   Zip Codes

For the zip code experiment, a "0" detector is trained on 1,000 zeros from the NIST data set. Due to an erroneous setting of the scaling of the training set, the detector was produced for a "0" half the size of the standard 32×32. This detector is therefore hitting loops and parts of loops in the larger images. The detector is run on a subset of 20,000 images from the NIST data set from all classes to produce the data for training the classification trees. In this case, the edges and not the edge arrangements were used for classification. Twenty randomized classification trees were trained. Some results of detection and classification on zip code images are shown in figure 10.12. This does not represent the final analysis of a zip code, merely the classification of the detections of the "0" detector.

In some of these images, one could have easily implemented a prior segmentation using some simple principle. This is not always the case, and any bottom-up segmentation of zip codes must be able to identify the misleading cases. One example is shown in figure 10.13. Here, some digits are joined together. We purposefully show all the detections in this image with no clustering to illustrate the fact that there is information to be obtained from all detections not just those that end up representing a cluster.

There are still plenty of errors in these initial detection-and-recognition experiments—less so if tested on isolated digits. For example, the same procedure was applied to 10,000 USPS digits. On each USPS image, all detections are classified and

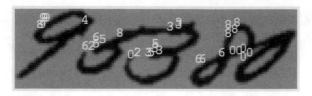

Figure 10.13   All classified detections on a zip code with no clustering.

if any one of them is correct, the digit is counted as correctly classified. Of the 10,000 images, there was a detection in 7,416 and of these, 93% were correctly classified in this manner. The large number of detections of the "0" detector is due to the fact that the model was trained for zeros half the standard size. With the lower threshold, any part of a loop is detected—for example, the upper part of a "4." It appears that we have used something between a global model for a particular object and a local feature. The "0" detector trained on the smaller scale can be viewed as a generic part that appears in many classes; however, when detected, this part helps determine the location and scale of the object as opposed to a local feature, which in itself can only loosely indicate location.

Bear in mind that these results are produced through direct implementation of the detection and classification procedures. Both the detection and the classification models are trained on relatively small samples of the NIST and are being tested on the more variable USPS database. Thus there appears to be some promise in such a top-down approach in which scene analysis is guided by some form of sparse object model that facilitates useful groupings of local features. It is important to recall that no prior segmentation is performed to identify objects, and the computation time is on the order of one second or less.

10.3   Object Clustering

A fundamental question arises in this context. How should the sparse-detection models be constructed so that on one hand, all elements of all classes are detected by at least one detector, and on the other hand, the number of detectors and the number of false positives on *generic background* is minimized? This can be formulated as a clustering problem. We want to form object clusters that cover the entire population, minimizing the number of clusters on one hand, and the "diameter" of the clusters on the other. Here the term *diameter* is used figuratively. Clusters with a large diameter will yield detectors with many hits and false positives. Note that there is no particular need for the clusters to be disjoint. However, it is obviously wasteful to detect the same object class multiple times.

Another question is how to produce the final scene interpretation. As we have seen, the detectors hit different parts of the object and the same object can be classified in several ways. Some classified detections will be inconsistent, as can be observed in the top-left zip code image of figure 10.12. There needs to be a clearly defined mechanism to generate candidate *scene interpretations* from the set of classified detections and to rank them according to some cost function. An interpretation involves making decisions regarding inconsistent classifications, deciding which objects are occluded, and so on. This also requires deciding exactly what are the "on-object" pixels for a particular classified detection and is closely related to final processing, perhaps using some of the deformation algorithms described in earlier chapters. Solutions to the second question of scene interpretation are beyond the scope of this book, although it is hoped that the array of tools we have presented can contribute to the solution. In the discussion section, we briefly mention some scene interpretation methods dedicated to "linear" scenes, such as zip codes and other images of text.

In the next section, we offer some suggestions for dealing with the problem of object clustering. We describe two possible approaches: In the first, we do not assume all classes are presented from the start—classes are learned sequentially. In the second approach, we assume all examples are present at the initial stage, and clusters are created using classification trees.

10.3.1   Sequential Object Clustering

Classes are presented sequentially in some predetermined order. A sparse model for the first class is trained and the detection algorithm corresponding to this model is applied to samples from a number of new object classes, as demonstrated in the previous section. Those data points from the training set that are hit form a cluster. The cluster is entirely defined in terms of the detector and the threshold used. A lower threshold produces a larger cluster. The training data can be used to estimate the conditional probabilities on class within this cluster.

Some classes will be fully detected and need not be addressed further—the original "0" detector serves as their detector as well. Other classes are partially detected and will need an additional detector to fully cover all samples. One approach is to produce a detector for a class that is poorly detected by the "0"—for example, the "4" (we skip the "1" because it has very little structure). Run the identical procedure with this detector, identify the training data in the new cluster, and produce appropriate classifiers. There will be overlaps between the two clusters, meaning that some data will be hit by the two detectors and may even be classified in two different ways. In the second histogram in figure 10.10, we show the distribution over the 62 classes of the number of training examples (out of 32) hit by the "0" *or* the "4" detector—namely, the union of the two clusters. Some progress has been made in terms of covering the entire population. The third and fourth histograms show the same information for the union of the "0," "4," "7" detectors and of the "0," "4," "7," and "a" detectors.

One hopes that the number of models needed to cover the entire population grows more slowly than the number of classes. In the context of view-based 3D object detection and recognition, each object is represented by a number of 2D models, namely, each 3D object generates a number of 2D classes, corresponding to different viewpoints. If the number of models grows linearly with the number of 2D classes, we are headed toward an explosion in the number of required models. It is hoped that different views of different objects will merge into common clusters, and this explosion can be avoided.

This clustering approach does not require having all the training data for all the classes available ahead of time and can be viewed as a crude way to mimic sequential learning of new classes. However, it is very redundant in that many data points will be hit by more than one detector. In other words, the clusters are far from disjoint.

10.3.2   Tree-Based Class Clustering

An alternative approach to creating the clusters is using the classification tree machinery introduced in chapter 9. We start with a simplifying assumption that all detectors are produced with a fixed set of feature types—for example, all two-edge arrangements such as those defined in chapter 9. Grow a classification tree (or an unsupervised tree, ignoring class labels; see section 9.1) of moderate depth on the training data, using absolute arrangements, as described in chapter 9. Each terminal node of the tree defines an object cluster. These are images of various classes that have answered the same way to a sequence of queries and hence necessarily have certain similarities in terms of shape. They all carry the same absolute arrangement. In fact, the queries along the path to the terminal node can serve as *part* of the model that is subsequently derived for the cluster. More than one tree can be used to obtain a more robust covering of the population.

Once a model is determined for the data at a terminal node, a classifier is trained to discriminate between the classes in the cluster. The detector is applied to each of the training images, the labeled data is registered to the reference grid in terms of the detected pose, and then multiple randomized classification trees are used to produce a classifier. Note that in this context the depth of the clustering tree determines the number of clusters. By definition, the set of terminal nodes of the tree covers the entire training set. This is in contrast to the previous clustering method where there was no way to predetermine the number of clusters. The deeper the tree, the larger the number of clusters on one hand, but then the associated models are more specific, and one would expect a smaller number of false positives from this collection of models. The hard task is to find the appropriate balance between these two variables.

It is interesting to note that this approach closes the loop between sparse models and classification trees based on arrangements of local features. A detection model is based on a cluster defined by a classification tree, and the registered data around a detection is subsequently classified with additional classification trees.

10.4   Bibliographical Notes and Discussion

In this chapter, no model is presented for the layout of the objects in the scene or their number. Typically, there is more contextual information that can be exploited. Zip codes are a very clear example wherein there is a fixed number of objects in the scene, and there are very clear constraints on how the objects are arranged. Given a set of multiple trees trained to classify among the digits, any candidate slice of the zip code image can be classified and also assigned a "confidence level" according to the magnitude of the mode of the aggregate distribution $A_N(c)$ (see equation 9.4). A range of slices covering some locations and slants is determined for each of the five digits. Dynamic programming based on the confidence levels of the slices finds the optimal set of five slices. The labels assigned to these slices have already been recorded and provide the outcome—this is the outline in the approach taken in Wang (1998). In LeCun and colleagues (1998), a much more sophisticated version of this idea is implemented. A bottom-up oversegmentation of the image is performed, with certain segments possibly containing subsets of the digits. Dynamic programming is now performed on possible individual segments or consecutive pairs. The system is improved by training classifiers with "parts" of other digits in the image, as well as training the weighting of the different components of the cost functions of the dynamic programming using labeled zip codes, where the answer is known. Another interesting idea suggested in this work is using the classifier to determine candidate segments. The classifier is run on the entire scene, and locations with high confidence become candidate segments for the dynamic programming. Other ideas on the use of high-level knowledge on the layout of the scene have been extensively exploited in the document analysis community (see Nagy 2000).

Typical images that our visual system encounters do not have such clear structure. Humans can quickly and successfully parse a scene with digits scattered about randomly with various sizes, shapes, and occlusions. It is therefore of interest to pursue the issue of scene analysis using models less restrictive than the "linear" ones described above.

It is important to reiterate that each detection carries with it much more information than has actually been used—for example, the precise locations of those features detected by the detector. So far, we have classified by registering *all* features found in the region of interest to the reference grid. It may be that there is useful information in the particular features found by the detector. Other information comes in the form of a match to a deformable model. In chapter 8, we showed how more-detailed models can be matched to the object following detection. Quantities measured in terms of these matches may be useful in pruning out false positives and making final determinations in classification.

The sparse models used here are quite successful in detecting objects with reasonable numbers of false positives. These models make a "leap" directly from the local features to the global models. With hundreds of possible local features and hundreds of possible locations on the reference grid, the number of possible models is enormous. The question is whether a relatively small number of models can cover a large collection of object classes without being too "trivial" in the sense that these models end up having numerous false positives. In chapter 8, we mentioned the ideas proposed in Biederman (1995), whereby objects are represented as coarse arrangements of generic parts. It may be that an intermediate level is necessary, involving a rather small number of generic-shape models, much like the "0" model used for the zip codes, which effectively detects small loops. These generic-shape models are then used to produce the entire library of object models. The object models could be even coarser than the current sparse models, because the components are more complex. For example, they could be defined on a much coarser reference grid. The chance of a particular configuration of these components occurring at random is very small. It is possible that detection is then limited to very simple configurations of these generic shapes. The difficult question is what price is paid in terms of false positives, if these generic components are to be stable on the objects.

11   Neural Network Implementations

There are fundamental differences between the form of computation performed in a serial computer and that performed in a massively parallel system of very primitive computational units. On a computer, we can learn a model for faces or any other object using our favorite technique, the model is stored using whatever complex data structures we need, and then by brute force, using the power of random-access memory, the model can be applied at every shifted location and scale to decide if an object is present there or not. In a parallel system, which mirrors the visual scene with a unit or multiple units for every pixel location, processing the data in its neighborhood, the question is how to *shift* a model learned and stored in some central location to all other locations in the system.

The dominant paradigm for learning in neural systems is through modification of the value of the connections between pairs of units. If, say, the connections at the central location of the system have been modified to classify face versus nonface, we can hardly imagine the values of these connections being shifted in some mysterious way to all other locations of the system. Moreover, what happens when we want to detect a clip and not a face? How does the entire parallel system know to change so as to detect clips and not faces?

Turning to classification, assume that the connections at the central location have been modified so that we can classify among the ten handwritten digits. What if a digit appears at a shifted location? The visual system can still recognize the digit without actually directly looking toward it, as long as it is not too far out in the periphery. Again we ask, how does the classifier encoded in the central location get shifted? One possibility is that the classifier is learned separately at each location—the appropriate connections are modified at each location in the system using training data presented at that location. This is not a viable solution, because we can very well learn an object model or a classifier at one location and scale and then recognize it anywhere else in the scene.

Both the sparse-detection models and the recognition algorithms described in the previous chapters are based on simple computations in terms of simple binary local features. In this chapter, these ingredients will be used to construct a parallel system able to overcome the difficulties described above. The system will integrate learning of individual object models for detection, learning of classifiers, and the implementation of detection and recognition over the entire visual scene. Neurons and their synaptic connections are modeled at a very simplistic level, avoiding the detailed complexities of their operation; however, the entire system does offer a "global" hypothesis as to how the visual system learns objects and detects them and how different object classes are recognized. After describing this network architecture, some analogies to the architecture of the biological visual system will be discussed.

11.1   Basic Network Architecture

11.1.1   Neurons and Synapses

The building block of the model is a binary neuron v receiving input from binary neurons u_i through directed synapses with efficacies J_{ij}, as illustrated in figure 11.1. The input connections from the neurons u_i are called *afferent* connections of v_j. Each neuron can either be on or off, denoted 1 and 0, respectively, and has an associated threshold θ. The neuron is on if the local field of the neuron, namely, the weighted

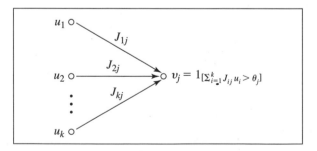

Figure 11.1 k presynaptic units feeding into v. The output of all units is binary 0/1. The output of v_j is obtained by taking the thresholded sum of the output of the units u_i.

sum of its inputs, is above the threshold θ. Specifically,

$$v_j = \begin{cases} 1 & \text{if } \sum_{i=1}^{k} u_i J_{ij} > \theta \\ 0 & \text{Otherwise} \end{cases} \tag{11.1}$$

The local field h_j of the neuron j is defined as

$$h_j = \sum_{i=1}^{k} u_i J_{ij} \tag{11.2}$$

11.1.2 Layer Connections

The network architecture has the form of layers of neurons feeding into other layers. Different neurons can have different thresholds; however, in order to maintain the simplicity of the system, neurons of the same layer all have the same threshold. In the material presented below, there are no connections within a layer—known as recurrent connections. Such connections are a crucial component of the real neural system and have a very important role to play in stabilizing the system and enabling consistent memory recovery, but they are beyond the scope of this chapter. Material on recurrent mechanisms can be found in Amit (1989) and Brunel, Carusi, and Fusi (1998).

In figure 11.2, we see a schematic diagram of a number of layers with connections between them. The arrows represent synaptic connections and indicate the direction in which information is flowing. Given two layers, A and B, we denote by $A \rightarrow B$

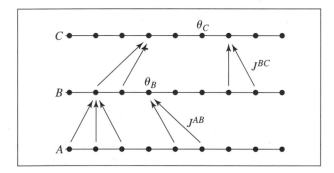

Figure 11.2   A schematic diagram of layers of neurons feeding into other layers. The efficacies of $A \rightarrow B$ synapses are all fixed at J^{AB}, and efficacies of $B \rightarrow C$ synapses are all J^{BC}. Neuron thresholds in B are all θ_B and in C are all θ_C.

synapses, those directed from layer A to B. We will also assume that the maximal synaptic efficacy for $A \rightarrow B$ synapses is constant at J^{AB}.

Input presented at some point in the system—for example, layer A in figure 11.2, is assumed to propagate in an orderly fashion from layer to layer one step at a time. This is a gross oversimplification, because the actual dynamics of a neural system are much more complex and chaotic, with neurons typically firing asynchronously at random times.

11.1.3   Visual Input: Edges and Edge Arrangements

The visual input layers are organized *retinotopically,* meaning that they form a two-dimensional grid corresponding to the entire image lattice L. These layers will consist of coarse-oriented edge detectors of the same type described in chapters 5 and 6. For any retinotopic layer B, we write $B(x) = 1/0$ according to whether the unit in B corresponding to location $x \in L$ is on or off. We thus have eight retinotopic layers $E_e, e = 1, \ldots, 8$, where a unit $E_e(x) = 1$ if an edge of type e is found at location x in the image.

The next system of layers will be wired to compute the locations of all $N = 256$ two-edge arrangements consisting of a center edge and one additional edge, as described in section 6.4. This particular collection of simple two-edge arrangements was also used as input to the classification trees in chapter 9. Let $\mathcal{R} = \{R_1, \ldots, R_m\}$ be the collection of regions used to define the edge arrangements (see section 6.4). For each edge type e, define a system of retinotopic layers $C_{e,k}, k = 1, \ldots, m$. A unit $x \in C_{e,k}$ receives input from the region $x + R_k$ in E_e. It is on (i.e., $C_{e,k}(x) = 1$) if any unit in $x + R_k$ is on in E_e, namely, if

$$\max_{y \in x + R_k} E_e(y) = 1$$

Let the synaptic efficacies between layers E and C all be of value J^{EC}, and let the threshold of all neurons in C be $\theta_C = J^{EC} - \epsilon$. This implies that input from only *one* presynaptic neuron is sufficient to activate the neuron in C.

The two-edge local features are computed in retinotopic layers $F_\alpha, \alpha = 1, \ldots, N$. Each feature α is defined by a triple (e, e', R_k), where e denotes the type of the center edge and e' the second edge, which is required to be present somewhere in the region R_k relative to the location of e. Each $x \in F_\alpha$ receives input from $x \in E_e$ and from $x \in C_{e',k}$ and is on only if *both* are on,

$$F_\alpha(x) = \min(E_e(x), C_{e',k}(x))$$

Let $J^{EF} = J^{CF} = J$, and for the neurons in the F layers, set the threshold to

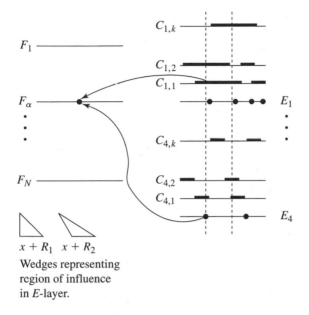

Wedges representing
region of influence
in E-layer.

Figure 11.3   Retinotopic layers for detecting two-edge arrangements. Four E layers detect edge locations. For each E_e layer there is a $C_{e,k}$ corresponding to each $R_k, k = 1, \ldots, m$. All in all $4 \times m - C$ layers. There is an F layer for each local feature. For feature $\alpha = (4, 1, R_1)$ each location x in the F_α layer receives input from *the same location x* in $C_{1,1}$ and in E_4.

$\theta_F = 2J - \epsilon$. In this case, two presynaptic neurons need to be on for the unit in the F layer to be on. The full system of E, C, and F layers is shown in figure 11.3.

11.2   Hebbian Learning

The prevailing assumption regarding synaptic modification, formulated in Hebb (1949), is that it depends only on the state of the presynaptic neuron a and that of the postsynaptic neuron b. There are many possible ways to implement this general principle (see, for example, Hopfield 1982; Kohonen 1984; Amit 1989; Fusi and colleagues 2000). In the current context, we employ a simple version of the methods used in Amit and Brunel (1995). Information learned by the system is coded exclusively in internal states of the synapses denoted S_{ab}, for a synapse connecting neurons a and b. The activity of the two neurons produces modifications in the internal synaptic states that then translates through a transfer function into the synaptic efficacy.

If both neurons are on, *synaptic potentiation* occurs, namely, the internal state increases by c_+. If the presynaptic neuron is on but the postsynaptic neuron is off, *synaptic depression* occurs, namely, the internal state decreases by c_-. The values of S_{ab} are always restricted between 0 and S_{max}. This is written in compact form as

$$\Delta S_{ab} = c_+ u_a u_b - c_- u_a (1 - u_b), \quad \text{if } 0 \leq S + \Delta S_{ab} \leq S_{max} \tag{11.3}$$

otherwise, $\Delta S_{ab} = 0$.

The synaptic efficacies are simple functions of this internal state—that is, $J_{ab} = J(S_{ab})$ where

$$J(S) = \begin{cases} 0 & \text{for } S \leq L \\ \frac{S-L}{H-L} J^{AB} & \text{for } L < S < H \\ J^{AB} & \text{for } S \geq H \end{cases} \tag{11.4}$$

for some positive $L \leq H$ and J^{AB}, which is the maximal value of the efficacy of a synapse connecting two layers A and B. If $H = L$, the synaptic efficacies are binary with values 0 and J^{AB} only. If $L < H$, there is a ramp between the low value 0 and the high value J^{AB}.

11.3   Learning an Object Model

Images from a training set for a particular object class are now presented to the system, registered to the reference grid G. Think of G as a subgrid placed at the center of the image grid L. Those parts of the F layers corresponding to the region G feed directly into a module M. This component of the network is no longer assumed to be retinotopic and is therefore called a module. Each unit in M receives input from one unit in the G subregion of the F layers. Thus M has a unit for each pair consisting of local feature α and a location $z \in G$, namely, $N \times |G|$ units. In our particular example, we will be using a 32×32 reference grid and 256 two-edge features so that the number of units in M is $N_M = 262, 144$. A unit $m = (\alpha, z) \in M$ is on if $F_\alpha(z) = 1$.

Also feeding into M is an "abstract" module A that we use to code object classes. For each class c, there is a class subset A_c of A, which is randomly selected, of fixed proportion P_A. The set A_c is used to code for class c. While the system is learning the model for class c, there is some hidden "teacher" that is able to activate the subset A_c through channels outside the visual system. Each unit in M receives input from some *random* collection of units in A, of proportion P_{AM}. We place random connections because these modules are *not* retinotopically organized, and there is no preference

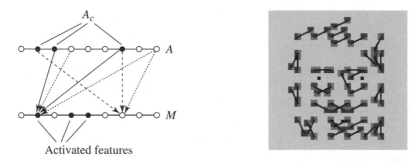

Activated features

Figure 11.4 (Left) Learning the object model. A_c units are activated at the same time data from class c is presented to F and replicated in M. Dark solid arrows: potentiating synapses (pre- and postsynaptic neurons on.) Dark dashed arrows: depressing synapses (presynaptic neuron on, postsynaptic neuron off.) Dotted arrows: no change in synaptic state. (Right) An object model learned for faces using two-edge features.

for any particular connection. During training, the local features from a registered image of class c are computed in F and the corresponding units are turned on in M. At the same time, the units in A_c are turned on in A (figure 11.4).

Let $m = (\alpha, z)$ be an activated unit in M. About $P_A \cdot P_{AM} \cdot |A|$ units $a \in A_c$ are feeding into m and all are on. The synaptic state S_{am} from each such unit is increased by c_+, as prescribed in equation 11.3. The synaptic state of any synapse connecting a unit $a \in A_c$ to a unit $m \in M$, which is *not* on, is decreased by c_- (figure 11.4). As examples of objects of class c are presented, the internal state of each synapse, connecting a unit $a \in A_c$ to some unit $m \in M$, is performing a random walk. The mean increment of this walk is given by

$$\delta_{am} = c_+ p_{m,c} - c_-(1 - p_{m,c})$$

where

$$p_{m,c} = P(F_\alpha(z) = 1 \mid Y = c)$$

is the probability of feature α occurring at location z for object class c. Let $\sigma = c_-/c_+$, then, after a large number of presentations, for those units m with

$$\frac{p_{m,c}}{1 - p_{m,c}} > \sigma, \quad \text{or} \quad p_{m,c} > \frac{\sigma}{1 + \sigma} \doteq \rho \tag{11.5}$$

The synaptic state S_{am} will tend to have a value closer to S_{max}, otherwise, the synaptic state will have a lower value closer to 0. If the efficacies are binary, it is possible to set the value of $L = H$ in equation 11.4 in such a way that when $p_{m,c} > \rho$, the synapse J_{am} will be enabled with high probability. This system is learning an object model as prescribed in the learning stage of the sparse model described in section 6.4. For each training image, all two-edge arrangements are computed and detected at all locations on the reference grid. Those above some probability are recorded as part of the model. This learning mechanism is schematically described in figure 11.4. The efficacy J^{AM} is set so that the input into a unit m from afferent units in A_c is above threshold only if most of these units are on. Thus we take $J^{AM} \sim (\theta_M - \epsilon)/(P_A \cdot P_{AM} \cdot |A|)$, for some small $\epsilon > 0$.

We have already defined the visual low-level input obtained in the layers of oriented edges E_e. High-level input, telling the system which object to look for, is given through external activation of a particular subset A_c, which in turn, after training, will cause the activation of the elements $m_i = (\alpha_i, z_i)$, $i = 1, \ldots, n_c$, belonging to the model for class c. Ultimately, this evoked model will drive a detection system that is capable of applying the model at every location in the image. This is described in section 11.5. On the right panel of figure 11.4, we show a model based on two-edge features trained on the face data. A schematic diagram showing the connections between A, M, F, and E is shown in figure 11.5.

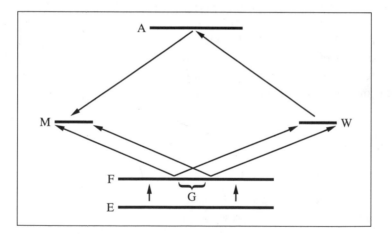

Figure 11.5 Network architecture. E layers—oriented edge detection on visual input. The two-edge arrangements are computed in the F layers. The center part corresponding to the reference grid G is replicated in the M and W modules. The M module receives input from the "abstract" A module. The $A \rightarrow M$ synapses are used to learn object models. A receives input from W and the $W \rightarrow A$ synapses are used to learn classifiers.

In the sequel, it will be important that the same number of features/location pairs m_i are activated for each object model. However, different object classes may have different numbers of activated model units, corresponding to feature-location pairs m with probability $p_{m,c} > \rho$. If all models are expected to have a fixed number n of features, using inhibitory units that receive input from the M layer and feed back into it, it is possible to ensure that only a random subset of size n of the total collection of n_c units remains active. We will not describe the details of such a mechanism here, because it requires introducing some real dynamics into the system.

11.4   Learning Classifiers

The previous section presented a mechanism for learning object models by activating the units A_c at the same time that examples from class c are presented at the reference grid. The two-edge arrangements in the central area of the F layers are computed and activate the corresponding units in M. Now we turn to the problem of recognition or classification, which involves discriminating between different object classes.

While the object models are being learned, the same visual information is copied from the F layers into another module W, similar to M, which again has a unit (α, z) for every feature/location pair (i.e., $N \times |G|$ units). A unit $w = (\alpha, z)$ is on if any unit in some neighborhood of $N_s(z)$ of z in F_α is on. The radius s of the neighborhood determines the degree of "spreading," which was introduced in chapter 9 and is important to ensure geometric invariance of recognition over local deformations and some range of linear transformations. The W module is also connected to A, but now the synapses are directed from W into A (see figure 11.5). Each neuron in A receives connections from a random subset of proportion P_{WA} in W.

11.4.1   Hebbian Learning

When an image from class c is presented in the reference grid, and the neurons in A_c are activated, those synapses connecting activated neurons in W to neurons in A_c are potentiated. If w corresponds to a high probability unit for class c, those synapses connecting w to units in A_c will all tend to have a high internal state after several presentations of samples from class c. When an object from another class d is presented to the system, a different subset A_d is activated in module A. If w also corresponds to a high probability unit in class d it will tend to be on during presentations of class d, but the corresponding units in A_c will be off. This is precisely the setting in which the synapses connecting W to elements in A_c get depressed—that is, the internal state decreases.

For each unit $w = (\alpha, z)$, let $p_{w,c}$ denote the probability of feature α in the neighborhood of z on class c

$$p_{w,c} = P\left(\max_{y \in N_s(z)} F_\alpha(y) = 1 \mid Y = c \right)$$

We introduce an additional quantity $q_{w,c}$, which is the probability of feature α at location z on the set of images *not* of class c

$$q_{w,c} = P\left(\max_{y \in N_s(z)} F_\alpha(y) = 1 \mid Y \neq c \right)$$

Let $P(c), c = 1, \ldots, K$ denote the prior distribution on object classes. Finally, let

$$\tilde{p}_{w,c} \doteq p_{w,c} P(c), \quad \tilde{q}_{w,c} \doteq q_{w,c}(1 - P(c)) \quad \rho_{w,c} \doteq \frac{\tilde{p}_{w,c}}{\tilde{q}_{w,c}} \tag{11.6}$$

The mean synaptic change for a synapse connecting a unit w to a unit $a \in A_c$ is given by

$$\delta S_{wa} = c_+ \tilde{p}_{w,c} - c_- \tilde{q}_{w,c}$$

With a large number of training examples for each class, S_{wa} will move toward one of the two reflecting barriers 0 or S_{max} according to whether the probability ratio

$$\rho_{w,c} > \sigma = \frac{c_-}{c_+} \tag{11.7}$$

or not. The resulting synaptic efficacies will then be either 0 or J^{WA}, respectively. This is in contrast to the situation for $A \to M$ synapses, where the only relevant information is the probability $p_{m,c}$ (except for the case where $a \in A_c \cap A_d$, which we ignore).

After learning is completed, presenting an image from class c at the reference grid will bring about the activation of units in W, which in turn will cause the activation of units in A. The goal is to have the number of units activated in the set A_c to be larger than the number activated in other sets, thus signaling the presence of class c, or the fact that the system has recognized the input as being from class c. The number of units activated in each class subset A_d will depend on the value of J^{WA}, on the threshold θ_A of units in A, on the statistics $\tilde{p}_{w,d}, \tilde{q}_{w,d}$ of the units w, and on the particular image presented. In real data sets, the distribution of the quantities

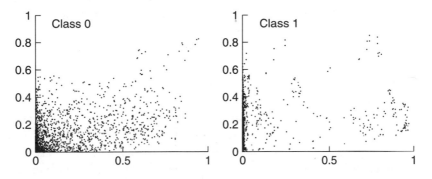

Figure 11.6   *pq* scatter plots for classes '0' and '1' in the NIST dataset. Each point corresponds to one of the feature/location pairs $= (\alpha, z)$. The horizontal axis represents the on class p-probability of the feature, and the vertical axis is the off class q-probability.

$\tilde{p}_{w,c}, \tilde{q}_{w,c}, w \in W$, and hence of $\rho_{w,c}$, is highly variable among different classes. See, for example, figure 11.6, where we show the 2D distribution of these *pq* probabilities for classes "0" and "1" of the NIST data set with which we worked in chapter 9.

The ratio θ_A / J^{WA} determines how many enabled units $w \in W$ need to be on in order to activate a unit in $a \in A_c$. These are, necessarily, units for which $\rho_{w,c} > \sigma$, (defined in equation 11.7); otherwise, the efficacy $J_{wc} = 0$. As an example, take $\theta_A / J_M^{WA} = 10$—that is, input from ten afferent units is sufficient to activate a unit in A. Assume that in class c there are 64 out of 262,144 units satisfying $\rho_{w,c} > \sigma$. For each unit in $a \in A$, let W_a be the set of afferent units of a and suppose that $P_{WA} = .5$ so that W_a is half the size of W (i.e., $|W_a| = 131,072$). Because W_a is a random subset, the expected number of units from W_a satisfying $\rho_{w,c} > \sigma$ is 32 (one half of 64), and the corresponding synapses will have efficacy J^{WA}. Assume that for each such unit $p_{w,c} > .5$. Then, upon presentation of an image of class c, the expected number of these units that are activated is 16. Taking the various random fluctuations into account, the actual number of activated units will be greater than 10, so that with high probability, most units in A_c will be activated.

If, on the other hand, in class d there are only 32 features satisfying the inequality, there is high chance that upon presentation of an image of class d, only a small number of units of A_d will be activated. There is a significant probability that the number of units activated in A_d will be less than the number activated in some other subset $A_{d'}$, leading to a high error rate for class d. Lowering σ in equation 11.7 will enable more synapses from class d to have nonzero efficacy, but then units in A_c will tend to be activated too easily. One solution is to adapt the threshold of the units in A_c to the particular statistics of class c. This, however, would require quite a wide range of thresholds and violates our assumption that neurons in the same module have the same threshold.

11.4.2   Field-Dependent Hebbian Learning

An alternative is to modify the learning rule to depend on the local field of the postsynaptic neuron, which is recomputed for each training image. When the subset A_c is activated together with the presentation of an image from class c, potentiation of an afferent synapse occurs only if the local field h_a, as defined in equation 11.2, is below $\theta(1 + k_p)$, where θ is the threshold of a and $k_p > 0$. Formally, the internal synaptic state is modified as follows.

$$\Delta S_{wa} = \begin{cases} c_+, & \text{if } h_a < \theta(1 + k_p) \quad \text{and} \quad u_w = 1, u_a = 1 \\ -c_-, & \text{if } u_w = 1, u_a = 0 \\ 0. & \text{otherwise} \end{cases} \tag{11.8}$$

The transfer from internal synaptic state to synaptic efficacy, $J_{wa} = J(S_{wa})$, needs to be computed at every update step of training in order to calculate the local field $h_a = \sum_{W_a} J_{wa} u_w$.

Assume that for some $a \in A_c$, at some stage of training, there are K afferent units $w_k \in W_a, k = 1, \dots, K$ for which the internal state $S_{w_k,a} > H$. The efficacies of these synapses are at the maximum value J^{WA}. If $K = \theta(1 + k_p)/J^{WA}$, and if the particular units $w_k, k = 1, \dots, K$ are activated by the current presented image of class c, the field h_a will be at least $\theta(1 + k_p)$. This prevents the internal states of *any* synapse feeding into a from increasing at this presentation, not only those at high internal state. Other images of the same class c may not activate all the units $w_k, k = 1, \dots, K$. The resulting field on a could be smaller. For those units w that are activated by such images, potentiation *can* occur on S_{wa} (figure 11.7). In contrast to regular Hebbian learning, this form of learning is not entirely local at the synaptic level due to the dependence on the field of the neuron.

The main purpose of field constraints on synaptic potentiation is to ensure that after training, the average field at a unit $a \in A_c$ is at approximately the same level upon presentation of an example of class c, irrespective of the specific class distribution of feature probabilities.

For example, after field-dependent training is completed for the NIST database, a certain distribution on the local field of units in A_0 and A_7 will be observed for examples from the correct and incorrect class. This is illustrated in the left panel of figure 11.8. The top panels show the distribution of the field for 0 and 7, respectively

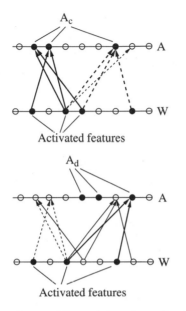

Figure 11.7   Training of classification network. (Top) Class c is presented. (Bottom) Class d is presented. Activity on the same synapses is compared. Thin solid line arrows: nothing happens in these synapses. Thick solid line arrows: potentiating synapses (the local field is not too large.) Thick dashed arrows: local field at neuron is high (three incoming enabled synapses) hence no potentiation, although both pre- and postsynaptic neurons are on. Thin dashed arrows: depressing synapses, presynaptic neuron is on, postsynaptic neuron is off.

when the correct class is presented. The bottom two panels show the distributions for the incorrect class. It is clear that the average fields are very similar for both cases. This allows us to use a *fixed* threshold for all neurons in A. Note that the separation between the correct and incorrect class distributions does not reflect on the classification rate of the network as a whole, as will emerge from the discussion below. For comparison, in the right panel of figure 11.8 we show the histograms of the fields when standard Hebbian learning is employed, all else remaining the same. The large variation in the location of these histograms between the two classes precludes the use of a fixed threshold for both classes.

Field-Dependent Hebbian Learning and Feature Statistics

An interesting question is Which synapses does the field-dependent Hebbian learning tend to enable? There is some form of competition over "synaptic resources" and if there are many units w connected to a unit $a \in A_c$ with a high value of $\rho_{w,c}$, not all

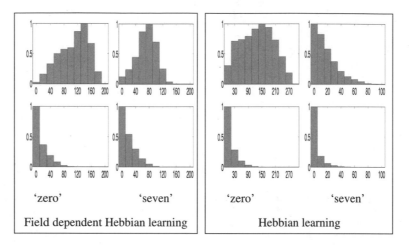

Figure 11.8   (Left) Field dependent Hebbian learning. (Right) Hebbian learning. In each panel the top two histograms are of fields at neurons belonging to class '0' on the left, class '7' on the right, when data points from the *correct* class are presented. The bottom row in each panel shows histograms of fields at neurons belonging to class '0', '7' when data points from the *other* classes are presented.

will be enabled. On the other hand, if there is only a small number of such units, the learning rule will tend to employ more features with lower ratios. In all cases, those synapses coming from units with a higher $\rho_{w,c}$ have a higher chance of being enabled after presentations of examples from class c. Those with higher on-class probability $p_{w,c}$ may get potentiated sooner, but synapses with low $p_{w,c}$ but large $\rho_{w,c}$ gradually get potentiated as well.

If the $W \to A$ synapses are binary, the outcome of the potentiation rule can be approximated quite well as follows: Sort all units according to their $\rho_{w,c}$ ratio. Let $p_{(w),c}$ denote the sorted probabilities on class c in decreasing order of ρ. Pick as many features from the top of the sorted list as are necessary to obtain an expected field of $\theta(1 + k_p)$.

$$\sum_{(w)=1}^{g_c} J_m^{WA} p_{(w),c} \sim \theta(1 + k_p) \tag{11.9}$$

The number g_c depends on the class c.

If the transfer function $J(S)$ is not a simple step function but has a "ramp," the situation is somewhat more complex. However, this allows the network greater flexibility and the classification rates are better.

11.4.3   Classification with Multiple Randomized Perceptrons

After training is completed, each unit $a \in A_c$ has a number of afferent connections (approximately g_c as defined in equation 11.9) from the set $W_a \subset W$ that have been enabled. Due to the randomized connections from W to A, these subsets W_a are different. Now each unit $a \in A_c$ can be viewed as a simple classifier P_a, which discriminates between class c and all the rest.

$$P_a = \begin{cases} 1 & \text{if } \sum_{w \in W_a} J_{wa} u_w > \theta_A \\ 0 & \text{otherwise} \end{cases} \qquad (11.10)$$

In other words, unit a is a simple two-class linear classifier, also known as a *perceptron* (see Minsky and Papert 1969; Duda and Hart 1973). It is a very simple and constrained perceptron in that the weights on the synapses are all positive and bounded by J^{WA}. The classical perceptron can have negative weights on the connections. Because there are many units in A_c, and because W_a is selected randomly, we have produced a large number of such simple classifiers with different sets of enabled synapses.

Visual input is presented at the reference grid and activates units in the W module through the E and F layers. The W layer then causes certain units in A to be activated. Classification is represented by the set A_c, with the largest number of activated neurons—namely, the class that received the most votes from its set of perceptrons.

This classifier, based on multiple randomized perceptrons that are aggregated by voting, is based on the same principle that led to the production of multiple randomized trees in chapter 9. The difference is that each of the classifiers employed here distinguishes only between one class and all other classes joined together. This aggregation of simple classifiers yields surprisingly good results, given the limitations imposed on each of the individual classifiers. For example, on the NIST data set, with 10,000 training samples, a network with 3,000 neurons in the A layer, taking A_c to be of size 300, and $P_{WA} = .2$, $J^{WA} = 10$, $\theta_A = 100$, and in equation 11.8, $k_p = .2$, $c_+ = 4$, and $c_- = 1$, the classification rate is higher than 94%. If several such networks are used with a simple boosting procedure, we observe classification rates of 97.4%. Even for the LaTeX database, with 293 classes, such networks can reach classification rates near 80%, which, although much less than that achieved with trees, is still very encouraging. Note that currently there is no neural analogue of the boosting procedure. For more details on the performance of such networks and the incorporation of attractor dynamics in the A layer, see Amit and Mascaro (2001).

11.5   Detection

We now construct a network for implementing the first step of the counting detector described in chapter 8. Recall that all features used in any object representation come from a predetermined pool $\mathcal{F}$ of 256 features, and the image locations of each feature in $\mathcal{F}$ are detected in the arrays F_α, $\alpha \in \mathcal{F}$. A location x in F_α is on if local feature α is present at location x in the image.

When a particular class A_c is activated in A, the corresponding units $m_i = (\alpha_i, z_i)$, $i = 1, \ldots, n$ of the model are activated in M. This is a result of the learning procedure for the object representation. Step I of the counting detector described in chapter 8 involved counting at each location $x \in L$ how many of the regions $x + B_{z_i}$ contained an instance of the feature α_i for $i = 1, \ldots, n$ (see section 8.1). To implement this in a network, we define, for each local feature array F_α, $\alpha \in \mathcal{F}$, a system of retinotopic layers $Q_{\alpha,z}$ indexed by the locations z in the reference grid G. A unit at location $x \in Q_{\alpha,z}$ receives input from the region $x + B_z$ in F_α and is responsible for checking whether feature α is present in $x + B_z$.

For each unit $m = (\alpha, z)$ in M there is a corresponding $Q_{\alpha,z}$ array. In order for $x \in Q_{\alpha,z}$ to be activated, both $m = (\alpha, z) \in M$ must be on *and* at least one unit in the region $x + B_z$ in F_α. Thus the model evoked in M *primes* the appropriate $Q_{\alpha,z}$ layers to a point where they *could* be activated if the appropriate input comes from below (i.e., the F_α layer). In terms of synaptic efficacies, this can be achieved by having a very strong connection $J^{MQ} = \theta - \delta$ from $m = (\alpha, z)$ to each unit in $Q_{\alpha,z}$ but very weak connections J^{FQ} of order δ such that $|B_z|\delta < \theta$. Input from the region $x + B_z$ in F_α alone cannot activate $x \in Q_{\alpha,z}$. It is necessary for $Q_{\alpha,z}$ to also receive input from $m = (\alpha, z)$. This form of "priming" is rather unrealistic because it assumes a very strong input from one unit $m \in M$ to an entire Q layer of units. One solution is to have a population of units corresponding to each $(\alpha, z) \in M$ that collectively increases the input to all units in $Q_{\alpha,z}$. The system of Q layers sum into a retinotopic detection layer S. A unit at location $x \in S$ receives input from *all* $Q_{\alpha,z}$ arrays at location x, and is on if

$$\sum_{\alpha \in \mathcal{F}} \sum_{z \in G} Q_{\alpha,z}(x) \geq \theta_S$$

where $\theta_S = \tau$ is the threshold for step I of the counting detector. Because the only units active in the Q layers are those corresponding to a count for the specific sparse model activated in M, the active units in the S layer are precisely those locations detected by step I of the counting detector.

Note that if we traverse the $Q_{\alpha,z}$ layers at a fixed location x, those units that are primed by input from M constitute a *shifted* copy of the object model to the region $x + G$. Thus the Q layers are the means by which the model learned in the central M module gets shifted to all locations. Because the detector is a simple thresholded sum with uniform weights, all that needs to be "shifted" is the information on the features and their relative locations, and as we see, this can be achieved by a fixed wiring. No connections need to be changed. If the detector was more complex, even involving a weighted sum, it is not at all clear how the weights in the sum could be shifted in a simple and transparent manner.

This detection network is described in figure 11.9. This is a clear example of location selection driven by top-down flow of information. If a unique location needs

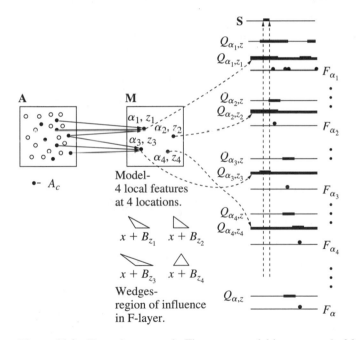
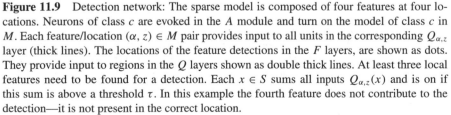

Figure 11.9 Detection network: The sparse model is composed of four features at four locations. Neurons of class c are evoked in the A module and turn on the model of class c in M. Each feature/location $(\alpha, z) \in M$ pair provides input to all units in the corresponding $Q_{\alpha,z}$ layer (thick lines). The locations of the feature detections in the F layers, are shown as dots. They provide input to regions in the Q layers shown as double thick lines. At least three local features need to be found for a detection. Each $x \in S$ sums all inputs $Q_{\alpha,z}(x)$ and is on if this sum is above a threshold τ. In this example the fourth feature does not contribute to the detection—it is not present in the correct location.

to be selected, say, for the next saccade (eye movement), then picking $x \in S$ with the highest sum seems a natural choice and can be achieved through competitive mechanisms within S using recurrent connections.

11.6   Gating and Off-Center Recognition

The visual system is able to recognize objects that are not present in the center of the visual field. So far, our recognition scheme assumed that the data was present in region G, located at the center of the F layers, and fed directly into W. We now introduce an intermediate system of layers between F and W whose role is to translate data from subregions of the size of the reference grid to the center. The main assumption is that all the information needed for recognition is stored in the synaptic connections between W and A and cannot be physically transferred to other regions of the image lattice.

For every possible location $y \in L$, define a layer U_y of units corresponding to feature/location pairs $(\alpha, z), \alpha \in \mathcal{F}, z \in G$, as in W. A unit $(\alpha, z) \in U_y$ receives input from the neighborhood $N_s(z + y)$ in F_α. Each of the U_y layers also receives input from the corresponding unit y in the detection layer S. The unit $(\alpha, z) \in U_y$ is on if any of the units in a neighborhood $N_s(z + y)$ of $z + y$ is on in F_α, so that U_y replicates the information in the F layers, in a window the size of the reference grid centered at y.

The input to W no longer arrives directly from F. Rather, we set $w = (\alpha, z) \in W$ to be on if the unit (α, z) is on in *any* of the U_y layers. Thus the activity in W at (α, z) is the *union* of activities of (α, z) in all U_y layers. In the absence of any gating of activity in the U system, a complex image will generate a large amount of incoherent activity in W, because each unit $(\alpha, z) \in W$ is on if the corresponding unit is on in *any* of the U_y layers, it is on if feature α is present *anywhere* in the visual field.

Only when a particular location is selected for attention, namely, a particular unit in S is activated, does order emerge. If a particular location y is activated in the detection layer S, there is an increase in input to U_y through priming mechanisms similar to those suggested for the Q layers. At the same time, any activity in S will activate a pool of inhibitory neurons that feeds into the entire system of U layers. This inhibitory input weakens the input to all neurons in U, and the only ones surviving with inputs above threshold are the units in U_y, corresponding to the selected location, which also received input from the F layer. We will not describe the details of such mechanisms but refer the reader to Amit and Brunel (1997) and Mascaro and Amit (1999), where inhibitory units are employed to achieve similar results.

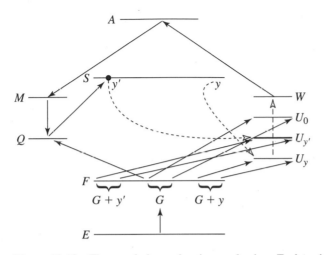

Figure 11.10   The translation and gating mechanism. Each region $G + y$ is replicated in the layer U_y, which also receives input from $y \in S$. The W module takes in all the activity in the U layers. y'—selected location in S, primes $U_{y'}$ and suppresses the other U layers. The activity in W is then a copy of $U_{y'}$. The system of Q layers is shown as one line with the arrows representing the direction of information flow. The F layers feed into the Q layers. The object model in M primes Q, and the detected location y' in S is obtained by summing and thresholding the Q layers at each location.

Now the only input into W is therefore a translation of the data in the neighborhood of the activated location $y \in S$. This is a *gating* procedure that singles out a particular spot in the scene for classification. Whereas the Q layers are primed by the detection model in M in terms of which *local features* should be attended to, the U layers are primed by S in terms of which *location* to attend to. This network is shown in figure 11.10. Note that if y is close to y', the windows $G + y, G + y'$ can have significant overlaps, hence the need for replication. Otherwise, the priming could occur directly in the F layers.

The location y in S can be selected through the detection process described earlier, which is initiated with a top-down flow of information through the model evoked in M. As discussed in chapter 10, this may be a coarse model representing an *object cluster,* and further classification is needed. Once W is activated by the translated data from U_y, the connections from W to A produce a classification of the data. This is essentially equivalent to the detection and classification scheme proposed in chapter 10.

Alternatively, the selected location in S can be the outcome of very primitive bottom-up processing. For example, if only one object is present in the scene, its location pops out easily as a "blob" at very low resolution and perhaps there is a separate mechanism whereby S gets activated by such simple blob detections, as suggested in Olshausen, Anderson, and Van Essen (1993). During learning, only one example of the object is presented in the image at each presentation. This simple form of bottom-up selection provides a mechanism whereby the information gets properly translated into W. Because only one object is present in the scene, there is no ambiguity. Another mechanism to overcome ambiguity during the learning phase is motion. If the learned object is moving against a static background, again, a simple mechanism is able to detect the location of interest.

11.7   Biological Analogies

The system described above provides a possible answer to the main questions posed at the outset. Learning is achieved in a central module. The object models are simple lists of binary features at particular locations on the reference grid. This allows for simple mechanisms for transmitting model information to the entire field of view. Those units coding for the features appropriately shifted are primed and detection is achieved by simple counting at the S layer. Implicitly, we have achieved the implementation of a centrally stored classifier (object/nonobject) at every place in the scene, because all it requires is counting and thresholding. It would be very hard to do so for more-complex types of classifiers.

Recognition is achieved by selecting a particular location for processing and translating the data to the central recognition module. One could argue that detection can also be achieved by simply shifting every reference grid window to the center and classifying object/nonobject. This would be prohibitive in time, because the windows would have to be processed sequentially, whereas detection occurs very fast. The system also has interesting analogies to the biological visual system, which we describe below.

11.7.1   Labeling the Layers

Analogies can be drawn between the layers defined in the network and existing layers of the visual system. Edge-detector layers $E_e, e = 1, \ldots, 8$ correspond to *simple* orientation-selective cells in layer V1. As noted in the Introduction, these layers represent a schematic abstraction of the information provided by the biological cells. However, the empirical success of the algorithm on real images indicates that not much more information is needed for the task of detection and recognition.

The $C_{e,z}$ layers correspond to *complex* orientation-selective cells in layer V1. One could imagine that all cells corresponding to a fixed-edge type e and fixed-image location x are arranged in a cortical column. The only difference as one proceeds down the column is the region over which spreading (or-ing) is performed, namely, the receptive field. In other words, the units in a column are indexed by the displacement region R_k. Indeed, any report on vertical electrode probings in V1, in which orientation selectivity is constant, will show a variation in the displacement of the receptive fields (see Hubel 1988; Zeki 1993).

The local-feature layers F_α correspond to cells in layer V2 that respond to more-complex structures, as reported in von der Heydt (1995) and Hedgé and Van Essen (2000). The Q and the U layers may correspond to layer V4 cells. These have much larger receptive fields, and the variation of the location of these fields as one proceeds down a column is much more pronounced than in V1 or V2—it is on the order of the size of the reference grid.

Alternatively, it may be that the Q and U layers are within V2. Without a hypothesis on the particular shifting function of the neurons in these layers, one would not be able to distinguish the behavior of Q- or U-layer neurons from F-layer neurons. They all respond to more-complex features, perhaps with some differences in the size of the receptive field. The difference would then be in terms of their projections to higher levels of the system. Under this hypothesis, V4 is simply a collection of even-more-complex features, perhaps generic parts such as the "loop" encountered in chapter 10. These are hardwired retinotopically because they are useful in constructing object models and classifiers. Furthermore, associated Q and U layers exist within V4 as well.

11.7.2   Learning

Hebbian learning is the dominant paradigm in the neural network literature (see Hebb 1949; Hopfield 1982; Amit 1989; Oja 1989; and Durtewitz, Seamans, and Sejnowski 2000). The idea that synaptic potentiation is modulated as a function of the local field or firing rate of the postsynaptic neuron is still speculative, although some form of regulation of synaptic activity as a function of the postsynaptic neural activity is reported in Abbott and Nelson (2000). The attractive aspect of the simple classification network described above, together with the field-dependent Hebbian learning rule, is that real data can actually be successfully classified with such a system. High classification rates on character recognition have been achieved with two-layer feed-forward networks LeCun and colleagues (1998), but the training procedure for such networks is not local and depends on the optimization of a global function of all the synaptic weights.

The "abstract" module A, which codes for the classes, could well be in parts of the cortex that are not directly involved in processing visual input, or it could be present in higher levels of inferotemporal cortex (IT). It could fit in a location that integrates inputs from diverse sensory modules, such as prefrontal cortex, or receive input from such a location. The external activation of the units corresponding to a class, during training, could be enabled by a nonvisual stimulus that is well recognized. This can be viewed in the context of reward-type stimuli, arriving from some other pathway (auditory, olfactory, tactile), as described in Rolls (2000), potentiating cues described in Levenex and Schenk (1997), or mnemonic hooks introduced in Atkinson (1975).

11.7.3   Interaction Between Bottom-Up Processing and Top-Down Information Flow

Top-down and bottom-up processing are explicitly modeled. Bottom-up processing is constantly occurring in the simple cell arrays E_e, which feed into the complex cell arrays $C_{e,z}$, which in turn feed into the F-V2 type arrays. The priming from the M module or from the S layer determines which components of the data flowing up from the bottom will be processed at higher stages. The object class that is evoked in the main memory module A activates the object representation in M and this determines which of the Q arrays will have enhanced activity toward their summation into S. Thus the final determination of the candidate locations is given by an interaction of the bottom-up processing and top-down information flow. The active location in the S layer determines which data flows from the U layers to the W module to be ultimately classified in the A module.

11.7.4   Gating and Invariant Detection

The summation array S serves as a gating mechanism for visual selection through its input into the U layers. This could provide a model for the somewhat puzzling behavior of IT neurons in delay match to sample (DMS) experiments (see Chelazzi and colleagues 1993; Desimone and colleagues 1995). Two objects are selected and neurons in IT are identified that respond to the first and not to the second and vice versa. The subject is then presented with one of the two objects as a target to be detected—the sample. After a delay period, an image with both objects is displayed, both displaced from the center. The subject is supposed to saccade to the sample object. After presentation of the test image, neurons responsive to *both* objects become active. About 100 milliseconds later, and a few tens of milliseconds prior to the saccade, the activity of the neurons selective for the nonsample object decays. Only those neurons selective for the sample object remain active.

At first glance, the fact that both types of neurons are active at the start could be interpreted as the brain having very quickly recognized the two objects, as well as having identified their location. In other words, two detection and recognition tasks had already been performed. This explanation is quite unlikely if, as discussed above, we preclude the possibility of many classifiers operating simultaneously in parallel across the scene.

Alternatively, this experiment can be explained in terms of the network described above. Assuming the recordings were made in A, at the outset there is no gating, and all information from all U layers flows into W. Sets of features characteristic of the two objects, and probably many others, are activated and subsequently activate quite a number of class populations in A. This activation is essentially meaningless and conveys very little information to the higher processing centers of the brain. However, once the object model, which was evoked in M at the sample presentation stage, is detected through the S layer, the detected position gates the activity from the U layers. Now the resulting activity in W comes from a particular window in the field of view, which contains the target. The only activity persisting in A corresponds to the subset coding for that object. This corresponds to the weakening of the activity of the nonsample neurons in the DMS experiment. Indeed, this weakening signals that the information conveyed by the A layer, IT in this context, has become meaningful and represents recognition of the sample object.

11.8 Bibliographical Notes and Discussion

Detailed descriptions of the human and primate visual systems can be found in Hubel (1988), Zeki (1993), and Tovee (1996). Recent physiological experiments on object recognition and detection in primates are summarized in a number of reviews (see Tanaka and colleagues 1991; Desimone and colleagues 1995; Desimone and Dyuncan 1995).

The detection and recognition networks described in this chapter were proposed in Amit (2000) and Amit and Mascaro (2001). In the use of simple/complex layers, there are important similarities with Fukushima (1986) and Fukushima and Wake (1991). Indeed, in both papers, the role of or-ing in the complex cell layers as a means of obtaining invariance is emphasized. However, there are major differences. In the detection model presented here, training is only done for local features. The global integration of local-level information is done by a fixed architecture, driven by top-down flow of information. Therefore, features do not need to get more and more complex, as in Fukushima and Wake (1991)—namely, there is no need for a long sequence of layers. Robust detection occurs directly in terms of the local feature level that has only the oriented edge level below it. With large numbers of learned complex features it is not clear how invariant detection can take place.

The ideas behind the translation mechanism in the U layers are very similar to that of Olshausen, Anderson, and Van Essen (1993). Here, translation is simply done through replication. By contrast, in Olshausen, Anderson, and Van Essen (1993), a more complex mechanism is proposed involving control neurons that directly affect synaptic connections and allow for an orderly translation of data directly from the F layer to W. The proposal in Olshausen, Anderson, and Van Essen (1993) for *selecting* a location for translation is limited to very low resolution "blob" detection. This could be useful for direct bottom-up selection, but cannot accommodate top-down selection due to a specific target object.

The network learning mechanism proposed above consists of an input module coding for feature/location pairs feeding into an "abstract" classification module. The main activity during learning involves updating the synaptic weights of the connections between the input module and the classification module. Such simple networks have recently been proposed both in Riesenhuber and Poggio (1999) and in Bartlett and Sejnowski (1998). In the former, the classification module is a classical output layer with individual neurons coding for different classes. This is insufficient for classification in relatively simple problems such as character recognition. Populations of large numbers of perceptrons are essential.

In Riesenhuber and Poggio (1999), the input layer computes *large range or-ing,* or MAX operations, of complex features that are in turn conjunctions of pairs of "complex" edge-type features. In an attempt to achieve large range translation and scale invariance, the range of or-ing is the *entire central visual field,* corresponding more or less to the reference grid. This means that objects are recognized based solely on the presence or absence of the features, *entirely ignoring their relative locations.* With sufficiently complex features, this may well be possible, but then the combinatorics of the number of necessary features appears overwhelming. It should be noted that in the context of character recognition studied here, we find a significant drop in classification rates when the range of or-ing or maximization is on the order of the reference grid size—see, for example, the experiments reported in section 9.6 in the context of classification trees. This trade-off between feature complexity, combinatorics, and invariance is a crucial issue that has yet to be systematically investigated.

In the architecture proposed in Bartlett and Sejnowski (1998), the input features are again edge filters. Training is semisupervised—not directly through the association of certain neurons to a certain class, but through the sequential presentation of slowly varying stimuli of the same class. Hebbian learning of temporal correlations is used to increase the weight of synapses, connecting units in a recurrent layer responding to these consecutive stimuli. At the start of each class sequence, the temporal interaction is suspended. This is a very appealing alternative form of supervision that employs the fact that objects are often observed by slowly rotating them in space. This network employs continuous valued neurons and synapses, which can in principle achieve negative values, and learning is not really local and incremental. It would be interesting to study whether field-dependent Hebbian learning can lead to similar results without use of such global operations on the synaptic matrix.

The field-dependent learning rule is motivated on one hand by work on binary synapses in Amit and Fusi (1994) and Mattia and Del Giudice (1999), where the synapses are modified stochastically *only* as a function of the activity of the pre- and postsynaptic neurons. Here, however, we have replaced the stochasticity of the learning process with a continuous internal variable for the synapse. This is more effective for neurons with a small number of afferent synapses. On the other hand, there is a close connection to the work in Diederich and Opper (1987), where Hopfield-type nets with positive and negative valued multistate synapses are modified using the classical Hebbian update rule, but modification stops when the local field is above or below certain thresholds. There exists ample evidence for local synaptic modification as a function of the activities of pre- and postsynaptic neurons (Bliss and Collingridge 1993, Markram and colleagues 1997). However, at this point we can only speculate whether this process can be somehow controlled by the activity of the postsynaptic neuron.

The network described above is based on a fixed set of hardwired two-edge features. In Amit (2000), it is shown how more-complex features can be used for detection. These are no longer hardwired and are adapted to the detection task at hand. Again, top-down priming plays a central role. In this context, it is operating at the lower level of the C layers. The complex edge arrangements are detected in certain F layers. These will be responding to different features, depending on the detection task at hand and the models evoked in the M module.

The suggested architecture provides an explanation to a variety of physiological experiments and also performs well on detection and recognition tasks involving real data (i.e., detection of objects in gray-scale images, and classification of shapes from a large number of classes). There are many aspects that may turn out to be biologically impossible, such as the particular connections required between M and Q or between S and U, or even whether U- and Q-type neurons exist. Yet it appears to be a productive framework for formulating hypotheses on the mode of operation of higher-level functions of the visual system.

12 Software

This chapter provides some information regarding the software and data sets that accompany this book. The important data structures as well as the most commonly used parameters are described. More information can be found in the documentation written in the source files and the script files. There is no guarantee attached to this software (it is not too hard to make it crash), nor is any support to be expected. A certain level of proficiency in C++ is essential to understand the program, and some experience with Unix and an X11-based window manager are necessary to get things running smoothly.

12.1 Setting Things Up

The source code provided here will compile on Linux.
Download

```
detect.tgz
```

from

```
http://galton.uchicago.edu/~amit/book.
```

to a directory whose full path will be called base for further reference.
Type

```
tar xvfz detect.tgz.
```

The following must be set for things to work:

- Set an environment variable $DETDIR to base.

  In csh add the line

  ```
  setenv DETDIR base
  ```

to your .cshrc file.

In bash add the line

DETDIR=base

to your .bashrc file.

- Add base/bin and base/bin/script to your path.

  In csh add the line setenv PATH "$PATH:base/bin:/base/bin/script"

  In bash add the line

  PATH="$PATH:base/bin:/base/bin/script"

- Add the bash shell program to your /bin directory. All the scripts are written in bash and assume it is in directory /bin

In directory* base *you will now see several directories.

- source. Contains the code with graphic options. cd into source and type
  make

  The program will compile and face will be written to base/bin

- sourcenox. Contains the code with no graphic options. cd into sourcenox and type
  make

  The program will compile and facenox will be written to base/bin

- bin. Contains the compiled executables, face and facenox, and a subdirectory scripts where all the script files written in bash are stored.

- book. This directory has subdirectories corresponding to the chapters of the book (*chap1, chap2, ...*), as well as a subdirectory data. Within each subdirectory corresponding to a particular chapter are parameter files that more or less reproduce the figures in that chapter. Running these scripts is a good way to begin getting acquainted with the program and the relevant parameters.

  The subdirectories of data are the following.

  - FACES. Contains a subdirectory train with three hundred 110×96 images of faces from the Olivetti data set, ten images per person. These are used to train the detectors. There is an additional directory test with hundred faces from the same data set. The directory pgm contains a number of pgm images on which detectors can be tested. The directories filt1, filt_d2, filt_from_edges contain different sparse models trained using different parameters.

- HEART. Contains ultrasound images of heart ventricles in directories pat1, pat2, pat3, and a couple of angiograms in directory ang.
- BRAIN. Contains two directories of axial MRI brain scans, train and test, as well as a directory filt3 which contains a sparse model for these images and a directory grmtch containing parameters for a sparse model of these scans for detection with dynamic programming.
- LATEX. Contains a directory protos with the prototypes of all the 293 LaTeX symbols, and a subdirectory latex_0 with a sparse model for the symbol 0 as well as a classifier for the hits of this detector (see chapter 10). Subdirectories latex_1, latex_4, latex_7 contain models for the 1, 4 and the 7.
- ESCR. Contains a sparse model and various templates for the $\mathcal{E}$ used in chapter 2—also, the classifier for hits of this detector on other script-style symbols.
- CLIP. Contains a sparse model for the clip shown in chapter 8.
- CHESS. Contains the sparse model and classifiers for the chess pieces.
- NIST. Contains one set of classification trees trained on the NIST data set and a small sample of 10,000 NIST digits for testing. The full data set is very large but can be obtained upon request.

12.1.1   Running the Program

The program face can receive input from a parameter file, from the command line, or from the parameter file and the command line. The general form for running face from the command line is

```
face file par1=n1 par2=n2 ...
```

or

```
face par1=n1 par2=n2 ...
```

The parameter file, if used, must come first. Parameters set on the command line override values set in the parameter file. Among the parameters, opt must be set to a particular option that tells the program what routine to use.

If no graphics are needed, then facenox can be run the same way. The list of parameters needed for each of the algorithms is detailed in section 12.4.

In each subdirectory of book, with a name corresponding to a chapter, are prepared parameter files for the figures in that chapter. Type `face f.par`

on the command line to obtain the corresponding figure.

12.1.2   Graphics

The program will show results of the algorithms as they are computing, as well as the final result, depending on parameter settings. Often the program will show one or several windows and will not continue until prompted by the user. This is done by typing c inside the active window which is highlighted by the window manager. Typing q kills the window and the program. Typing n magnifies the window to n times the original size of the image.

12.2   Important Data Structures

In this section, we provide a brief summary of the important C++ templates and classes used in the program. More details are to be found in the corresponding `.h` files. All classes come with some I/O functions for reading, writing, and printing information.

12.2.1   Grid

The `grid`, defined in `grid.h`, is a template for arrays of all types. It contains functions for allocating memory, accessing coordinates, copying, copying subarrays, and so on; `dgrid`, `igrid`, `ucgrid` are particular instantiations of this template for the types `double`, `int`, and `unsigned char`.

12.2.2   Image

The class `image`, defined in `image.h`, is a friend class to `ucgrid` (unsigned character grid). This class has various image-processing-type member functions.

The program reads in images from `Images_n` files $n = 0, 1, \ldots, N$. These files contain up to 100 images. If $N > 0$, then all files for $n < N$ contain exactly 100 images and the last one may contain less. Multiple images created in the program can also be written in to such files. There is a function that takes a sequence of pgm images called `pic0.pgm`, `pic1.pgm`, ..., `picN.pgm` and translates them into `Images_n` files. The corresponding script is call `pgmtoIm`. Images are stored with 1 byte per pixel, allowing for 256 gray-scale values. The only exception is the NIST data, which is stored with 1 bit per pixel. To view an image from such a data set, which is located in directory `IM`, type

```
face opt=40 dataset=IM first=10 numdigits=30
```

Each image will appear, and you will need to type "c" in the window to proceed to the next (see script `viewim`). To see a collection of images at once, type

```
face opt=41 dataset=IM first=10 numdigits=30 last=10 scale=32
```

This will put up the 30 images starting from the tenth, 10 images per row, each taking up a 32 × 32 box. If viewing NIST data, add `datadepth=1` to the command line.

12.2.3 Viewport

The `viewport`, defined in `viewport.h`, manages the interface between the images and the X11 graphics and has various graphics functions such as line, point, and text drawing on images. It is used in conjunction with `xobject`, defined in `xobject.h`. An `image` or `ucgrid` is attached to a `viewport` and then the `viewport` is displayed with all the relevant information on `points`, `lines`, and so on. The display is interactive; the window can be magnified by typing the magnification digit on the window, q kills the entire process, c continues the program, r reverses the video.

12.2.4 Landmarks

The class `landmarks`, defined in `landmark.h`, is a class for storing locations of detected local features of several types. The type is coded by an increasing index from 0, 1, 2, and so on. Functions are included to obtain the number of instances of each type and the coordinates of each instance of each type. The `landmark` (without an s) class is a structure used within the programs to record two coordinates and a type. These are accumulated during the actual detection process. Then a member function of `landmarks` called `setup_from_lmarklist` takes the array of `landmark` - s and arranges them in one `landmarks` class. For the use of various training procedures, `landmarks` for large numbers of images are stored in files Lands_n, organized like the Images_n files in batches of 100. The member functions for reading and writing `landmarks` from these files are provided. To dump the `landmarks` of an image, see script `dumplandmarks`.

12.2.5   Tree

The `tree` template is defined in `tree.h` and includes definitions needed to create binary trees with quite general nodes. The main component is the `treeiterator`, which has built-in functions for moving up and down the tree, creating children nodes, and so forth. The information in each node, denoted `data`, is defined for particular instantiations of this template, such as an `ltatree` defined in `ltatree.h`.

- `ltatree`. LTA stands for `local tag arrangement`, where local tag refers to any local feature such as an edge, a microimage code, ridge-detector, and so on. This class is used to construct and store trees with relational and absolute arrangements of local features, as described in chapter 9, as well as the local-edge arrangements. The local-edge arrangements can be viewed as relational trees with only a small number of yes answers, all the relations being with respect to the first edge, and all edges constrained to be near the center edge.

    Class `ltadata` is used for the `data` entry. The `ltadata` class codes for the additional relational question asked at the current node using the `question` class, it codes for the list of data points at the node while growing the tree and the histogram of frequencies, also used for growing the tree. To view an `ltatree`, use script `dumpltatree`.

- `carttree`. Another `tree` example is `carttree`, defined in `carttree.h`. The query at each node is simply a pair (f, s), where f is a predictor index, and s is a threshold for the value of the predictor. The query is whether $X_f > s$. When using binary local features, $s = 0$, and the size of the predictor vector is $dx \cdot dy \cdot N$, where dx, dy are the dimensions of the image, and N is the number of local features. The class `cartdata` is where the information for simple cart-type questions (coordinate and threshold) are stored as well as the list of data points and the histogram also used in training. There is some duplication in that `carttrees` do exactly what `ltatrees` with absolute arrangements do. For various reasons, the former are used for postdetection classification: classifying one class against the rest of the world, and then among several object classes. The latter is used in the experiments on isolated object recognition. To view a `carttree`, use script `dumpcarttree`.

12.2.6   Detection

The `detection` class is defined in `detection.h`. The important data entries are the `scale`, which records at which resolution the detection was found, and `tripts`, the coordinates of the detection triangle; `cartprobs`, `cartprobs2`, and `cartprobs3` are used to record the output from the various classification stages; `counts` is used to store the number of hits from the counting detector and other related information; and `locs` is an `igrid` for storing the coordinates of the instantiation. The number of points depends on the particular application.

12.3 Local Features

All routines for detecting binary local features in an image can be found in the file `edge.C`. Below, we list the different types together with the relevant parameters and how they can be computed and displayed.

12.3.1 Edges and Ridges

Edges and ridges are computed through the `detectedges` subroutine, which loops through disjoint blocks of size `EdgeSizeBlock` in the image, calls a routine to find all binary features in that block, sorts these detections according to some criterion, and keeps the top `EdgeNumberOfPixels`. The final detected features are stored in a `landmarks` structure. To view the edges on an image (say no. 3) in `Image_` files in directory *IM,* run

```
face parfile opt=53 dataset=IM showedges=1 first=3 last=4
```

with `parfile` set according to one of the parameter sets defined below. To create a database of local features. Do

```
mkdir LF
face parfile opt=44 onlyedges=1 dataset=IM numdigits=num
landdir=LF
```

with parfile set according to one of the parameter sets defined below. See also script `getedges`.

`EdgeType=0`. 0—detect edges defined in section 5.4 using `find_edge_in_block` subroutine. 1—Detect ridges with values on the ridge higher than outside. 2—values on the ridge lower, (see section 4.1). Last two use `find_ridg_in_block` subroutine.

`EdgeNumberOfPixels=2`. Keep the top two edges found in each disjoit block, in terms of absolute value of the differences.

`EdgeSizeBlock=2`. Use disjoint 2×2 blocks.

`EdgeRadius`. The value of distance along ridge for comparisons, μ_a in section 4.1.

`EdgeEpsilon=.03`. Minimal edge threshold is $255 \times .03$

edgeinc=1. Use all eight oriented edges. edgeinc=2, use only vertical and horizontal.

primitiveedges=0. Use polarity-sensitive edges. primitiveedges=50, use polarity insensitive edges (so only four types: horizontal, vertical, and two diagonals).

EdgeGoodTests=5. Number of inequalities defining an edge (in equation 5.11) that are satisfied is greater than 5. Total number is 6. Lower values make more-robust and more-frequent edges.

12.3.2 Local Edge Arrangements—LTAs

Local edge arrangements are chosen through training for a particular object (see below), or a fixed pool can be defined. The individual trees containing the information for each of the local-edge arrangements are all stored in a file ltatrees in a directory (say, treesgood). These arrangements are detected in the routine edges_to_ltas, which is called from extract_landmarks. The number of local-edge arrangements is also stored in this file. To view the locations of local-edge arrangements on an image (say, no. 3), do

```
face parfile opt=53 onlyedges=0 showltas=2 ltatreedir=treesgood
first=3 last=4
```

where parfile contains the parameter settings for the edge extraction, as described in the previous section, which must precede the computation of local-edge arrangements. The locations of each local-feature type are shown in sequence. Press c to proceed. To create a database of local edge arrangements, do

```
mkdir LF
face parfile opt=44 onlyedges=0 merge=0 dataset=IM numdigits=num
landdir=LF ltatreedir=treesgood
```

If merge=1, the edge information is appended after the local feature information in the landmarks structure. See script getedges.

12.3.3 Hardwired Edge Pairs

A special case is local-edge arrangements with only two edges and 8 possible boxes defining the relative location of the second edge (as opposed to wedges). The advantage of these is the speed of computation. All 256 are computed in one loop based on an initial edge extraction, in detectpairs, which is called from extract_landmarks.

```
face parfile opt=53 onlyedges=0 ltausedepth=0 showltas=1
spread=1 EdgeRadius=2 first=3 last=4
```

spread—radius of the box, *EdgeRadius*—the distance of the box center from the center edge of the arrangement. For storing the information in files, do

```
mkdir LF
face parfile opt=44 onlyedges=0 merge=0 dataset=IM numdigits=num
landdir=LF
```

See also script getedges.

12.3.4   Comparison Arrays

The comparison arrays defined in section 6.3 are computed in detect_masks using a file masks.asc that has the masks used by the current model and the minimal thresholds for the -1 and +1 regions. The format for this file is defined through the mask class in mask.h. The file directory is given in maskdir. Also in this directory is a parameter file defining the graph to be used and the hard constraints on the angles and lengths in the triangles composing the graph. The format for this file is defined in the graph class in graph.h.

12.3.5   Microimage Codes

These are features used exclusively for recognition of binary images. (see chapter 9). The training procedure is described below. The quantization tree is stored in a carttree structure in a file called codes.tree. The microimage codes in the image are computed in detecttags. To store the codes in Lands_, codes.tree must be in the current directory. Then do

```
mkdir LF
detecttags dataset=IM newlanddir=LF
```

12.4   Deformable Models

In each subsection is a list of the parameters used for a particular algorithm, some possible values, a short description, and references to the notation used in the corresponding chapter. Further information can be obtained in the documentation within each program. Each of these algorithms can either be run directly on an image, as described in this section, or following a detection of the sparse model, as described in the next section.

12.4.1   Deformable Contours

These parameters refer to the deformable-contour algorithms described in chapter 3. The program file is `defcont.C`.

`opt=113`. Option number.

`tempfile=snake.circ`. File with a list of coordinates for model. If `tempfile=""` then the program prompts the user to point out the curve by hand and writes it to `defcont.temp`.

`detfile=detout`. File for writing out `detection` class with coordinates of final curve in the `locs` entry.

`dumpdetections=1`. Dump the detection info to command line.

`curve_length=128`. Length of curve to work with, can be larger or smaller than model, in which case the program interpolates to the desired size.

`dataset=IM`. The directory containing the `Images_` files.

`inside=0`. The average value of the inside $\mu_{in} \geq 0$. If `inside = -1`, the on-line estimation of the parameters is enabled.

`outside=.1`. The average value outside μ_{out}.

`dt_scale_factor=1`. A scaling factor for the computed time step.

`base=5`. Wavelet basis to use in expanding curve—`base=1`—Haar, up to `base=6`—smoothest.

`numiters=10000`. Number of iterations.

`post=.3`. Scaling of model curve.

`minenergychange=.001`. If change in coefficients is below this value, add more coefficients for optimization or exit if at maximal number of coefficients.

`FIRSTDIM=1`. Initial number of coefficients updated $\mathcal{N}_1$, for each curve component.

`LASTDIM=16`. Final number of coefficients to update $\mathcal{N}_A$.

`prior_fac=0`. Factor multiplying the prior term.

`first=3`. Index number of first image to run.

`imrange=.2`. For graphic purposes, reduces gray-value range of image display.

`basecol=10`. Color of the curve, `basecol=0`—red, `basecol=10`—white.

`displayinter=100`. Display result every 100 iterations.

`point1x=79`. Initial points, if `point1x=-1` (default), the user provides the initial point by pointing with the mouse.

`point1y=67`.

12.4.2   Deformable Curves: Dynamic Programming

This algorithm is described in section 4.2. Only the simpler model of equation 4.9, which involves only two parameters, p_o and p_b, has been implemented. The program file is `curve_dyna.C`.

`opt=112`. Option number.

`tempfile=dyna.escr`. File name with coordinates of model curve. If `tempfile=""`, user is prompted to pick points on displayed image. When finished, type c inside image. Points will be written to default file `dyna.temp`.

`detfile=detout`. File for writing out `detection` class with coordinates of final curve in the `locs` entry.

`dyna_dis=2`. Distance of comparison pixels in the orthogonal direction to the curve for determining `ridg`-type features; μ_a in equation 4.1; ν_a is taken to be half μ_a.

`prior_angle=10`. Factor on prior term penalizing changes in angle of segment relative to model curve; A in equation 4.10.

`prior_length=30`. Factor on prior term penalizing changes in length; B in equation 4.10.

`dyna_regionsize=10`. Radius of a square neighborhood around each pixel of model curve. This is the radius of each of the S_i neighborhoods (see section 4.2).

`inside=.95`. Probability of getting $X_a = 1$ for curve of angle a (i.e., p_o in equation 4.9).

`outside=.05`. Probability of getting $X_a = 1$ otherwise (i.e., p_b in equation 4.9).

`dataset=IM`. Data set with images to process.

`first=3`. First image to process.

`revvideo=0`. Reverse video graphic display.

`dumpdetections=3`. How much information to dump on screen and show. If value is 3, show each step of the dynamic programming. If value is 1, only show final result.

`imrange=.3`. Gray-level value range.

`basecol=10`. Color for showing curve.

`pixsize=2`. Size of pixel in display.

`point1x=43`. Two initial points determining location, rotation, and scale of curve.

`point1y=23`.

`point2x=43`.

`point2y=33`.

12.4.3   Deformable Curves: Tree-Based Algorithm

This algorithm is described in section 4.3. The data structure needed for this algorithm is very similar to the `tree` template, except it is ternary—three children for each node—and is defined in `curve_tree.h`. The algorithm is coded in `curve_tree.C`.

`opt=117`. Option number.

`dataset=IM`. Directory with images.

`inside=.7`. Probability p_o of getting $X_a = 1$ on segment with angle a.

`outside=.4`. Probability p_b of getting $X_a = 1$ otherwise.

`LEN=10`. Length of each arc.

`ORTHLEN`. Length orthogonal to arc for testing μ_a (same as *dyna_dis* above).

`deg=10`. Degree of change allowed from one arc to the other (β).

`ZSTAR=.999`. Above which posterior to declare an arc on the curve and restart algorithm.

`mindepth=3`. Minimum depth of arc with posterior above ZSTAR to allow reinitialization (the top arcs quickly reach a posterior of over ZSTAR and are not so interesting).

`numtrack=10`. Number of times to reinitialize with high posterior arc.

`numiters=10000`. Maximal number of arc testings in each reinitialized run.

`first=0`. First image to process.

`last=1`. Last image to process.

`pixsize=2`. Image magnification.

`imrange=.3`. Gray-value range (imrange $= 0$) maximal range.

`basecol=10`. Color of curve.

`point1x=43`. Two initial points determining first arc. If any of these is negative, user is prompted to provide initial two points.

`point1y=98`.

`point2x=41`.

`point2y=112`.

12.4.4 Deformable Images: Gaussian Data Model

This corresponds to the algorithm described in 5.3, based on the least-squares data term and the linearized algorithm described in section 5.5. These are implemented in `defimage_gaus.C`. Only a wavelet expansion of the deformation is coded. Because of this, the dimensions of the image need to be a power of 2. If they are not, the program embeds the image in the smallest power of 2 larger than the dimensions.

`opt=111`. Option number.

`tempdataset=TEMPIM`. Data set with template.

`tempnum=45` Template image number.

`dataset=IM`. Data set with images.

`first=123`. Data image number.

`post=1`. Factor multiplying data term.

`prior_fac=.3`. Factor multiplying prior term. Relative weighting of prior on coefficients λ_k is computed as in equation 5.6, with $\rho = 2$.

`minenergychange=.01`. Minimum total change in coefficients to increase dimension $\mathcal{N}_a$ to $\mathcal{N}_{a+1}$ by factor of two or stop, if $a = A$.

`linear_elas=0`. Regular deformation algorithm. `linear_elas=1` uses iterations of linearization step described in section 5.5. Starts solving at FIRSTDIM and increases dimension at each iteration.

`FIRSTDIM=1`. First level of coefficients to be updated. This is half of $\mathcal{N}_1$.

`LASTDIM=8`. Last level of coefficients to be updated. This is half of $\mathcal{N}_A$.

`dt_scale_factor=1`. Factor multiplying computed time step.

`numiters=1200`. Maximum number of iterations.

`pixsize=4`. Magnification

`displayinter=100`. Display result every 100 iterations.

`arrow_spacing=2`. Spacing of arrows in display of displacement field.

`imrange=.2`. Range of gray levels.

`basecol=10`. Color for displaying arrows.

12.4.5   Image Warping with Bernoulli Model

This implements the Bernoulli model for deformable images described in section 5.4.

Training

The probabilities of the edges on a reference grid of size `DIMX` by `DIMY` are saved in a file `edgetemps`. The training is implemented in routine `get_edgetemps` in `trainstat.C` (see script *getedgetemps*).

`opt=28`.

`DIMX=64`. Dimensions of the reference grid to which the extracted local features are registered.

`DIMY=64`.

`point1x=25`. Coordinates of three reference points p_1, p_2, p_3, to which the anchor points in each training image are mapped

`point1y=32`.

`point2x=40`.

`point2y=32`.

`point3x=32`.

`point3y=46`.

`dataset=train`. Data set with training images.

`num=300`. Number of training images in data set.

`rt=.4`. Downsampling ratio to apply to each image (this is the ratio used for the faces).

`onlyedges=1`. Only use edge features. `onlyedges=0` together with an `ltatreedir` will extract edge arrangements and then register. Edge parameters are below.

`EdgeEpsilon=.03`.

`edgeinc=1`.

`EdgeGootTests=4`.

`EdgeNumberOfPixels=2`.

EdgeSizeBlock=1.

spread=1. Radius of box into which each detected edge is spread.

tempfile=edgetemps. File for writing out the frequencies.

showtriangles=1. Show images with the frequencies.

Detection

Implemented in defimage_ber.C.

opt=115. Option number.

dataset=IM. Data set with face images of more or less the correct size (DIMX by DIMY) with faces more or less centered so that the eyes are about 14 pixels apart. Significant variation is tolerated.

tempfile=edgetemps. Name of probability map file produced in training.

minval=.3. Background edge probability. All areas where the edge probabilities p_b are less than minval are set to minval.

first=0. First image to process.

last=10. Last image to process.

eyex=32. Use these dimensions of the data around the middle point. Allows use of smaller windows for matching.

eyey=32.

shift=5. Range of shifts $(+/-)$ in brute-force search for optimal shift and scale.

lowscale=.6. Lower and upper bounds of scaling in brute-force search for optimal scaling.

highscale=1.4.

spread=1. Amount of spread of detected edges in data.

dt_scale_factor=1. Factor multiplying computed time step for gradient-descent stage.

minenergychange=.01. As in Gaussian model.

FIRSTDIM=1. First level of optimized coefficients. $\mathcal{N}_1 = 2 \times FIRSTDIM \times FIRSTDIM$

LASTDIM=4. Last level of optimized coefficient. $\mathcal{N}_A = 2 \times LASTDIM \times LASTDIM$

numiters=20. Number of iterations of gradient descent.

prior_fac=.01. Factor of prior term.

post=1. Factor of data term.

pixsize=1. Magnification.

displayinter=10. Display every 10 iterations.

imrange=0. Gray-level range.

basecol=10. Color for dots and lines.

12.5   Sparse Models

12.5.1   Dynamic Programming

There is no routine for identifying the comparison arrays and thresholds for the chosen landmarks on the training sample. All we provide is an existing model that is encoded in two files: masks.asc, containing the masks being used with the corresponding thresholds, and tempfile, containing information on the graph and model locations. The algorithm is implemented in sparse_dyna.C. The corresponding scripts are to be found in directory chap7 and the files in BRAIN/grmtch.

opt=116.

maskdir=grmtch. Directory where masks.asc is found as well as the tempfile.

usemasks=1. If set to 0—use ltas defined in ltatreedir

dataset=test. Images data set.

first=2. First image.

last=30. Last image.

ratio=.5. Downsampling ratio to apply to image.

pixsize=2.

dumpdetections=1. Show final result. 2—show each step in dynamic programming. 3—show template and locations of local features.

tempfile=PRM1a.asc. File containing graph information.

imrange=.3.

basecol=10.

12.5.2 Counting Detector—Running an Existing Detector

A trained detector stored in directory `filt` consists of some subdirectories and one parameter file `pars`:

All edge parameters.

`ltatree1x, ltatree1y, ltatree2x, ltatree2y, ltatree3x, ltatree3y`— coordinates of the anchor points.

`hits, acchits`. The thresholds τ and τ_e for steps I and II of the counting detector.

`numcarts=20`. Number of classification trees—object against false positives. 0—no classification.

`fnumcarts=20`. Number of classification trees among detected classes. 0—no classification.

`numratios=6`. Number of resolutions at which to run detector.

`testrotations=1/0`. Whether to estimate rotations.

`boxcluster=5`. How close are two detected triangles (3 reference points) for them to be clustered.

`ltatreedir=treesgood`. Contains a file `ltatrees` with information regarding the LTAs and their coordinates in the reference grid.

`edgetreedir=treesedge`. Contains a file `ltatrees` with information regarding the edge model for step II. This model is used to adjust scale if parameter `edgesforscale=1`. If `edgesforscale=0` the LTAs are used to adjust for scale and `treesedge` is not needed.

`carttreedir=treescart`. Contains classification trees to classify detections of steps I and II as object or not-object. If `numcarts=0`, no classification is performed, and this directory is not needed.

`carttreedir=facecart`. Contains classification trees to classify detections of steps I and II among different classes. If `fnumcarts=0`, no classification is performed, and this directory is not needed.

`showtriangles=1`. Show detection triangles; 2—show only vertices of triangle.

`dumdetections=1`. Print out some information as detection proceeds; 2—print out all information on all detections, dump the detection structures.

If there is a list of `pgm` files in file `image_list` and the detector parameters are in directory `filt` run:

```
test_pgm_list image_list filt first=3 last=20
```

If the images are in a directory `image_data` in `Images_` format,

    test_imaged 3 20 filt

will run the detector on images 3–20.

12.5.3   Running a Deformable Model Initialized
with a Sparse-Model Detection

The parameter `templatestyle`, if greater than 0, determines which deformable model is run. Depending on the model, the appropriate parameters (defined earlier) must be included in the parameter file.

`templatestyle=1`. Apply deformable contour directly on image—the pose a_p of the detection is applied to the template contour to produce initial contour.

`templatestyle=2`. Apply deformable curve dynamic programming algorithm directly on image—the pose a_p of the detection is applied to the template curve to produce initial curve.

`templatestyle=3, 4, 5, 6`. The region of interest around the detection is registered to a reference grid. This reference grid could have different dimensions and the reference points could be different from those of the sparse model. The dimensions of the reference grid are set in `defsizex`, `defsizey`, and the three reference points in the reference grid are given by `defpoint1x`, `defpoint1y`, `defpoint2x`, `defpoint2y`, `defpoint3x`, `defpoint3y`. The detection triangle `det.tripts` is mapped to these three points, determining the affine map for registration.

The registered image is then processed with a deformable model as follows:

`templatestyle=3`. Deformable image—Gaussian model.

`templatestyle=4`. Deformable image—Bernoulli model.

`templatestyle=5`. Deformable contour.

`templatestyle=6`. Deformable curve—dynamic programming.

12.6   Sparse Model—Counting Detector: Training

Here we describe how to train models for step I and step II of the counting detector described in chapters 6 and 8.

Assume we are in directory `object` with `numtr` training images in directory `train`, and `numte` training images of the object in directory `test`. These images are used to adjust the two thresholds τ and τ_a. In both directories, there is supposed to be a `coords` file with the coordinates of the three anchor points for each image, marked beforehand, three rows per image, two coordinates per row. The training procedure is implemented with the script `doitob`. The parameters defining the edge detection are set in `doitob` and can be changed. Also, two parameters defining the wedges for the edge arrangements—numang=16 number of wedges. The angle of each wedge is 360°/numang (see section 6.4.); near=4 is the radius of the neighborhood containing the wedges. The script `doitob` is run from the command line with eight arguments—for example:

```
doitob 32 20 3 2 3 .5 1
```

1. Number of training data.
2. Number of LTAs to use in final model.
3. Complexity of edge arrangements, number of edges (n_r).
4. The features used for the classification trees of object against the false positives: 0—normalized and registered gray levels, 2—edges, 3—edge arrangements.
5. Size of disjoint blocks in which only one edge arrangement is chosen—typically, 3×3.
6. In each block, the highest frequency edge arrangement is found. It is taken only if its probability is higher than `objprop`; ρ—in algorithm 6.1.
7. By what factor to downscale the training images before edge extraction.
8. If greater or equal to 0, the classification trees are made of this object class against false positives obtained by the detector. Otherwise, classification trees are made between the different class labels of the detections of the detector. The false positives for this step are found on images in directory `../trainall`, which contains training images from all object classes.

The steps in `doitob` are the following:

1. Write edge extraction parameters to `pars`.
2. Obtain three reference points either from user (written in `newbasis`) or by taking averages of anchor points in training images.
3. Extract edges from data in `train`.
4. Register the edge locations to reference grid, anchor points get mapped to reference points; script—`register_edges`.
5. Find high-probability edge locations ($>$`objprop`) and store them in `treesedge/ltatrees`. Assume `nume` are found; script—`choose_edgelocs`.

6. Find high-probability edge arrangement locations (> objprop) and store them in treesgood/ltatrees. Assume numl are found; script—make_ltas.

7. Find thresholds for two steps of counting detector using test set. First find τ by starting at τ=numl/2 and incrementing by one until a test point is missed. The estimated τ is assigned to variable hits. Write hits to pars; script—findhits.

8. Then with this τ find maximal τ_a for step II of counting detector in the same way. Assigned to variable acchits. Write acchits to pars; script—findacchits.

9. Classification trees (optional). Script findnewp.
findnewp 0 cartstyle classlabel
The parameters inside findnewp are described in section 12.10.

(a) Extract detections from data set ../trainall, using parameter file pars. The detection triangle is recorded in file detcoords. Each detection in an image is reported in one line with eight numbers, two coordinates of three points, the image number, and class number of that image. If no detections occur in the image, there is a line with −1s and the image number. Several detections are possible in one image.

(b) Loop over images of ../trainall, extract data (gray level, edges, or edge arrangements), and register using affine map determined by detection triangle in detcoords. Data is stored in file ftrraw.

(c) Read in data in ftrraw and train multiple randomized classification trees using the carttree structure.
If these trees classify object against the rest of the world, set numcarts to number of carttrees and write to pars. Store carttrees in directory treescart.
If these trees classify among detected object classes, set fnumcarts to number of carttrees and store trees in directory facecart.

12.7   Example—LaTeX

In directory LATEX, the subdirectory protos contains images of the 293 LaTeX symbols. Synthetic deformations of any number of these are obtained using the parameters bellow; script—make_train. These synthetic deformations also create a coords file, mapping the three reference points marked on the prototype according to the generated random map.

`opt=47.`

`dataset=protos.`

`ratio=1.0.` What scaling to apply to each prototype.

`first=0.` First prototype to be deformed.

`last=292.` Last prototype to be deformed.

`randomize=1.` Produce random deformations.

`rotate=.3.` Sample uniformly from $\pm.3$ radians (about 18°). (0—do not rotate)

`scale=3.` Sample uniformly from log-scale $\pm(.5/3)$ giving approximately $\pm20\%$. (0—do not scale)

`skew=3.` Sample uniformly from log-skew (ratio of x-scaling and y-scaling) $\pm(.5/3)$ giving approximately $\pm20\%$. (0—do not skew)

`numdigits=50.` Number of random samples per prototype.

`synthesize=1.` Generate random nonlinear deformations. Using random Gaussian wavelet coefficients with exponential decay in variances. (0—do not deform)

`base=3.` Daubechies wavelet basis to use, the coefficients for 2–6 are stored in the program.

`LASTDIM=4.` $2 \times LASTDIM \times LASTDIM$ is the number of randomly generated coefficients to use in wavelet expansion.

`latexdim.` Dimension of image in which to put the randomly perturbed prototypes; default is 32.

   The images are written to the directory in which `face` is called. The above parameters would create fifty randomly deformed images for all 293 classes. These can be stored in a directory `trainall`.

   The script `makedet` is called to create a directory for a particular class, create training and test sets for this class, train the detector using `doitob`, and run the classification on false positives obtained from the data set `../trainall` using `findnewp`, which is called from `doitob`.

`makedet latex_n n 32 20 3 2 3 .5 1.`

The parameters to `makedet` are:

1. Name of directory that contains the object information.

2. Index number of prototype from `protos` to use.

3. Number of synthetic training data to produce.

4. Maximal number of local features to create in model.

5. Complexity of local features (number of edges).

6. Type of features for the classification trees (0, 2, 3).

7. Size of disjoint regions in each of which at most one local feature is found.

8. Proportion of training data required to keep a local feature.

9. Scaling to apply to each training image before edge extraction.

The parameters determining the type of deformations to apply to create training and test sets are written in the file `makedet` and can be changed.

The steps taken in `makedet` are the following. Assume directory name is `object`.

1. `mkdir object. cd object`.

2. Creates a `train` directory—`cd` to `train`; apply `make_train`; `cd` back to `object`.

3. Creates a `test` directory—`cd` to `test`; applies `make_train`; `cds` back to `object`.

4. Runs `doitob` with the parameters given to `makedet`.

12.8   Other Objects with Synthesized Training Sets

We outline the steps for making object models for a collection of objects where we assume one image of each object is taken on a flat background. (This prevents training to incorporate background information in the object model.)

1. Make a base directory `objects`.

   ```
   mkdir objects
   cd objects
   ```

2. Take images of objects such as the clip or the chess pieces shown in chapters 8 and 10. Convert to `pic0.pgm, pic1.pgm, ..., picN.pgm` (assuming N objects).

3. Make a `protos` directory

   ```
   mkdir protos
   mv pic*.pgm protos
   cd protos
   ```

4. Convert to `Images_` format.

   ```
   pgmtoIm numdigits=N
   ```

5. Choose anchor points by clicking on three points in each prototype image with the left mouse button. The coordinates of the three points get stored in `coords`.

```
face opt=40 numdigits=N dataset=./ >> coords
```

6. Go back to `objects` directory and make `trainall` directory.

```
cd..
```

and prepare a `trainall` directory with, say, 50 randomly deformed images of each prototype:

```
mkdir trainall
cd trainall
make_train 50 first=0 last=N latexdim=40 dataset=../protos
rotate=.3 skew=3
cd..
```

For parameters of random deformations, see above.

7. To make a model for object "n" with 32 training images:

```
makedet object_n n 32 20 3 2 3 .5 1
```

12.9   Shape Recognition

In `base/NIST` there is a subdirectory `trees` with 100 classification trees trained on the NIST data base with absolute arrangements. The directory `test` has 10,000 NIST test images on which to try the trees.

```
face par.online
```

will classify the 10,000 images using the trees, computing the landmarks on the fly.

Similarly in `base/LATEX/CLASS` is a subdirectory with trees made with relational arrangements. The data for testing can be made by going to subdirectory `test` and running `make-lands`. The data is classified by returning to `base/LATEX/CLASS` and running

```
face par.rel
```

To see some of the arrangements detected on an image and other images in the same terminal node run

```
face par.show.
```

12.9.1   Extracting Features

The first step is creating the feature files for the training data and the test data.

cd train (or cd test)

face pars opt=44

- Generic edge-based features
  The file pars should contain the parameters defining the type of features.

  ratio=1. What downscaling to apply to image before feature extraction.

  onlyedges=1. Extract only edges; 0—extract edge arrangements defined in base/all.

  merge=1. Merge the edge features with the edge arrangements.

  ltatreedir=base/all. Directory with definition of predetermined collection of edge arrangements.

  dataset=./

  numdigits=10. Number of data points.

  EdgeParameters: See above for parameters defining the type of edges being extracted.

- Microimage codes
  First a cart tree describing quantization of the microimages must be made. It is written to codes.tree. The training images are assumed binary. For the NIST data set they are stored with 1 bit per pixel and datadepth must be set to 1.

  opt=48

  datadepth=1 For NIST image set to 1.

  codesize=4 Size of subimages to code.

  maxdepth=5 Maximum depth of tree.

  numdigits=100 Number of images from which to extract random codesize subimages.

  numperts=5 Number of random subimages to extract from each image.

  nist=1 Preprocess binary image:
  − Run median filter to eliminate little spots.
  − Blur image with Gaussian filter.
  − If any dimension of image is greater than scale downsample to size scale. Default value for scale is 32.
  − Threshold image at fraction threshold of maximal value. Default value is .2.

For extracting code labels for all subimages of all training images.

`opt=1000`

`numltas=62` Total number of microcodes.

`datadepth=1` Binary images.

`ltacluster=6` Size of blocks for clustering features of the same type.

`numdigits=100` Number of training images.

12.9.2 Training and Testing Trees

Assume the training landmark files are in subdirectory `train`

`opt=148`.

`nist=48`. Class labels of NIST data are in ASCII code, so, need to substract 48.

`althistsize=10`. How many classes to keep in terminal node. This is useful for problems with many classes (i.e., LaTeX). Stores only top `althistsize` classes in the terminal node.

`numcarts=100`. Number of trees to grow.

`class_tree=2`. Absolute arrangements; 1—relative arrangements.

`cartsizex=32`. Dimension of grid on which absolute locations are defined. Must be the same for all if `class_tree=2` (absolute arrangements); `cartsizey=32`.

`cartspread=1`. If absolute arrangements are used, locations of features can be down-sampled to coarser grid by factor `cartspread`. Warning: `cartspread*cartsizex` should equal true dimension of images.

`near=8`. Radius of box of spread for each feature, $s = 2 * (\text{near} - 1) + 1$.

`numland=62`. Number of local feature types.

`maxdepth=20`. Maximum depth of the tree.

`numtreedata=100000`. Number of data to use.

`landdir=train`. Directory with landmark data.

`numclass=10`. Number of classes.

`numquesask=200`. Number of random questions to sample at each node.

`mindata=0`. Minimum amount of data for splitting a node.

`modetwo=3`. Minimum amount of data at second largest class to stop splitting.

`boost=1`. Use boosting.

`alpha=1`. Extra factor to multiply boosting factor.

`carttreedir=./`. Directory to write the trees.

`useques(5)=1`. In case of relational trees, use questions 5 and 6; 5—asks for the first two features with a relation; 6—asks for an additional feature in relation to one existing in the pending graph.

`useques(6)=1`.

Testing is achieved as follows:

`opt=147`. 147—loops through test points and then through all the trees, and reports aggregate classification rate at the end; 149—Loops by tree and reports aggregate rate after each tree.

`nist=48`.

`numtreedata=10000`. Number of test data points.

`landdir=test`. Directory with landmark data.

`numclass=10`. Number of classes.

`carttreedir=./`. Directory with trees.

12.10   Combining Detection and Recognition

The same scripts used above for creating a detector for a particular class and classifiers for the object against false positives obtained from `trainall` will produce classifiers among the classes detected by the detector. The only change is to run

`findnewp 0 cartstyle -1` and set the parameters inside `findnewp`.

`nd=3100`. Number of data to use from `trainall`.

`ncl=62`. Total number of classes.

`npcl=50`. Number of elements per class (usually 50).

`acf=.8`. The factor to apply to the threshold `hits` to lower it and thereby obtain more detections in other classes.

`numcarts=50`. Number of classification trees.

`cartdepth=10`. Maximal depth of a tree.

`nq=200`. Number of random questions to sample.

`crtsp=2`. The radius of spreading for a binary feature used in the classification trees.

The program creates a file good, showing how many of each class are detected. In order for the program to know how to label detected and classified objects, a file with labels for the classes must be appended to pars

```
facenames(0) = marx
facenames(1) = lenin.
```

When classification trees for multiple classes are produced, they are written to a directory called facecart and are used if the parameter fnumcarts is positive. Otherwise, they are ignored and regular unclassified detection is performed.

Bibliography

Abbott, L. F. and Nelson, S. B. (2000). Synaptic plasticity: taming the beast. *Nat. Neurosci.,* *3* (suppl), 1178–1183.

Amit, D. J. (1989). *Modelling brain function: The world of attractor neural networks.* Cambridge: Cambridge University Press.

Amit, D. J. and Brunel, N. (1995). Learning internal representations in an attractor neural network with analogue neurons. *Network, 6,* 261.

Amit, D. J. and Brunel, N. (1997). Model of global spontaneous activity and local structured (learned) delay activity during delay periods in cerebral cortex. *Cereb. Cortex, 7,* 237–252.

Amit, D. J. and Fusi, S. (1994). Dynamic learning in neural networks with material synapses. *Neural Computation, 6,* 957.

Amit, Y. (1994). A non-linear variational problem for image matching. *SIAM J. Sci. Computing,* *15*(1), 207–224.

Amit, Y. (1997). Graphical shape templates for automatic anatomy detection: application to MRI brain scans. *IEEE Trans. Med. Imaging, 16,* 28–40.

Amit, Y. (2000). A neural network architecture for visual selection. *Neural Computation,* *12,* 1059–1082.

Amit, Y. and Geman, D. (1997). Shape quantization and recognition with randomized trees. *Neural Computation, 9,* 1545–1588.

Amit, Y. and Geman, D. (1999). A computational model for visual selection. *Neural Computation, 11,* 1691–1715.

Amit, Y. and Kong, A. (1996). Graphical templates for model registration. *IEEE Pattern Anal. Machine Intell., 18,* 225–236.

Amit, Y. and Mascaro, M. (2001). Attractor networks for shape recognition. *Neural Computation, 13,* 1415–1442.

Amit, Y. and Blanchard, G. (2001). Multiple randomized classifiers: MRCL. Technical report, Dept. of Statistics, University of Chicago.

Amit, Y., Geman, D., and Jedynak, B. (1998). Efficient focusing and face detection. In H. Wechsler and J. Phillips, eds., *Face recognition: From theory to applications,* NATO ASI Series F. Berlin: Springer-Verlag.

Amit, Y., Geman, D., and Wilder, K. (1997). Joint induction of shape features and tree classifiers. *IEEE Trans. Pattern Anal. Machine Intell., 19,* 1300–1306.

Amit, Y., Grenander, U., and Piccioni, M. (1991). Structural image restoration through deformable template. *J. Am. Stat. Assoc., 86*(414), 376–387.

Arbter, K., Snyder, W. E., Burkhardt, H., and Hirzinger, G. (1990). Application of affine invariant fourier descriptors to recognition of 3D objects. *IEEE Trans. Pattern Anal. Machine Intell., 12,* 640–647.

Atkinson, R. (1975). Mnemotechnics in second-language learning. *Am. Psychol., 30,* 821–828.

Bajcsy, R. and Kovacic, S. (1988). Multiresolution elastic matching. *Comput. Vis. Graphics Image Processing, 46,* 1–21.

Ballard, D. H. (1981). Generalizing the Hough transform to detect arbitrary shapes. *Pattern Recognit., 13,* 111–122.

Bartlett, M. S. and Sejnowski, T. J. (1998). Learning viewpoint-invariant face representations from visual experience in an attractor network. *Network: Comput. Neural Syst., 9,* 399–417.

Bertele, U. and Brioschi, F. (1969). A new algorithm for the solution of the secondary optimization problem in non-serial dynamic programming. *J. Math. Anal. Appl., 27,* 565–57.

Biederman, I. (1995). Visual object recognition. In S. M. Kosslyn and D. N. Osherson, eds., *Visual cognition.* Cambridge: MIT Press, pp. 121–166.

Bienenstock, E., Geman, S., and Potter, D. (1997). Compositionality, MDL priors, and object recognition. In M. C. Mozer, M. I. Jordan, and T. Petsche, eds., *Advances in neural information and processing systems,* vol. 9. Cambridge: MIT Press, pp. 834–844.

Binford, T. O. and Levitt, T. S. (1993). Quasi-invariants: theory and exploitation. In *Proc. Image Understanding Workshop.* Washington, D.C.: pp. 819–828.

Bishop, C. M. (1995). *Neural networks for pattern recognition.* New York: Oxford University Press.

Blake, A. and Issard, M. (1998). *Active Contours.* New York: Springer-Verlag.

Blake, A. and Yuille, A. (1992). *Active Vision.* Cambridge: MIT Press.

Bliss, T. V. P. and Collingridge, G. L. (1993). A synaptic model of memory: long term potentiation in the hippocampus. *Nature, 361,* 31.

Bookstein, L. F. (1991). *Morphometric tools for landmark data: Geometry and biology.* Cambridge: Cambridge University Press.

Bottou, L., Cortes, C., Denker, J. S., Drucker, H., Guyon, I., Jackel, L. D., LeCun, Y., Muller, U. A., Sackinger, E., Simard, P., and Vapnik, V. (1994). Comparison of classifier methods: a case study in handwritten digit recognition. In *Proceedings of the IEEE international conference on pattern recognition,* pp. 77–82.

Breiman, L. (1994). Bagging predictors. Technical report 451, Department of Statistics, University of California, Berkeley.

Breiman, L. (1998). Arcing classifiers (with discussion). *Ann. Stat., 26,* 801–849.

Breiman, L., Friedman, J., Olshen, R., and Stone, C. (1984). *Classification and regression trees.* Belmont, Calif.: Wadsworth.

Brooks, R. A. (1981). Symbolic reasoning among 3D models and 2D images. *Artif. Intell., 17,* 285–348.

Brunel, N., Carusi, F., and Fusi, S. (1998). Slow stochastic Hebbian learning of classes of stimuli in a recurrent neural network. *Network, 9,* 123–152.

Burl, M. C., Leung, T. K., and Perona, P. (1995). Face localization via shape statistics. In M. Bichsel, ed., *Proceedings of the international workshop on automatic face and gesture recognition,* pp. 154–159.

Burl, M., Weber, M., and Perona, P. (1998). A probabilistic approach to object recognition using local photometry and global geometry. In *Proceedings of the fifth European Conference on Computer Vision, ECCV '98.*

Camion, V. and Younes, L. (2001). Geodesic interpolating splines. In *EEMVCPR.*

Caselles, V., Kimmel, R., and Sapiro, G. (1997). Geodesic active contours. *Int. J. Comput. Vis., 22,* 61–79.

Caselles, V., Kimmel, R., Sapiro, G., and Sbert, C. (1997). Minimal surfaces based object segmentation. *IEEE Trans. Pattern Anal. Machine Intell., 19,* 394–398.

Chalidabhongse, J. and Kuo, C.-C. J. (1997). Fast motion vector estimation using multiresolution-spatio-temporal correlations. *IEEE Trans. Circuits Syst. Video Technol., 7,* 477–488.

Chelazzi, L., Miller, E. K., Duncan, J., and Desimone, R. (1993). A neural basis for visual search in inferior temporal cortex. *Nature, 363,* 345–347.

Chesnaud, C., Réfrégier, P., and Boulet, V. (1999). Statistical region snake-based segmentation adapted to different physical noise models. *IEEE Trans. Pattern Anal. Machine Intell., 21,* 1145–1157.

Christensen, G., Rabbitt, R. D., and Miller, M. I. (1996). Deformable templates using large deformation kinematics. *IEEE Trans. Image Processing, 5,* 1435–1447.

Chuang, G. and Kuo, C. (1996). Wavelet description of planar curves: theory and applications. *IEEE Trans. Image Processing, 5,* 56–70.

Cohen, I. and Cohen, L. D. (1993). Finite element methods for active contour models and balloons for 2D and 3D images. *IEEE Trans. Pattern Anal. Machine Intell., 15,* 1131–1147.

Cohen, I., Cohen, L. D., and Ayache, N. (1992). Using deformable surfaces to segment 3-D images and infer differential structures. *CVGIP: Image Understanding, 56*(2), 242–263.

Cohen, L. D. (1991). On active contour models and balloons. *CVGIP: Image Understanding, 53,* 211–218.

Cootes, T. F. and Taylor, C. J. (1992). Active shape models—smart snakes. In *Proceedings of BMVC.* pp. 267–275.

Cootes, T. F. and Taylor, C. J. (1996). Locating faces using statistical feature detectors. In *Proceedings of the second international workshop on automatic face and gesture recognition.* IEEE Computer Society Press, pp. 204–210.

Cover, T. M. and Thomas, J. A. (1991). *Elements of information theory.* New York: John Wiley.

Daubechies, I. (1988). Orthonormal bases of compactly supported wavelets. *Comm. Pure Appl. Math., 41,* 909–996.

Desimone, R. and Dyuncan, J. (1995). Neural mechanisms of selective visual attention. *Annu. Rev. Neurosci., 18,* 193–222.

Desimone, R., Miller, E. K., Chelazzi, L., and Lueschow, A. (1995). Multiple memory systems in visual cortex. In M. S. Gazzaniga, ed., *The cognitive Neurosciences.* Cambridge: MIT Press, pp. 475–486.

Diederich, S. and Opper, M. (1987). Learning correlated patterns in spin-glass networks by local learning rules. *Phys. Rev. Lett., 58,* 949–952.

Dryden, I. L. and Mardia, K. V. (1998). *Statistical shape analysis.* New York: Wiley.

Duda, R. O. and Hart, P. E. (1973). *Pattern classification and scene analysis.* New York: John Wiley.

Durtewitz, D., Seamans, J. K., and Sejnowski, T. J. (2000). Neurocomputational models of working memory. *Nat. Neurosci., 3* (suppl), 1192–1198.

Elder, J. and Zucker, S. W. (1996). Computing contour closure. In *Computer vision—ECCV.* New York: Springer, pp. 399–412.

Figueiredo, M. and Leitao, J. (1992). Bayesian estimation of ventricular contours in angiographic images. *11,* 416–429.

Fischler, M. A. and Elschlager, R. A. (1973). The representation and matching of pictorial structures. *IEEE Trans. Comput., 22,* 67–92.

Fleuret, F. (2000). Détection hiérarchique de visages par apprentissage statistique. Ph.D. thesis, L'úniversite Paris 6.

Fleuret, F. and Geman, D. (2001). Coarse-to-fine visual selection. *Int. J. Comput. Vis., 41*, 85–107.

Forsyth, D., Mundy, J. L., Zisserman, A., Coelho, C., Heller, A., and Rothwell, C. (1991). Invariant descriptors for 3-D object recognition and pose. *IEEE Trans. Pattern Anal. Machine Intell., 13*, 971–991.

Freund, Y. and Shapire, R. E. (1997). A decision-theoretic generalization of on-line learning and an application to boosting. *J. Comput. Syst. Sci., 55*, 119–139.

Friedman, J., Hastie, T., and Tibshirani, R. (2000). Additive logistic regression: a statistical view of boosting. *Ann. Stat., 28*, 337–374.

Friston, K., Ashburner, J., Frith, C. D., Poline, J.-B., Heather, J. D., and Frackowiak, R. (1995). Spatial registration and normalization of images. *Hum. Brain Mapping, 3*, 165–189.

Fukushima, K. (1986). A neural network model for selective attention in visual pattern recognition. *Biol. Cybern., 55*, 5–15.

Fukushima, K. and Wake, N. (1991). Handwritten alphanumeric character recognition by the neocognitron. *IEEE Trans. Neural Netw.*

Fusi, S., Annunziato, M., Badoni, D., Salamon, A., and Amit, D. J. (2000). Spike-driven synaptic plasticity: theory, simulation, VLSI implementation. *Neural Comput., 12*, 2227.

Garris, M. D. and Wilkinson, R. A. (1996). *NIST special database 3. Handwritten segmented characters.* Gaithersburg, Md: NIST.

Geiger, D., Gupta, A., Costa, L., and Vlontzos, J. (1995). Dynamic programming for detecting, tracking, and matching deformrable contours. *17*, 294–302.

Geman, D. (1990). Random fields and inverse problems in imaging. In *Lecture notes in mathematics,* no. 1427. Springer Verlag.

Geman, D. and Jedynak, B. (1996). An active testing model for tracking roads from satellite images. *IEEE Trans. Pattern Anal. Machine Intell., 18*, 1–15.

Geman, S. and Geman, D. (1984). Stochastic relaxation, Gibbs distributions, and the Bayesian restoration of images. *IEEE Trans. Pattern Anal. Machine Intell., 6*, 721–741.

Geman, S., Potter, D. F., and Chi, Z. (1998). Composition systems. Technical report, Division of Applied Mathematics, Brown University.

Gersho, A. and Gray, R. M. (1992). *Vector quantization and signal compression.* Boston: Kluwer Academic.

Gold, S. and Rangarajan, A. (1996). A graduated assignment algorithm for graph matching. *IEEE Trans. Pattern Anal. Machine Intell., 18*, 377–388.

Grenander, U. (1970). A unified approach to pattern analysis. *Adv. Comput., 10,* 175–216.

Grenander, U. (1978). *Pattern analysis: Lectures in pattern theory I–III.* New York: Springer-Verlag.

Grenander, U. (1993). *General Pattern Theory.* Oxford: Oxford University Press.

Grenander, U. and Miller, I. M. (1998). Computational anatomy: an emerging discipline. *Q. Appl. Math., LVI*(4), 617–694.

Grenander, U., Chow, Y., and Keenan, D. (1991). *A pattern theoretical study of biological shape.* New York: Springer Verlag.

Grimson, W. E. L. (1990). *Object recognition by computer: The role of geometric constraints.* Cambridge: MIT Press.

Hallinan, P. L., Gordon, G., Yuille, A. L., Giblin, P., and Mumford, D. (1999). *Two- and three-dimensional patterns of the face.* Natick, Mass.: A. K. Peters.

Haralick, R. M. and Shapiro, G. L. (1992). *Computer and robot vision,* vols. 1–2. Reading, Mass.: Addison Wesley.

Hastie, T. and Simard, P. Y. (1998). Metrics and models for handwritten character recognition. *Stat. Sci.,*

Hastie, T., Buja, A., and Tibshirani, R. (1995). Penalized discriminant analysis. *Ann. Stat., 23,* 73–103.

Hebb, D. O. (1949). *The organization of behavior.* New York: Wiley.

Hedgé, J. and Van Essen, D. C. (2000). Selectivity for complex shapes in primate visual area v2. *J. Neurosci.,*

Hinton, G. E., Dayan, P., Frey, B. J., and Neal, R. (1995). The wake-sleep algorithm for unsupervised neural networks. *Science, 268,* 1158–1161.

Ho, T. K., Hull, J. J., and Srihari, S. N. (1994). Decision combination in multiple classifier systems. *IEEE Trans. Pattern Anal. Machine Intell., 16,* 66–75.

Hopfield, J. J. (1982). Neural networks and physical systems with emergent selective computational abilities. *Proc. Natl. Acad. Sci. USA., 79,* 2554–2558.

Horn, B. K. P. and Schunck, B. G. (1981). Determining optical flow. *Artif. Intell., 17,* 185–203.

Hough, P. V. C. (1962). Methods and means for recognizing complex patterns. *U.S. Patent, 3069654.*

Huang, T. S. and Tsai, R. Y. (1981). Image sequence analysis: Motion estimation. In T. S. Huang, ed., *Image sequence analysis.* New York: Springer-Verlag.

Hubel, H. D. (1988). *Eye, brain, and vision.* New York: Scientific American Library.

Ishikawa, H. and Geiger, D. (1998). Segmentation by grouping junctions. In *Proceedings of the IEEE computer vision and pattern recognition.*

Ishikawa, H. and Geiger, D. (1999). Mapping image restoration to a graph problem. In *Proceedings of the IEEE-EURASIP workshop on non-linear and signal and image processing.*

Jermyn, I. and Ishikawa, H. (1999). Globally optimal regions and boundaries. In *Proceedings of the seventh IEEE international conference on computer vision (ICCV '99).*

Joshi, S. (1997). Large deformation diffeomorphisms and Gaussian random fields for statistical characterization of brain submanifolds. Ph.D. thesis, Department of Electrical Engineering, Washington University.

Kass, M., Witkin, A., and Terzopoulos, D. (1987). Snakes: active contour models. *Int. J. Comput. Vis.,* 321–331.

Kim, B., Boes, J. L., Frey, K. A., and Meyer, C. R. (1997). Mutual information for automated unwarping of rat brain autoradiographs. *NeuroImage, 5,* 31–40.

Kohonen, T. (1984). *Self-organization and associative memory.* Berlin: Springer Verlag.

Kwok, S. W. and Carter, C. (1990). Multiple decision trees. In R. D. Shachter, T. S. Levitt, L. Kanal, and J. F. Lemmer, eds., *Uncertainty and artificial intelligence.* North-Holland, Amsterdam: Elsevier Science Publishers.

Lamdan, Y., Schwartz, J. T., and Wolfson, H. J. (1988). Object recognition by affine invariant matching. In *IEEE international conference on computer vision and pattern recognition.* pp. 335–344.

LeCun, Y., Bottou, L., Bengio, Y., and Haffner, P. (1998). Gradient-based learning applied to document recognition. *Proc. IEEE, 86*(11), 2278–2324.

Levenex, P. and Schenk, F. (1997). Olfactory cues potentiate learning of distant visuospatial information. *Neurobiol. Learn. Mem., 68,* 140–153.

Malik, J. and Perona, P. (1990). Preattentive texture discrimination with early vision mechanisms. *J. Opti. Soc. Am. A, 7,* 923–932.

Malladi, R., Sethian, J. A., and Vemuri, B. C. (1995). Shape modeling with front propagation. *IEEE Trans. Pattern Anal. Machine Intell., 17,* 158–176.

Mallat, S. (1989). A theory for multiresolution signal decomposition: the wavelet representation. *IEEE Trans. Pattern Anal. Machine Intell.,* 674–693.

Markram, H., Lubke, J., Frotscher, M., and Sakmann, B. (1997). Regulation of synaptic efficacy by coincidence of postsynaptic ap's and epsp's. *Science, 375,* 213.

Marr, D. (1982). *Vision*. W. H. New York: Freeman and Company.

Marr, D. and Hilderith, E. (1980). Theory of edge detection. *Proc. R. Soc. Lond. B Biol. Sci., 207*, 187–217.

Marr, D. and Nishihara, H. K. (1978). Representation and recognition of the spatial organization of three-dimensional shapes. *Proc. R. Soc. Lond. B Biol. Sci., 200*, 269–294.

Mascaro, M. and Amit, D. J. (1999). Effective neural response function for collective population states. *Network, 10*, 351–373.

Mattia, M. and Del Giudice, P. (1999). Asynchronous simulation of large networks of spiking neurons and dynamical synapses. Submitted for publication to *Neural Computation*.

Meyer, Y. (1990). *Ondelettes et operateurs*. Paris: Herman.

Miller, M., Christensen, G., Amit, Y., and Grenander, U. (1993). A mathematical textbook of deformable neuro-anatomies. *Proc. Nat. Acad. Sci., R90*, 11944–11948.

Minsky, M. and Papert, S. (1969). *Perceptrons*. Cambridge: MIT Press.

Mumford, D. (1994). Pattern theory: a unifying perspective. In *First European congress of mathematics, vol 1*. Birkhausër, pp. 187–224.

Mundy, J. L. and Zisserman, A. (1992). *Geometric invariance in computer vision*. Cambridge: MIT Press.

Nagel, H. H. (1983). Displacement vectors derived from second-order intensity variations in image sequences. *Comput. Vis. Graph. Image Processing, 21*, 85–117.

Nagy, G. (2000). Twenty years of document analysis in PAMI. *IEEE Trans. Pattern Anal. Machine Intell., 22*, 38–62.

Oja, E. (1989). Neural networks, principle components, and subspaces. *Int. J. Neural Syst., 1*, 62–68.

Olshausen, B. A., Anderson, C. H., and Van Essen, D. C. V. (1993). A neurobiological model of visual attention and invariant pattern recognition based on dynamic routing of information. *J. Neurosci., 13*, 4700–4719.

Parida, L., Geiger, D., and Hummel, R. (1998). Junctions: detection, classification, and reconstruction. *IEEE Trans. Pattern Anal. Machine Intell., 20*, 687–698.

Petrocelli, R. R., Elion, J. L., and Manbeck, K. M. (1992). A new method for structure recognition in unsubtracted digital angiograms. In *Proceedings of computers in cardiology*. IEEE Computer Society, pp. 207–210.

Plamondon, R. and Srihari, S. N. (2000). On-line and off-line handwritten recognition. *IEEE Trans. Pattern Anal. Machine Intell., 22*, 63–84.

Press, W. H., Teukolsky, S. A., Vetterling, W. T., and Flannery, B. (1995). *Numerical recipes in C, The art of scientific computing,* 2nd ed. Cambridge: Cambridge University Press.

Quinlan, J. R. (1986). Induction of decision trees. *Machine Learn., 1,* 81–106.

Rabiner, L. and Juang, B.-H. (1993). *Fundamentals of speech recognition.* Englewood Cliffs, N.J.: Prentice Hall.

Rangarajan, A., Chui, H., and Bookstein, F. (1997). The softassign procrustes matching algorithm. In J. Duncan and G. Gindi, eds., *Information processing in medical imaging.* Springer, pp. 29–42.

Reiss, T. H. (1993). Recognizing planar objects using invariant image features. In *Lecture notes in computer science,* no. 676. Berlin: Springer Verlag.

Revow, M., Williams, C. K. I., and Hinton, G. E. (1996). Using generative models for handwritten digit recognition. *IEEE Trans. Pattern Anal. Machine Intell., 18,* 592–606.

Rice, J. A. (1995). *Mathematical statistics and data analysis,* 2nd ed. Belmont, Calif.: Duxbury Press.

Riesenhuber, M. and Poggio, T. (1999). Hierarchical models of object recognition in cortex. *Nat. Neurosci., 2,* 1019–1025.

Riesenhuber, M. and Poggio, T. (2000). Models of object recognition. *Nat. Neurosci., 3* (suppl), 1199–1204.

Ripley, B. D. (1994). Neural networks and related methods for classification. *J. R. Stat. Soc. B, 56,* 409–437.

Rojer, A. S. and Schwartz, E. L. (1992). A quotient space Hough transform for scpae-variant visual attention. In G. A. Carpenter and S. Grossberg, eds., *Neural networks for vision and image processing.* Cambridge: MIT Press.

Rolls, E. T. (2000). Memory systems in the brain. *Annu. Rev. Psychol., 51,* 599–630.

Rose, D. J., Tarjan, R. E., and Leuker, G. S. (1976). Algorithmic aspects of vertex elimination on graphs. *Siam J. Comput.,* pp. 266–283.

Rowley, H. A., Baluja, S., and Kanade, T. (1998). Neural network-based face detection. *IEEE Trans. Pattern Anal. Machine Intell., 20,* 23–38.

Sandor, S. E. and Leahy, R. M. (1995). Towards automated labelling of the cerebral cortex using a deformable atlas. In Y. E. A. Bizais, ed., *Information processing in medical imaging.* Netherlands: Kluwer Academic Press, pp. 127–138.

Schapire, R. E., Freund, Y., Bartlett, P., and Lee, W. S. (1998). Boosting the margins: a new explanation for the effectiveness of voting methods. *Ann. Stat., 26*(5), 1651–1686.

Shapiro, L. G. (1980). A structural model of shape. *IEEE Trans. Pattern Anal. Machine Intell.,* *2,* 111–126.

Shi, J. and Malik, J. (2000). Normalized cuts and image segmentation. *IEEE Trans. Pattern Anal. Machine Intell., 22,* 888–905.

Simard, P. Y., LeCun, Y., Denker, J. S., and Victorri, B. (2000). Transformation invariance in pattern recognition—tangent distance and tangent propagation. *Int. J. Imaging Syst. Technol., 11,* 181–197.

Sung, K. K. and Poggio, T. (1998). Example-based learning for view-based face detection. *IEEE Trans. Pattern Anal. Machine Intell., 20,* 39–51.

Tanaka, K., Saito, H. A., Fukada, Y., and Moriya, M. (1991). Coding visual images of objects and the inferotemporal cortex of the macaque monkey. *J. Neurosci., 66*(1), 170–189.

Tarr, M. and Bülthoff, H. (1998). Image-based object recognition in man, monkey, and machine. *Cognition, 67,* 1–20.

Terzopolous, D., Platt, J., Barr, A., and Fleisher, K. (1987). Elastically deformable models. *Comput. Graph., 21,* 205–214.

Tovee, M. J. (1996). *An introduction to the visual system.* Cambridge: Cambridge University Press.

Trouvé, A. (1998). Diffeomorphism groups and pattern matching in image analysis. *Int. J. Comput. Vis., 28,* 213–221.

Ullman, S. (1996). *High-level vision.* Cambridge: MIT Press.

Van Rullen, R., Gautrais, J., Delorme, A., and Thorpe, S. (1998). Face processing using one spike per neuron. *Biosystems, 48,* 229–239.

Vapnik, V. N. (1995). *The nature of statistical learning theory.* New York: Springer Verlag.

Viola, P. and Jones, M. J. (2001). Robust real time object detection. to appear in *Int. J. Comput. Vis.*

Viola, P. and Wells, W. M. I. (1997). Alignment by maximization of mutual information. *Int. J. Comput. Vis., 24,* 137–154.

von der Heydt, R. (1995). Form analysis in visual cortex. In M. S. Gazzaniga, ed., *The cognitive neurosciences.* Cambridge: MIT Press, pp. 365–382.

Wang, S. C. (1998). A statistical model for computer recognition of sequences of handwritten digits, with applications to zip codes. Ph.D. thesis, Department of Statistics, University of Chicago.

Wang, Y. and Staib, L. H. (2000). Boundary finding with prior shapes and smoothness models. *IEEE Trans. Pattern Anal. Machine Intell., 22,* 738–743.

Wickerhauser, M. V. (1994). *Adapted wavelet analysis from theory to software.* Wellesley, Mass.: IEEE Press.

Wiskott, L., Fellous, J.-M., Kruger, N., and von der Marlsburg, C. (1997). Face recognition by elastic bunch graph matching. *IEEE Trans. Pattern. Anal. Machine Intell., 7,* 775–779.

Zeki, S. (1993). *A Vision of the brain.* Oxford: Blackwell Scientific Publications.

Zhu, S. and Yuille, A. (1996). Region competition: unifying snakes, region growing, energy/ Bayes/MDL for multi-band image segmentation. *IEEE Trans. Pattern Anal. Machine Intell., 18,* 884–900.

Zhu, S. C. and Mumford, D. (1997). Prior learning and Gibbs reaction-diffusion. *IEEE Trans. Pattern Anal. Machine Intell., 19,* 1236–1250.

Index

absolute arrangements, 26, 184, 196,
  201–208, 219, 230
aggregate classifier, 190, 192, 202–205
anchor points, 123, 163
angiogram, 76, 80
area integral, 39
arrangement of local features, 26, 184
  absolute, *see* absolute arrangements 181
  constraints, 113, 151
  relational, *see* relational arrangements 181
  star type, 184

backward transform, 41, 55, 89
  discrete, 42, 90, 91
basis coefficients, 33, 42, 85, 86, 88
basis functions, 32, 33, 38, 41, 42, 45, 53,
  85, 105
  Fourier, *see* Fourier basis 33
  linear, 92
  principal components, 54
  wavelets, *see* wavelet basis 33
Bayes classifier, 8
Bayes' rule, x, 17
Bayesian modeling, x, 11, 18
Binomial distribution, 68, 128, 135
boosting, 191, 192, 203–205
bottom-up processing, 1, 7, 215
brain, 101, 173
  activity, 101
  matching, 101
  ventricle, 109–111, 120

brute force search, 153, 154, 156

chess piece, 45, 216
  classification, 216
Cholesky decomposition, 98
classification tree, x, 25, 185, 186, 188, 196,
  215, 230, 236
  depth, 185, 187, 203
  multiple, *see* multiple classification
    trees 181
  node
    empirical distribution, 186
    query, 185, 186, 189
  predictors, 25
  purity measure, 186
  recursive partitioning, 26
  relational arrangements, 198
  split, 186, 200
  stopping rule, 186, 203
  terminal node, 186, 187
    class distribution, 187
    class distribution estimates, 187
  testing, 187
  training, 26, 185, 186, 200
clutter, 45, 57, 64, 76, 79, 207, 208, 219
coarse to fine
  computation, 34, 45, 53, 87, 89, 93, 99,
    145, 180
  object model, 180
  sparse model, 145
comparison arrays, 110, 118, 119

compositional models, 11
computer vision, 1, 2, 40
conditional independence, 16, 36, 53, 57, 61,
    69, 72, 95, 115, 128
conjugate gradient, 45, 91
continuum, 57, 84, 87
continuum formulation, 32, 36, 37, 49, 53, 81
correspondence space search, 5, 148
cost function, 18, 57, 112
    deformable contour, 37
    deformable image, 95
    non-linear, 41, 107
covariance matrix, 54

data model
    deformable contour, 35, 48
    deformable curve, 59, 68
    deformable image, 84, 93
    sparse model, 114
Daubechies wavelet, 33, 100
decomposability, 140
deformable contour, 4, 19, 40, 51, 53, 57, 78,
    88, 179
    algorithm, 42, 46
        coarse to fine, 45, 47, 53, 89
    computation, 41
    cost function, 37
    data model, 35, 37, 48
    deformations, 31, 32, 34, 54, 88
    detection, 169
    discretization, 42
    edge model, 40, 53
    initialization, 79
    inside-outside model, 31, 36, 55, 88
    instantiation, 32, 42, 48, 54
    lattice parameterization, 53
    likelihood, 36, 37
    parameter estimation
        off-line, 48, 52
        on-line, 48, 51, 52
    posterior, 35, 36, 48, 49
    prior, 32, 35
    shape, 31, 174
    sparse model initialization, 169, 171, 174

spectral parameterization, 33, 53
    template, 32, 79
    time step, 42, 44
    variational analysis, 37
deformable curve, 4, 20, 78, 116, 179
    algorithm
        dynamic programming, 63–66, 78, 80
        tree based, 67, 74, 78, 80
    background model, 59, 68
    backtracking, 76
    computation time, 64
    data model, 57, 59, 61, 62, 68
    deformations, 57
    detection, 169
    image transform, 58
    initialization, 79, 80
    instantiation, 57, 60, 62, 67, 79
    jump ahead, 76
    likelihood, 59–61, 68
    local features, 58
    model, 62, 63
    parameter estimation, 61
    posterior, 62, 71
        partial, 71, 73, 74
    prior, 57, 62, 80
        tree structured, 67
    shape, 67
    template, 57, 62, 79
deformable image, 21, 101, 105, 179
    algorithm, 101
        coarse to fine, 89, 99, 101, 104
    Bernoulli model, 4, 85, 93, 97, 105, 112,
        121, 168, 179
    background, 96
    image transform, 94
    computation time, 100
    cost function, 87, 88, 95
        linearization, 92, 97, 98, 100, 101
    deformations, 81–83, 87, 88, 93, 95,
        101, 105
    discretization, 90
    displacement field, 84, 85, 87, 93, 99
    flow models, 104
    Gaussian model, 84, 97, 112

image transform, 85
initialization, 92
instantiation, 84, 95, 96
lattice parameterization, 92, 100, 104
likelihood, 84, 87, 95
parameter estimation, 85, 96, 105
pose parameters, 92
posterior, 87, 95
prior, 85, 87
prototype image, 84, 88, 96, 104
regularizing term, 87
sparse model initialization, 168, 180
spectral parameterization, 85, 87, 93, 98, 104
template, 82
time step, 91
training, 96
deformable models, x, 3, 6, 19, 24, 111
automatic initialization, 163, 166
instantiation, 161
sparse model initialization, 180
user initialization, 19
deformations
deformable contour, 31, 32, 54
deformable curve, 57
deformable image, 81–83, 87, 88, 93, 95, 101, 105
dynamic programming, 17, 57, 63, 67, 117, 140, 151
deformable curve, 63, 148
sparse model, 148
state space, 63, 142, 148, 149

edge arrangements, 7, 113, 121, 122, 125, 128, 157, 163, 184, 194, 206, 216, 221, 224
background density, 129–131, 133
complexity, 121, 129–131
subregions, 121, 129
two-edge arrangements, 123, 194, 236, 240
wedges, 121, 122, 128
edge maps, 128, 161, 162
edges, 93, 94, 113, 121, 184, 194, 219, 236
background density, 129–131, 136, 160

entropy, 69, 72
conditional, 70, 186
joint, 69
Euler equations, 100

face, 128, 132, 162, 163, 168
deformations, 81, 82
detection, 97, 125
detector, 161–163
edge arrangements
frequencies, 125
edges
frequencies, 125
instantiation, 96
matching, 82
sparse model, 125, 126, 155
Fast Fourier Transform, 42
feed forward neural net, 185, 196, 253
Fisher, 185
forward transform, 38, 41, 50, 55, 89, 95
discrete, 42, 90, 91
Fourier basis, 35, 42, 86, 87

Gaussian, 35, 37, 48, 52, 84, 85, 93
generative models, 11
geometric invariance, 10, 26, 118, 122, 184, 193, 212, 241
geons, 178
global optimization, 57
global optimum, 55, 79
gradient descent, 17, 31, 41, 57, 84, 88, 89, 92, 95, 99, 100, 112
gradient flow, 38, 41, 91
Green's theorem, 39, 50

handwritten digits, 181, 202, 233
heart, 51
heart ventricle, 46
Hebbian learning, 29, 237, 241, 245, 253, 256
field dependent, 244, 245, 253, 257
Hessian, 44, 91, 100
high-level processing, 1
homeomorphisms, 104

Hopfield networks, 257
Hough transform, 6, 153–155
hypothesis, 128

image compression, 93
image deformation, 81
image grid, 13
image normalization, 9
image registration, 9
image segmentation, 1, 7, 11, 27, 53, 181,
    215, 227
image sequence analysis, 4, 100
image surface, 20, 41, 81
  local topography, 14, 109, 120
  topography, 81, 85
image synthesis, 5, 111
image transforms, 4, 16, 18, 21
images
  background, 129, 135, 161
  office, 136
inexact consistent labeling, 6, 148
initialization, 31, 55
  deformable contour, 79
  deformable curve, 78, 79
  deformable image, 107
instantiation
  deformable contour, 32
  deformable curve, 57, 79
  deformable image, 95, 96
  region of interest, 161, 162, 181
    registration, 161
  sparse model, 112, 116
interpolation, 160
  linear, 90

Laplacian, 100
LaTeX symbols, 201, 206, 247
  detection, 226
  prototype, 168
  random deformations, 168
  recognition, 226
  scene analysis, 224–226
  sparse model, 168
    detection, 170

local features, 168
  training, 168
least squares, 98, 100
level curves, 81
level set methods, 54
likelihood
  deformable contour, 36, 37
  deformable curve, 59
  deformable image, 87
  ratio, 60
  sparse model, 114, 115
linear discriminant analysis, 185, 196
local features, 16, 20, 24, 93, 112, 184, 221
  background density, 111, 128, 129,
    135–137, 145, 161
  background probabilities, 115, 118
  binary, 16, 21
  clustering, 158
  comparison arrays, *see* comparison
    arrays 118
  consistent arrangement, 5
  density, 149
  edge arrangements, *see* edge
    arrangements 121
  edges, *see* edges 93
  false positives, 109
  invariant, 112
  micro-image codes, *see* micro-image
    codes 184
  on class probability, 246
  pose invariance, 133
  registered, 216, 217, 219, 221
  ridges, *see* ridges 93
  spreading, 193, 196, 201, 206, 219, 241
  statistics, 111, 128, 245
low-level processing, 1

machine learning, 212
maximum likelihood, 48, 61
mean curvature, 41
medical imaging, 31
micro-image codes, 193, 202
minimal cut, 55
model shifting, 233

motion estimation, 93, 104
MPEG, 93
MRI, 31, 101, 109
  brain scan, 48, 58, 65, 66, 76, 77, 102, 106,
    109, 110, 144, 147
    instantiation, 174
    sparse model, 146, 173, 174
    ventricle, 109
  functional, 101
multiple classification trees, 27, 165, 189,
    202, 216, 217, 225
  aggregation, 189–191, 202
  boosting, 191, 192
    overfit, 204
  conditional covariance, 209
  conditional independence, 209
  experiments, 201
  mean margin, 210
  object recognition, 192
  randomized, 165, 185, 187, 189, 197,
    219, 247
  with absolute arrangements, 196
  with relational arrangements, 198
multiple objects, 116
mutual information, 71–73, 106

network, x, 12, 28
  abstract module, 238, 256
    class subset, 238
  architecture, 235, 255
  biological analogies, 252
  bottom-up processing, 254
  classification, 12, 29, 248
  detection, x, 12, 28, 252
  detection layer, 248–250
  gating, 250, 254, 255
  Hebbian learning, *see* Hebbian learning 241
  inhibitory units, 241, 250
  input
    high level, 240
    low level, 240
    visual, 236
  invariant detection, 254
  layers, 235

  learning, 12, 28, 253, 256
    classifier, 241
    object model, 238, 240
  location selection, 250, 252
    bottom-up, 251, 252
    pop-out, 252
    top-down, 249, 251
  module, 238
  priming, 248, 250–252
  recognition, x, 250, 252
    off center, 250
  retinotopic layers, 236, 248
  top-down information flow, 249, 251,
    254, 255
  training, 239, 244
  translation, 251, 252
  translation layer, 250
neural dynamics, 236
neural system, 235, 236
neuron
  afferent connections, 234
  afferent units, 240
  binary, 234
  local field, 234, 244
  output, 234
  post-synaptic, 237–239, 244, 257
  pre-synaptic, 234, 236–239, 257
  threshold, 234, 235
NIST database, 201, 228, 244
  misclassified digits, 202
  pre-processing, 201
non-linear deformations, 19, 158
normal equations, 98

object boundary, 31, 81
object cluster, 27, 215, 216, 228, 230, 251
object clustering, 228
  sequential, 229
  tree based, 230
object detection, ix, 3, 11, 18, 215, 219
  and recognition, 7, 27, 215, 219, 220,
    221, 229
  as classification, 25
  Bayesian approach, 13

object detection (*cont.*)
  model points, 14
  non-rigid 2d, 3, 7, 8
    deformable contour, *see* deformable
      contour 178
    deformable curve, *see* deformable
      curve 178
    deformable image, *see* deformable
      image 178
    sparse model, *see* sparse model 178
  rigid 3d, 5, 7, 178
    3d models, 178
    sparse model, 171, 172
    view based, 230
    view based models, 8, 171, 178
object model, 2, 241
  admissible instantiation, 15, 18
  coarse to fine, 180
  complexity, 14
  computation, 17, 18
  cost function, 17
  data model, 16
  efficient computation, 17
  image transforms, 16, 18
  instantiation, 14–17
  learning, 241
  likelihood, 16–18
  model points, 13, 14, 18
  one dimensional, 31, 81, 88, 107, 180
  parameter estimation, 18
  posterior, 16, 17
  prior, 15, 17, 18
  sparse, 109
  template, 3, 13, 15, 18, 179
  two dimensional, 88, 107, 180
object pose, 96
object recognition, ix, x, 8, 11, 25, 181,
    215, 219
  deformable models, 8
  local features, 193, 194
  multiple classification trees, 192
Occam's razor, 18
occlusion, 17, 23, 113, 151, 159
Olivetti data set, 163

optical flow, 100
or-ing, 10, 12, 113, 121, 193, 196, 256

parameter estimation
  deformable contour, 48
  deformable curve, 61
  deformable image, 96
  sparse model, 119, 122
parts, 214, 232, 253
pattern recognition, 212
peeling, 141, 142
perceptrons, 247
  multiple randomized, 247, 256
    voting, 247
photometric invariance, 4, 10, 16, 20, 58, 93,
    94, 105, 113, 118, 120, 184, 193
pose space search, 6
  coarse to fine, 6
positron emission tomography, 101
posterior
  deformable contour, 35, 48
  deformable curve, 62
  deformable image, 87, 95
  sparse model, 114–116
pq probabilities, 243
predictors, 185–188, 193, 196
  random subset, 186, 189
prefrontal cortex, 254
priming, 254
principal components, 35, 54, 106
prior
  deformable contour, 32
  deformable curve, 57, 62
  deformable image, 87
  sparse model, 114, 139
prototype image, 14, 17, 21, 82–84, 93, 111,
    133, 216

QR, 98
quasi-Newton, 92, 100

recurrent connections, 235
reference grid, 13, 57, 96, 111, 113,
    160–162, 173, 238

reference points, 123, 125
region growing, 53
region of interest, 215, 221
relational arrangements, 26, 184, 197–208
  as labeled graph, 198
  as query, 199
  instances, 198, 200
  minimal extension, 199
  partial ordering, 197, 198
  pending, 199, 200
ridges, 58, 93
road tracking, 78
rotation invariance, 133, 139, 213

saccade, 250
scale invariance, 62, 139, 144, 196, 201
scene, 13
scene analysis, x, 7, 10, 27, 215, 228
scene interpretations, 229
serial computation, 233
shape, 2, 45, 48, 53, 54, 81
shape classification, 184
smoothness penalty, 87
sparse model, 4, 7, 21, 23, 24, 111–113, 179,
    215–217, 224, 228, 229, 248
  admissible instantiation, 117, 135, 151
  as initialization, 163
  candidate centers, 117, 151, 154, 156,
    160, 249
    density, 159
  coarse to fine, 145, 151, 153
  computation time, 148, 153, 160, 179
  counting detector, 23, 28, 153, 155, 159,
    163, 172, 184, 248
    step I, 23, 154, 157, 159, 161, 164,
      169, 248
    step II, 23, 157, 159, 160, 163, 164,
      166, 169
  data model, 114
  detection, 152, 163, 251
  dynamic programming, 6, 23, 142–145, 148
  false negative probability, 135
  false positive density, 128, 135–137, 159
  false positives, 152, 157

final classifier, 161, 165, 169
image transform, 114
instantiation, 112, 114, 116, 128, 135, 145,
    147, 157, 158, 160, 200
  clustering, 158
landmarks, 109, 119, 122
  user defined, 109
likelihood, 114, 115
local features, 113, 117, 140, 151, 157, 220
  consistent arrangement, 111–113, 151,
    152, 184
  on object probabilities, 114, 128, 129,
    131–134, 153
multiple objects, 116
parameter estimation, 119, 122
pose detection, 147, 156, 168, 215, 217
posterior, 114–117, 135
prior, 114, 139
  decomposable, 23, 140
template, 113, 119
threshold, 117, 126, 128
training, 119, 122, 157, 224, 240
  edge arrangements, 124
splines, 35
statistical model, 40, 48, 53, 54, 104
statistical modeling, 18
support vector machine, 185
synapse, 234
  depression, 238, 242
  efficacy, 234–238, 240, 242, 244, 248
  internal state, 237–239, 241, 244
  potentiation, 238, 241, 244, 253
synaptic connections, 235
  directed, 235
synaptic modification, 237

template
  deformable contour, 32, 81
  deformable curve, 57, 81
  deformable image, 82
  sparse model, 119
test error rate, 187
thin plate splines, 160
tracking in time, 54

training error rate, 187
translation invariance, 196, 201

ultrasound, 46
unsupervised learning, 188
unsupervised tree, 188
  class distribution estimates, 188
user initialization, 3, 4, 57, 109, 149
USPS database, 202, 228

ventricles, 45
visual scene, 233
visual system, 7, 8, 233, 234, 250, 252, 253
  complex cells, 253
  cortical column, 253
  infero-temporal cortex, 254
  layers, 253, 254
  object detection, 234
  object recognition, 234
  orientation selectivity, 253
  receptive field, 253

wavelet basis, 33, 35, 42, 45, 86, 87, 100
  Daubechies, 33
  discrete transform, 34, 42, 43, 90
  packets, 35, 87, 106
  pyramid, 33, 86
  resolution, 34, 35, 86
  two dimensional, 86
    discrete transform, 90
weighted training sample, 191